SHADOW LORD

For Mum

Shadow Lord

Theobald Bourke
Tibbott-ne-Long
1567-1629

Son of the Pirate Queen, Grace O'Malley

ANNE CHAMBERS

ashfield
PRESS

Published in 2007 by
ASHFIELD PRESS • DUBLIN • IRELAND

ISBN 10: 1 901658 65 1
ISBN 13: 978 1 901658 65 1
EAN: 9781901658651

This book is typeset by Ashfield Press in 11 on 14.5 point Adobe Garamond
Designed by SUSAN WAINE
Printed in Ireland by ßETAPRINT LIMITED, DUBLIN

Contents

Acknowledgements   7

Map of Tibbott-ne-Long's Connaught   8

❧

CHAPTER ONE   *Chieftain to Knight*   9

CHAPTER TWO   *The De Burgo Ancestry*   14

CHAPTER THREE   *A Gaelic Chieftain 1567-1583*   25

CHAPTER FOUR   *Rebel in Arms 1583-1593*   49

CHAPTER FIVE   *The Hare and the Hounds 1593-1597*   67

CHAPTER SIX   *To Serve His Own Turn 1597-1601*   88

CHAPTER SEVEN   *A Knight of Property 1601-1612*   103

CHAPTER EIGHT   *The Gaelic Viscount 1612-1629*   119

CHAPTER NINE   *The Descendants 1629-1767*   139

CHAPTER TEN   *The Viscount Mayo Title 1767-1814*   166

❧

Appendices   176

Genealogy   191

References   196

Bibliography   205

Index   209

Granuaile: Ireland's Pirate Queen (Grace O'Malley) c. 1530 – 1603
Eleanor, Countess of Desmond c. 1545–1638
La Sheridan: Adorable Diva – Margaret Burke Sheridan, 1889–1958
The Geraldine Conspiracy (A NOVEL)
Ranji: Maharajah of Connemara
At Arm's Length: Aristocrats in the Republic of Ireland
Granuaile: Sea Queen of Ireland (BIOGRAPHY FOR CHILDREN)
Finding Tom Cruise and Other Stories (SHORT STORY COLLECTION)

Further information about the author and her published work is
available from the following websites:
www.graceomalley-annechambers.com
www.merlinwolfhound.com
www.collinspress.com
www.newisland.com
www.amazon.com
www.ashfieldpress.com

Acknowledgements

I T I S E V E R Y B I O G R A P H E R ' S dream to locate and access original source material related to the chosen subject. When that material consists of undeciphered and unpublished 16th- and 17th-century manuscripts, it is both a privilege and a pleasure. My sincere thanks to Lord Sligo for allowing me access to the manuscript collection at Westport House. The manuscripts contributed significantly to my research and this book could not have been written without them.

The research for this biography unearthed much fascinating and hitherto unknown material about Tibbott-ne-Long his life and his times. It also brought to light information about his descendants and the controversy that adheres to his title, Viscount Mayo, to this day.

I am indebted to Dr. K. Nicholls, University College Cork, for his extensive knowledge both of the period and of the genealogy of De Burgos, Bourkes and Burkes. His guidance and interest were much appreciated.

My thanks to the late Joe Kilmartin, Castlebar, for his assistance with the Latin translations; to Fergus Gillespie, Chief Herald of Ireland; Dr. T.K. Whitaker; Aileen Holmes; Paul Waldron and Stuart O'Malley-Dunlop and Tony Roche.

For their assistance and courtesy, I wish to thank the staffs of the National Library; the National Archives; the Genealogical Office; the Manuscripts Library, Trinity College; the Irish Folklore Commission, University College Dublin; the South Mayo Family Research Centre; Department of the Environment, Heritage and Local Government and the Public Record Office, London.

Much thanks also to my agent Jonathan Williams and to John Davey, Susan Waine and Judith Elmes at Ashfield Press.

N O T E : 'Burke' and 'Bourke' are two spellings used for that name. 'Bourke' is the most usual spelling for the Bourkes of Mayo, while 'Burke' is used for the Galway Burkes.

Tibbott-ne-Long's Connaught

To Scotland

SLIGO BAY

Sligo Castle

● SLIGO

INISHKEA

Moyne ✠

SLIGO

MAYO

ACHILL
ISLAND

LOUGH CONN

Ballymote

Rockfleet

Burrishoole

ROSCOMMON

Kildawnet

● CASTLEBARRY

CLARE
ISLAND

CLEW BAY

Castleleapry ✠
Cahernamart

Bellcarra

Murrisk ✠

● BALLYHAUNIS

Kinturk

To Dublin

Ballintobber ✠

Castlebourke

LOUGH
MASK

LOUGH CARRA

LOUGH
REA

Bunowen

● BALLINROBE

KILMAINE

● SHRULE

LOUGH CORRIB

GALWAY

ATHLONE ●

Athenry

GALWAY ●

GALWAY BAY

Shannon

ARAN
ISLANDS

● GORT

River

To Kinsale

LOUGH
DERG

CHAPTER ONE

Chieftain to Knight

O
N 21 SEPTEMBER 1601, some 3,400 Spanish troops sailed into Kinsale. They came to support the Ulster Gaelic chieftains in their struggle against the English Crown. Inadvertently they landed in the southernmost part of the country – the length of Ireland lay between them and their Gaelic allies.

In late October the Spaniards were besieged by a 7,000-thousand strong army, commanded by the English Lord Deputy in Ireland, Charles Blount, Lord Mountjoy. Ostensibly English, this army also included within its ranks hundreds of Irish 'royalists'.

In Ulster, Red Hugh O'Donnell, chieftain of Tirconaill, mustered his clansmen and tributary lords and set out to join the Spanish. In an incredible feat of human endurance, O'Donnell and his army out-marched and outmanoeuvred the forces sent by the English to bar their way on the long journey south to Kinsale.

At the end of November, after much deliberation and delay, his more cautious ally, Hugh O'Neill, Earl of Tyrone, and also led his army on the long trek south. With a combined army of 6,500 men, O'Neill and O'Donnell lay siege to the English besiegers.

At the beginning of December a flotilla of three galleys, carrying a well-armed and provisioned army of 300 men, sailed from Clew Bay on the west coast of Mayo and set its course southwards. It was commanded by a Gaelic chieftain, thirty-four years of age, whose actions over the previous decade had caused much confusion to both sides preparing to do battle at Kinsale.

O'Neill and Mountjoy awaited the arrival of this small armada with anticipation and apprehension. In the months of frantic preparation and intrigue which had preceded the battle, both leaders had tried to lure this chief to fight on their side. But he had led them a merry dance and remained uncommitted to the very last. Now, with the battle-lines finally drawn, it was still anybody's guess which way he would turn.

The chieftain was Theobald Bourke, better known by his sobriquet, Tiboíd-ne-Long (Tibbott of the Ships), chieftain of the Bourkes of Mayo. During the nine years of unprecedented political and social upheaval that had preceded Kinsale, his power and influence in Connaught had made him an alternately indispensable ally or formidable foe.

Earlier O'Neill had journeyed to meet him in Connaught in a last-ditch attempt to resolve an ongoing feud between Tibbott-ne-Long and O'Neill's confederate, O'Donnell, and to entice him to fight on the side of the Gaelic confederacy. The Mayo chieftain had listened to the terms O'Neill had offered but had given no indication of his intent. Mountjoy, too, through his spies and officials, had covertly sought Tibbott's alliance and had to pocket his anger and frustration at the chieftain's vacillations and duplicity. But Tibbott well realised his worth to both sides and kept them guessing right to the end.

At Kinsale, however, he finally made up his mind. He led his army past the banner of O'Neill and O'Donnell and stuck his standard alongside the army of Mountjoy.

The cast was assembled and the stage set for the final battle to decide the fate of Gaelic Ireland. The darkening December sky foretold 'the stormy conclusion of a stormy century, the lurid sunset of one of the wildest epochs of our history'.[1]

Much was at stake. A victory for O'Neill and O'Donnell would, at the very least, guarantee further aid from Spain and a defection from the Crown of the many Gaelic and gaelicised lords, who, like Tibbott Bourke, through fear, bribery or for personal gain, now supported Mountjoy. At most, it would free Ireland from the malevolent control of England. For Mountjoy, victory at Kinsale would destroy the power of the Ulster chieftains, stamp out the possibility of the confederacy spreading, and secure Ireland, once and for all, for the English crown.

Notwithstanding its numerical superiority, the Gaelic confederates were haunted by a sense of foreboding and inevitable doom. The threat stemmed not from any deficiencies in the leadership O'Neill or O'Donnell; they had already proved their military ability at previous engagements with the English at the Yellow Ford and the Curlew Mountains. The threat emanated rather from championing the cause of a culture and a way of life that, by the beginning of the 17th century, had become simply outmoded.

Gaelic Ireland was detached from mainstream European political and social development. It had never shared a common history with the Continent, being by-passed by the sweeping changes that had occurred there over the centuries; changes that had altered the social, political and religious fabric of mainland Europe. Gaelic Ireland had remained virtually unchanged since its Celtic origins. It had failed to produce a centralised government or monarchy, but instead had nurtured its fragmented and independent tribal kingdoms. In 16th-century Ireland, tribal loyalty and warfare, cattle-raiding and blood money were as much a part of daily life as they had been in the time of Queen Maeve and Cuchulain. Gaelic Ireland had failed to evolve from the Celtic conception of the individual ruler into the modern conception of a state. 'Such a life had been an anachronism in the medieval system and there was no place for it in Renaissance Europe.'[2]

What induced a Gaelic chief like Tibbott Bourke to fight on the side of the perceived enemy of his country? What strange metamorphosis had occurred in this leader which caused him to turn his back on his birthright, his nationality, his country and his culture in its most critical and momentous hour? What bizarre motivation caused him to ally with a regime at whose hands he had suffered imprisonment and deprivation, his life hanging on two occasions by the proverbial thread, as he faced torture and the gallows; a regime against which he had rebelled and intrigued so often in the past?

Tibbott-ne-Long's decision to fight on the side of the English Crown at Kinsale was based on that sense of inevitable doom. As well as nursing a personal grudge against one of the confederate leaders, Hugh O'Donnell, Tibbott also had the foresight to recognise that the cause of Gaelic Ireland was a lost one. Perhaps his mixed ancestry made it easier for him than for others to accept the futility of continuing to oppose a stronger and more progressive aggressor. As gaelicised Anglo-Norman and Gael lined up at Kinsale for the final showdown, each side had a claim to Tibbott's allegiance by right of ancestry.

His father, Richard Bourke, was a descendant of the Anglo-Norman De Burgos, who had conquered Connaught in the 12th century but who had, in the intervening centuries, become completely gaelicised. His origins through his mother, Grace O'Malley (Granuaile), were deeply rooted in the Gaelic world he had opted to destroy. Both his parents, by their actions prior to Kinsale, had set him an example in the art of survival which had moulded him into a pragmatic opportunist. And at Kinsale he chose the winning side.

After the battle, a new war commenced; a war waged over ownership of the land of Ireland, this time fought with weapons of parchment and ink, spurious claims and faulty deeds. Despite the defeat at Kinsale, at the beginning of the 17th century, the greater part of the land of Ireland was still in Gaelic hands. After Kinsale and the collapse of the Gaelic system, and following the flight from Ireland of the Ulster leaders in 1607, vast tracts were left unprotected and open to the hungry eyes of English planters, adventurers and entrepreneurs, armed with vague and suspect titles to the land and property of the Gaelic chieftains and their followers.

In this legal minefield, Tibbott's instinct for survival was to meet its greatest test. In this complex, new age and within an alien legal framework, he was to demonstrate his natural talent for survival and advancement, as he had previously done in the Machiavellian political and military arena. In the decades after Kinsale, Tibbott was the only Gaelic chieftain substantially to increase his patrimony. His success is even more extraordinary since it was achieved despite the well-founded doubts of the English about his loyalty and against the concerted efforts of the foreign speculators and adventurers, who, at the collapse of the Gaelic world of his birth, sought to establish claims to its unprotected lands.

The life of Tibbott-ne-Long Bourke, inheritor of both Gaelic and Anglo-Norman traditions, spans a period of radical change in Irish history. It was a period in which Gaelic chieftains, gaelicised Anglo-Norman lords and English crown administrators competed by sword and by stealth for control of Ireland. It was a period in which compromise and cunning were the essential weapons for survival.

Tibbott-ne-Long Bourke's story is a unique commentary on this period of immense change. His story is the story of every other Gaelic chieftain and lord who occupied the middle ground between the fixed battle-lines of two fundamentally incompatible protagonists – the old Gaelic and the new English systems. These chieftains and lords were trapped by events over which they had little control. Many became pawns in a momentous game of strategy and were duly sacrificed. A few, like Tibbott, plotted their own moves and, in a game within a game, became intrepid knights charting their own survival.

CHAPTER TWO

The De Burgo Ancestry

O N HIS PATERNAL SIDE, Tibbott's ancestry stretched back to the time of the Anglo-Norman invasion of Ireland in the 12th century and to the great De Burgo dynasty that had helped effect it. That he descended from such old 'English' stock was commented upon by English monarchs, administrators and military men on numerous occasions during his lifetime and offered as a reason why his support might be solicited and his advancement promoted. His bold, enterprising and acquisitive nature mirrored the traits of his early Anglo-Norman ancestors. The evolution of his ancestral background provides a window by which to view and understand his mind-set and actions.

In August 1167, Dermot Mac Murrough, the deposed King of Leinster, landed on the Wexford coast and with the help of a few score Anglo-Norman mercenaries, regained part of his former kingdom. These relatively minor events led ultimately to a dramatic change in the course of Irish history. Mac Murrough's allies from the Welsh marches were followed by hundreds of their brethren. In 1171, Strongbow, the Earl of Pembroke, landed near Waterford. He was accompanied by William de Burgo, founder of the De Burgo dynasty of Connaught, which later split into two great branches: the Upper MacWilliam Burkes of Galway and the lower MacWilliam Bourkes of Mayo – Tibbott's direct ancestors.

William de Burgo was first married to Elizabeth, daughter of King Edward I of England, by whom he had a son, Richard Mór. He married, secondly, the daughter of Daniel Mór O'Brien, the last King of Cashel. In 1179, King John of England granted William and his heirs overlordship of the entire province of Connaught. While De Burgo never attempted to gain an actual foothold in the province, the very existence of this grant was a source of the wars and dissension that were to plague Connaught for centuries.

The name most associated with the Anglo-Norman conquest of Connaught is that of Richard de Burgo, who inherited the lordship of Connaught from his father William, in payment to the Crown of a rent of 300 marks* for the first five years and 500 marks per year thereafter. The King retained five cantreds and the Episcopal investitures. This was the origin of the De Burgo lordship of Connaught, whereby they, and the Norman barons who accompanied them, established themselves within their fortified castles in the western province.

It was Richard de Burgo who first acquired the title 'Lord of Connaught'. In Mayo, one of the knights who accompanied him, Adam de Staunton, was granted lands in the barony of Carra. These same lands, 400 years later, were to change hands between Tibbott, De Burgo's descendant, and the descendant of de Staunton, Myles MacEvilly. Botiller (later to become Butler) was granted the O'Malley territory of Burrishoole. This territory was held by the Butlers until the end of the 14th century when they, in turn, were dispossessed by Tibbott's direct ancestors, the Bourkes of Burrishoole and Carra. Richard de Burgo died in 1243, his vast possessions passing to his eldest son, Richard II, who in turn was succeeded by his brother Walter. Walter was subsequently created Earl of Ulster, an event that was to prove significant.

---

* The value of the Irish 'mark' or pound against its English equivalent was unclear throughout the 16th century. In Connaught, according to the Composition of 1585, one Irish mark was equivalent to ten English shillings. After 1603, when a systematic attempt to regularise the chaotic Irish monetary system was undertaken, the official exchange rate was one Irish mark to fifteen English shillings.

During the succeeding decades the De Burgos continued to consolidate their position in Connaught at the expense of the former native kings, the O'Connors and the other Gaelic chieftains. In 1315, Edward Bruce arrived in Ireland. After a brief and unlikely alliance with the De Burgos, Felim O'Connor finally declared for Bruce. Bruce defeated Richard De Burgo at the Battle of Connor but in 1316 Sir William Liath (Grey) De Burgo and Richard de Bermingham defeated O'Connor's army at Athenry. Richard's grandson, William, became Earl of Ulster. He was assassinated by his own attendants at his castle of Carrickfergus, leaving a daughter, Elizabeth, to inherit his estates both in Ulster and in Connaught.

Rather than have the Connaught lordship inherited by an outsider through marriage to Elizabeth, the lords of the junior branches of the De Burgos in Connaught, Richard and Edmund Albanach (Scottish), usurped the authority and possessions of the lordship there. Knowing that English law 'wolde speedily evict them out of their possession ... they held it the best polity to cast off the yoke of English Law and to become Meere Irish ... so as from thence forth they suffered their possessions to run in course of Tanistry and Gavel-Kinde. They changed their names, language and apparel and all their civil manners and customs of living',[1] to embrace the laws and customs of the country they came to conquer, eventually becoming as Irish as the Irish.

Richard's successors adopted the title of MacWilliam Uachtarach (upper) and took control of the De Burgo possessions in Galway. The descendants of Edmund became known as the MacWilliam Íochtarach (lower) and established themselves in Mayo, with the tacit approval of the principal native clans of both counties. Richard secured the hand of the O'Flaherty's daughter, while in Mayo, Edmund married Sabina, daughter of the chieftain Dermot Mac Eoghan Mac Teig Roe O'Malley.

Elizabeth De Burgo, the legal heiress according to English law, eventually married Lionel, Duke of Clarence, the third son of King Edward III, who, in her name, became Earl of Ulster. From this union descended King Edward IV of England. Thus the De Burgo earldom of Ulster and the lordship of Connaught were, in theory, annexed to the Crown. Lionel, in right of his wife, laid claim to the usurped possessions in Connaught. However, through the denunciation by the two junior branches of the De Burgos of feudal law in favour of Gaelic or Brehon law, Connaught was divided between them. But in the background the shadowy claim of the English crown lingered on.

The Gaelic or Brehon laws were distinct to Ireland and had evolved from earliest times. In the 17th century, it was recorded that 'the customes of Ireland were anciently of two kindes; the one concerninage theyr behaviour, breedinge, and manner of life, the other touchinge theyr government in warre and peace.'[2] The system, in theory at least, catered for every conceivable contingency in Gaelic life. 'The early brehons maintained that it represented the law of nature, so that Christianity might add but not subtract from it.'[3] The pagan origins of the system were evident in many of its customs. Even as late as the 16th century, the inauguration ceremony of the Lower MacWilliam Bourke, for instance, continued to be held not in a church or monastery but at a pagan, prehistoric rath.

The Brehon system of jurisprudence differed from the common law of England in two distinct ways: succession and inheritance. The legal and social unit of the highly-regulated Gaelic society was the *deirbfhine*, a joint family and property-owning grouping, the limits of whose membership could be symbolised by the hand. The palm denoted a common ancestor; the fingers denoted the descendants, extended over five generations, to include the leader, his children, his father's brothers, his grandfather's brothers and his great-grandfather's brothers.

Unlike the feudal system, primogeniture was not part of the Brehon system of succession. Succession to the chieftainship could be contested by any male member from within the ruling family group, so that a brother could succeed a brother or a nephew an uncle, as much as a son could succeed his father. A candidate's success depended on his ability to defend his people and his *tuath* (lordship). Despite its apparently democratic basis, the system also contributed to violent disputes between the eligible candidates. To offset this defect, *tanistry* had been introduced by the 8th century, whereby a successor was chosen from the eligible candidates during the lifetime of the reigning chief.

In the beginning, in theory, the land belonged to the people and was vested in the chief, in an almost mystic bond, on their behalf. The kin-based system of land ownership that evolved meant that land was held in common by members of the *deirbfhine*. The chieftain or king had no claim to the ownership of the land other than to his personal estate. Land was inherited by all freeborn males within a particular clan. By a complex and highly flexible system of gavelkind – which differed not only from region to region, but also from clan to clan, dependent as it was on the political and social circumstances affecting individual families – the land was divided and transferred to co-heirs. This was done sometimes on the death of a co-heir or, in some areas, on an annual basis. Such freeborn inheritors and their co-heirs enjoyed fixity of tenure. So indestructible were these rights that land continued to be held by the same free-holding families for hundreds of years, down to the close of the 16th century.

As in every political system, there were those at the bottom of the social scale, who held land in varying degrees of insecurity and extortion from both chiefs and freeholders alike. They were known as *betagh*. Unlike their feudal counterparts, however, these Gaelic labourers or tenants-at-will were not bound for life to their chief. They constituted a highly mobile work force who could, and were wont, to abandon the land of their chief for another on more favourable terms.

Politically those in power were tied to those under them by a system of clientship, known as *célsine*. The laws legislated in great detail the rights and obligations of the chief to his client lords and vice versa. It was in the interest of the leader, *rí* (king), *úir-rí* (sub-king) or *tiarna* (chief), that he treated his clients according to what was agreed by arbitration. If he did not, they could seek redress from the law or the protection of his enemy, to whom they might transfer their allegiance. It was similarly in the interest of the client that he fulfil his obligations to his overlord, so that he might enjoy his protection from an enemy. Whether it was the number of cattle, sacks of corn or jars of honey, the level of hospitality or the number of fighting men he was contracted to provide, the specific amount and duties for which the client was indebted to his lord were clearly stipulated and agreed by both parties, as were the obligations of the lord to his client. They were not, as future English adventurers wilfully or ignorantly reported, to be at the chief's 'mere will and pleasure'.[4] This self-same system of clientship and tribute were an integral part of Tibbott's chieftaincy in the 16th century and formed the basis of his power and status.

While women were excluded from obtaining shares in redistributed land, they could own land in their own right. They were subject to the same law governing inheritance as their husbands, i.e. if a woman had sons, it descended to them before her daughters and if she had no sons, it descended to her daughters. Tibbott's mother, Granuaile, for example, inherited lands in her own right in the O'Malley lordship of Umhall from her mother, Margaret O'Malley. Safeguards were built into the system to ensure that land remained under the clan's control should a woman marry into another clan. In 1614, Tibbott contested and won a case in the Court of Chancery against the O'Malleys, by English law, to the lands inherited by his mother, which by Brehon law would have remained in possession of the O'Malleys.

The defects of the Brehon system were obvious and led to much dissension and bloodshed, which greatly increased when the English administration introduced primogeniture as a method of succession. 'The course of dynastic history in Ireland, at least from the 10th century onwards, reeks with bloodshed, disorder and internecine wars, resulting directly or indirectly from the succession system. The elected chieftain lacked one of the strongest incentives to work for posterity – the certainty that his son would inherit the government and perhaps perpetuate his policy.'[5] The Gaelic system could, however, also 'produce an organised, economically stable state such as Hugh O'Neill's lordship'[6] in Ulster in the late 16th century.

The Gaelic system recovered from the reversal it had suffered at the Anglo-Norman invasion by absorbing many aspects of feudal law. Yet English opposition to the fundamentals of a system which, they maintained, 'draweth the obedience of the subject from his prince unto the captain,'[7] continued. If the Gaelic system hoped to survive, it had to adapt to the changing political and social circumstances happening else-where in England and in Europe. If it stagnated and remained inflexible, then it could hardly hope to survive.

✤ ✤ ✤

The De Burgos of Connaught were foremost among the Anglo-Normans to fully adopt the Gaelic way of life but the transition was a gradual process. Succession to the Upper MacWilliamship title was accomplished according to English law until as late as the end of the 15th century, while succession to the Mayo MacWilliamship title fol-lowed the Gaelic method of election from as early as the latter half of the 14th century.

The descendants of the two MacWilliams, particularly the Upper MacWilliam, ostensibly acknowledged the English king's supremacy, but they intended to retain the lands they had acquired, whether con-sidered illegal or not by the king's law. 'Acceptance of their submission by the king seemed only to acknowledge their right to the territories and positions they had seized.'[8]

In the division of the Connaught lordship in 1340, all the Anglo-Norman lords in Mayo, with the exception of de Prendergast, sided with Edmund Albanach. The division was not accomplished entirely peacefully, as Edmund was forced to defend his position as the senior of the two De Burgo branches. During his reign, continual warfare raged between both factions and the 'pattern of alliances which came into existence at this date was to persist throughout the whole medieval history of Connaught; even in the late 16th century, the political alle-giances, centred on the two great factions ... were still a living thing.'[9] Edmund was successful in the main against the aspirations of the Upper MacWilliam and the Lower MacWilliam was acknowledged as the superior during most of the troubled decades until the beginning of the 15th century.

This period was also witness to the disappearance of the authority of the English kings in Connaught. In 1358, it was recorded that no rents could be collected for the Crown because of the on-going war between the two MacWilliams. 'An attempt two years later to recover them produced only 18 shillings 4 pence, of which meagre sum – along with his own clothes and possessions – the collector, who had not felt able to afford an escort, was robbed on his way back by the Irish of Ormond.'[10]

During his reign as the Lower MacWilliam, Edmund Albanach initiated a significant development in warfare in Connaught – the employment of Scottish mercenaries. Edmund, as his name Albanach (Scottish) implies, had spent many years in Scotland where he learned the value of professional soldiery and saw it in action at the Battle of Bannockburn in 1314. His own career showed much military ability and the introduction of the Scottish gallowglasses (*gallóglaigh*) into Mayo was a major contributory factor to his military success.

The MacDonnells were the mercenaries most associated with the Mayo MacWilliam. Initially they were paid for their services in money and livestock. Eventually they received land and so became settlers, their followers becoming their tenants. They were the nucleus of the local standing armies in the west and their numbers were replenished from time to time with additional troops from Scotland. The employment of Scottish mercenary troops in the wars and disputes in Connaught continued to the beginning of the 17th century and their importation by sea into the province from Scotland provided a lucrative business for Tibbott and his family in the closing years of the 16th century.

Edmund Albanach died in 1371. By the English law of primogeniture, his eldest son should have inherited his estate. Since he had chosen to rule according to Brehon law, however, the election of his successor was decided by septs of the Mayo De Burgos. They chose Thomas, the eldest surviving son of Edmund. It was an unfortunate choice qwing to Thomas's lack of experience and the emergence at this time of a formidable and effective military opponent in Ricard Óg as the Upper MacWilliam in Galway. Eventually he superseded Thomas as the 'superior' MacWilliam in Connaught. Mayo disintegrated into poverty and disorder because of Thomas's inability to control the tributory De Burgo septs and the barons and chieftains, and his failure to protect his territory from the ravages of his enemies.

A major event in the history of the Lower MacWilliam Bourkes occurred on his death. Thomas's estates were divided between his five sons. From two of these emanated the senior septs of the Mayo Bourkes from whom future MacWilliam chieftains were to be elected, until the disbandment of the title at the close of the 16th century. The senior septs were

1. Sept Walter or the Bourkes of Kilmaine; and
2. Edmund Féasóige (of the beard) or the Bourkes of Castlebar, subdivided into
    (a) Sept Ulick of Carra and Umhall (Tibbott and his father were of this sept);
    (b) Sept Richard of Castlebar and Tirawley; and
    (c) Sept of Thomas Rua in Tirawley and Umhall Íochtarach.[11]

Two categories of land were involved in the division of Thomas's land: his own personal estate and the lands pertaining to the MacWilliamship title. In the manuscript 'Historia et Genealogia Familiae de Burgo'__ the original mensal lands of the MacWilliamship in the barony of Kilmaine are stated to have consisted of three distinct 'pobbles' or districts. Together with his mensal lands, the MacWilliam was in receipt of substantial tributes and rents from almost every territory under his overlordship, ranging from a barrel of ale and a pot of honey from one area, to six bundles of oats and twelve white candles per quarter of land, from another.

The Composition of Connaught (1585) listed the lands then belonging to the MacWilliam, Tibbott's father (the substantial part of which was eventually acquired by Tibbott) as

1. the castle and manor of Ballinrobe with 1,000 profitable acres in demesne;
2. the castle and manor of Bally Lough Mask with 3,000 profitable acres in demesne; and
3. the castle and manor of Kinlough with 2,500 profitable acres in demesne.[12]

The MacWilliam was also in receipt of one penny per statute acre from all freeholders' lands in the barony of Kilmaine, which amounted to about 63,000 statute acres, and to 1½d per acre in the baronies of Tirawley, Carra and Burrishoole. A 'rising-out' (military aid) was the MacWilliam's sole entitlement from the O'Malley territory of Umhall. Little wonder that the power, wealth and prestige of the Mac Williamship made it the most coveted title in Connaught.

The supremacy of the Upper MacWilliam over the Lower MacWilliam was firmly established by Thomas's death in 1401. To the end of Thomas's reign as the Lower MacWilliam, the role of official representative of the English kings in Connaught had tended to alternate between the two MacWilliams. After his death, however, future Lower MacWilliams withdrew from all contact with the English administration, while their counterparts in Galway, the Clanrickards, 'continued to hold a shadowy sheriffdom in Connaught through the century'.[13]

But the history of the Mayo MacWilliams was not all bloodshed and disorder. Under their rule numerous stone castles, monasteries and abbeys were established throughout the county for orders such as the Dominicans, Carmelites and Augustinians. In 1469, Richard Bourke, the MacWilliam, granted 200 acres of land to the Dominican Order for the establishment of Burrishoole Abbey. Richard subsequently resigned the MacWilliamship and entered the abbey where he died in 1473. The foundation of Burrishoole, however, had been executed without the necessary papal dispensation, an action punishable by excommunication at the time. It was consequently necessary to appeal to Rome and finally, in 1484, the necessary dispensation was granted by Pope Eugene VIII. The abbey, situated on an inlet of Clew Bay, is in a ruined state, but appears to have been an extensive establishment.

Richard was succeeded in 1469 by his nephew, Richard O'Cuairsge (of the Bent Shield), who celebrated his election by an invasion of the Upper MacWilliam. His reign was marked by the increasing intervention of the O'Donnell chieftains of Tirconaill in the affairs of Connaught. A power struggle between Richard and O'Donnell for supremacy in Mayo continued to the close of the 15th century. This intervention by the O'Donnell chiefs surfaced again in the last years of the 16th century and lead to animosity between Hugh Roe O'Donnell and Tibbott which, in turn, lead to Tibbott's alienation from the Gaelic confederate cause at Kinsale.

Ulick Finn, a turbulent and aggressive chief, became the Upper MacWilliam of Galway in 1485. He sought to establish his authority over all Connaught, including Mayo. At first the powerful Earl of Kildare, Garret Mór, then Lord Deputy of Ireland, sought to curtail Ulick's ambition by giving him his daughter, Eustacia, in marriage. But Ulick entered a confederacy with O'Brien and the chieftains of Munster against Kildare. The Lower MacWilliam was only too willing to join forces with Kildare to suppress his ambitious neighbour. The two sides gave battle at Knockdoe in Galway on 19 September 1504. Ulick and his confederates sustained a heavy defeat. The result of the battle righted the balance of power once more between the two MacWilliams.

The Battle of Knockdoe was the final major confrontation in the long struggle for power between the two MacWilliams. After the battle, the Upper MacWilliams faded into obscurity for some decades until the arrival of the first English Lord Deputy in Connaught in 1536. In 1543, the Upper MacWilliam agreed to the 'surrender and regrant' policy of Henry VIII, was created Earl of Clanrickard and henceforth became the upholder of English law in the province.

The Lower MacWilliam, on the other hand, together with his neighbouring allies the O'Malleys and O'Flaherties, remained aloof from the gradual incursion of English law and administration into Connaught. They continued to rule their kingdoms according to the Gaelic or Brehon code. The only threat to their power came from the O'Donnells' sporadic incursions into their territory.

This involvement by the O'Donnell chieftains in the affairs of Mayo during the early part of the 16th century contributed significantly to developments at the close of that same century. Then the loyalties of the Mayo Bourkes, especially Tibbott-ne-Long, would become a major contributory factor in determining the outcome of the struggle for supremacy, not only between the English Crown and the O'Neill-O'Donnell confederacy, but between the crumbling medieval world of Gaelic Ireland and the aggressive, colonising tactics of Elizabethan England.

CHAPTER THREE

A Gaelic Chieftain
1567-1583

THEOBALD BOURKE, TIBBOTT-NE-LONG (Toby-of-the-Ships), was born in 1567. He was the only son of Grace O'Malley (Granuaile) by her second marriage to Richard Bourke (Richard-an-Iarainn), the Lower MacWilliam from 1581 to 1583. His was an unusual family background in so far that both his parents were established as principal actors on the political stage, his mother being the more powerful and influential partner of her marriage to Tibbott's father.

Granuaile was 'a most famous feminine sea captain', according to an English Lord Deputy, Sir Henry Sidney. She was born into the Gaelic ruling class, the only daughter of Owen, Dubhdara (Black Oak) O'Malley, chieftain of Umhall and leader of the O'Malleys, a clan uniquely different from others in one pivotal respect. The O'Malley association with the sea and seafaring was long established. The clan's maritime lifestyle comprised fishing, trading to Scotland and Spain, piracy and plunder, and mercenary work. They provided a pilot service for foreign vessels along the west coast of Ireland, asnd the ships for the importation of the gallowglass from Scotland.

Granuaile was married firstly to Donal-an-Chogaidh (of the battles) O'Flaherty, *tanaist* or heir-apparent to the chieftaincy of the O'Flaherty clan of Iar- (West) Chonnacht. She had two sons by O'Flaherty, Owen and Murrough, and a daughter Margaret. After Donal's death, Granuaile established herself as a figure of power and prominence in the province of Connaught. Based on Clare Island, she commanded an army of 200 followers and a fleet of galleys and continued her family's maritime business which she described as 'maintenance by the land and sea'.

Granuaile was a remarkable woman by the standards of any age. She was undisputed captain of her fleet and matriarch of the truculent mixture of clansmen – O'Flaherties, O'Malleys, Bourkes, O'Dowds, Conroys – over whom she held undisputed sway. They willingly sailed in her service, under her active command, in an age, environment and a social structure that made little allowance for female leaders. She was fearless by land and sea, a shrewd political pragmatist and able nego- tiator, matriarch and warrior. To find an analogy for this remarkable trailblazer one would have to go back in time to pre-history and to the Celtic warrior queens of her remote ancestors. At the time of her mar- riage to Richard Bourke in 1566, Granuaile had consolidated her position as a figure of power in Mayo in her own right. Richard was to become consort to his remarkable wife and participent in her political plans and ambitions.

Tibbott's father, Richard, was descended from the sept of the Bourkes of Umhall and Carra (one of the senior Bourke branches). He was the great-great-grandson of Edmund Féasóige de Burgo, the Lower MacWilliam from 1440 to 1458. His father, David, had been the MacWilliam until his death in 1558. His brothers were Walter Fada (Tall), William (nicknamed the 'Blind Abbot') and Ulick. Richard's sobriquet 'an-Iarainn' was possibly derived from the presence of iron mines on his property rather than, as popular legend would have it, from a suit of Norman armour he was said to have worn. Richard had three sons, Edmund, Walter and John, and a daughter, Caitríona, either by a previous marriage or illegitimately.

Tibbott was the only son of the marriage of Granuaile and Richard. Tradition holds that he was born on the high seas on board one of his mother's galleys, hence his unusual pseudonym. De Burgo's *Hibernia Dominicana* acknowledges this theory as the source of his sobriquet 'ne Long' and states *'bellatorem strenuum, et invictum, qui (sc Richardus) ex Grania, (aliis Grisella) O'Maly, Dynastae O'Flaherti Vidua, genuit Equitem Theobaldum (Ny Lung, id est, de Navibus, quia Mari in*

Navium Classe natum)...'[1] (… the mighty and invincible warrior [that is Richard] had by the wife Grania [alias Grisella] O'Malley of the O'Flaherty family, the knight Theobald ny Lung, of the Ships, because he was born in a fleet of ships at sea.)

Tibbott was born into a Gaelic world, the very foundations of which were being subtly but effectively undermined by England. The Tudor period is without parallel in the history of both Ireland and England. On a broader plane the period marks the transition of the western world from medieval to modern times. This was a gradual process which revolutionised every aspect of life from politics to religion, philosophy to art, the discovery and exploration of new countries and civilisations, bringing wealth and territorial riches to the discoverer and exploitation and tragedy to the discovered. Spain and England most clearly reflected the effects of this transition, particularly during the 16th century, in their expansionary and religious activities which eventually were to bring them into direct conflict.

It was in Ireland, however, that 'England's first steps towards empire were taken … Ireland was the first field for English enterprise and colonisation. Sir Walter Raleigh, Sir Humphrey Gilbert, Ralph Lane… the leaders of the early colonies in North America … all gained their first experience in Ireland. England learnt to establish herself beyond the Irish Sea before she leaped the Atlantic.'[2]

There were other reasons, however, apart from empire-building, which made Ireland loom large in Elizabethan policies and plans. Throughout the 16th century 'viewed from England, Ireland was a strategic risk, a pawn in the English political game: the great conflicts of sixteenth-century Ireland were inseparable from English strategic interests and ecclesiastical changes'.[3] Ireland, that hitherto distant island to the west of England, forgotten and overlooked by successive English kings, who yet maintained a shadowy claim to her ownership, was to emerge as England's principal problem. It became the key factor in ensuring England's own security – as the old proverb of the time held: 'he that will England win, first with Ireland must begin.'

By Tibbott's birth in 1567, the conquest of Ireland by England was well under way. It had been initiated in 1520 by Henry VIII, who introduced a policy of 'surrender and regrant' to win back his lost kingdom. Henry had been relatively successful with this policy of 'amiable persuasion'. By his death in 1547, some forty of the principal Gaelic chieftains and Anglo-Norman lords had surrendered and been re-granted their lands, together with an English title, on condition that they abide by English law and acknowledge Henry as their king. The king was less successful, however, on the matter of religious conformity, and the effects of the Reformation did not manifest themselves in Ireland until much later in the century.

The introduction into Ireland of English-born officials to take charge of the administration and to extend English control outside the Pale was another feature of English strategy in the 16th century. After the fall and the annihilation of the house of Kildare in 1535, future lords deputy and senior administrators in Ireland were henceforth to be English-born.

Henry's policies were furthered by his daughter, Mary, who in 1556, initiated 'plantation' as a method of subduing Ireland. By the plantation of Laois-Offaly, she sought to extend the area of the English Pale and subdue the native inhabitants who had become too daring in their attacks on loyal Palesmen.

Yet at the time of Elizabeth's accession to the throne in 1558, much had still to be accomplished before the Tudors could claim, with any degree of conviction that, as well as England, they ruled Ireland, too.

In Connaught, Henry VIII's policy of surrender and re-grant had made slow progress. In 1537, however, the Lord Deputy, Sir Leonard Grey, received a professed submission from the Upper MacWilliam and from the O'Flaherty and O'Madden chiefs. In 1541, the Upper MacWilliam attended parliament in Dublin. Two years later, in 1543, both the Upper and Lower MacWilliam, with O'Connor Roe and O'Connor Sligo, attended a Council of Ireland in Dublin. The result of these tentative contacts with the English Crown induced the Upper MacWilliam to surrender his Gaelic title and his lands to the Crown.

He was re-granted his lands in the king's name and created Earl of Clanrickard for his trouble. From henceforth he became an upholder of English law in Connaught.

There is no evidence of a submission by the Lower MacWilliam at this time, although ten years later, the Lord Chancellor, Sir Thomas Cusacke, could write (somewhat optimistically), 'MacWilliam Bourke, second Captain of most power in Connaught, is of honest conformity, and doth hinder none of the King's Majesty's subjects, and is ready to join with the Earl of Clanrickard and every other Captain to observe the King's Majesty in every place in Connaught.'[4]

Until the reign of Elizabeth I, the scope of English authority in Connaught was negligible. Apart from Clanrickard, the crown forces were not sufficiently strong to back the aspirations of any lord or chieftain who might wish to embrace English law. They were too weak to subdue the many lords and chieftains who regarded any extension of English authority as a threat to their individual power and status. 'Until the beginning of the reigne of Queen Elizabeth the ordinary justice of the Kingdome hadd little passage on Conaght, the English races remayninge under the rule of the chieffes of every particular septe',[5] a chronicler of the time observed.

When Elizabeth I became Queen of England, the re-conquest of Ireland took on a new urgency. It was a time of dangerous uncertainty for the new queen. There had been much plotting and intrigue to deny her the Crown and Elizabeth ascended the throne of England with the realisation that many of her own subjects had reservations about her right to it. The implementation of the provisions of the Reformation became imperative to the establishment of her right to rule, since strict Catholicism regarded her as illegitimate. Mary, Queen of Scots, Elizabeth's most likely successor, had married the Dauphin of Catholic France. The prospect of Scotland and France allied against her, and the fear of such an alliance spreading across from Scotland to involve Ireland, was a very real prospect. In order to strengthen her own position, Elizabeth sought to establish uniformity of religion within both England and Ireland. In England, fidelity to Catholicism became synonymous with disloyalty to Elizabeth, and in Ireland, with rebellion against her.

Elizabeth was initially content to continue her father's 'civil' policy to further the re-conquest of Ireland rather than resort to military means. 'Although the English determination to control Ireland increased, as the century progressed, not even Elizabeth, who was the strongest of the Tudors, abandoned, until the very end, the hope of achieving her purpose by negotiation, which was economical, rather than by force, which cost money.'[6]

A parliament assembled in Dublin in 1560 to establish the Queen's title and to reverse her sister's attempts to re-establish the old religion. But it was merely an outward show, an attempt to impress and overawe. Powerful chieftains, like Shane O'Neill in Ulster, successfully resisted English rule and continued to extend his authority into the territories of his neighbours. Such was O'Neill's strength that in 1563 Elizabeth was forced to make peace with him, acknowledge him as the O'Neill and withdraw the English garrison recently established at Armagh.

In Connaught the Earl of Clanrickard maintained a watching brief for the English government on the activities of the Bourkes of Mayo, who in 1550 had allied themselves with Shane O'Neill. In 1558, Tibbott's father, Richard-an-Iarainn, brought a force of 1,200 Scots under Donal and Donald MacAillin, cousins of the Earl of Argyle, into Connaught, where they plundered MacMaurice and Lord Athenry, allies of Clanrickard. Clanrickard subsequently defeated Richard and his Scottish mercenaries at Cloonee. The Scottish leaders and over 700 of their followers were slain. Richard hotfooted it back to the safety of Clew Bay where English law had yet to gain a foothold.

In 1566, the Lord Deputy, Sir Henry Sidney, sought to patch up the ongoing feud between Clanrickard and the Lower MacWilliam to prevent Shane O'Neill from taking advantage. The points at issue between the two lords involved the Brehon custom of *célsine* and related to complaints by MacWilliam that his protégé, the O'Connor Don, had been imprisoned by O'Connor Roe, the protégé of Clanrickard, during a time when a peace treaty had been in operation. MacWilliam further disputed the imprisonment of other persons by Clanrickard and also the Earl's claim to the castle Moyne, which MacWilliam claimed as his hereditary right. Hitherto, such disputes would have led automatically to armed hostilities between the two lords as the only method of settlement. Now an arbitrator in the person of an English Lord Deputy had emerged. English conquest of Connaught had taken another significant step.

Sidney toured Connaught in 1567 and introduced provisions for the direct government of the province by the appointment of commissioners to act in the place of the Lord Deputy. Leading a considerable army, Sidney procured a show of submission from most of the Connaught lords and chieftains. It was a submission unlikely, however, to be adhered to after his departure. At the same time, as one observor recorded the presence 'of the royal authority accustomed the lords to its recognition as more than an empty form'.[7]

Tibbott's father's property was confined to the Barony of Burrishoole, a territory situated on the north-eastern coast of Clew Bay. Prior to the Norman Conquest, Burrishoole, together with Umhall Uachtarach (Upper Umhall)), comprised the ancient kingdom of the O'Malleys. As a reward for his service in the invasion, John Butler (Bottiller) was granted Umhall Íochtarach (Lower Umhall). A strong castle was later built and the borough of Umhall established, hence the name Burrishoole, from the Gaelic '*Burgheis*' (town) and '*Umhall*' (territory). Later, the O'Malleys became tenants-in-chief to the Butlers at Burrishoole, while retaining sole chieftaincy of the other half of their lordship, Upper Umhall, later to become known as the Barony of Murrisk.

Based on the grant to John Butler, whose descendants became earls of Ormond, the Butlers continued to lay claim to Burrishoole. This uncertainty regarding title to land was typical of the 16th and early 17th centuries and was further complicated when the English system of inheritance began to replace Brehon law. Definition of title then became a matter merely of political expediency, as new re-grants of land, regardless of prior ownership, were issued as a method of bringing stubborn and troublesome chiefs under control.

After 1333, it was the De Burgos who gradually established themselves in Burrishoole at the expense of the Butlers, while the O'Malleys re-established themselves on Achill Island. There is no indication that the Butlers received any rents from either the O'Malleys or De Burgos and they were gradually superseded in the area by both clans.

The Sept of Ulick Bourke, headed by Tibbott's father, held Burrishoole under the MacWilliam. By the 16th century, under the chieftaincy of the sept Ulick, the barony of Burrishoole was inhabited by such septs of the Bourkes as MacPhilpins, MacTibbotts, MacMyler, MacWalter Boy, and also by the Clandonnells and the Clangibbons. The Sept Ulick, from whom Tibbott was descended, possessed the castles of Burrishoole, Newport and Carrickahowley (Rockfleet). The MacPhilbins had the castles of Aille and Doone, MacTibbott held Castleaffy, Clangibbons, Ballyknock Castle (as tenants to the O'Malleys), while the Clandonnells maintained the castles of Carrickennedy and Clogher.

While English law and custom was gradually finding a footing in the rest of Connaught, during Tibbott's childhood, it made little impact in Mayo. He was reared in a world that still adhered to Gaelic custom. Fosterage played an important role in Gaelic society and particularly so for young Tibbott Bourke, given that his mother, as well as his father, was an active leader and pursued a career hardly conducive to child-minding. 'The practice {of fosterage} was of considerable political importance, for the person so fostered could count on the adherence of his foster family throughout his life …. Conversely, the fosterers would also reap the benefits of support and protection.'[8] This system was to have a crucial impact on Tibbott in later life. With its propensity towards inter-tribal dependence and allegiances, fosterage, however, found little favour with the English, who considered that 'the cause of many strong combinations and factors do tend to the utter ruine of a Commonwealth',[9] an observation that was to prove particularly true in the case of Tibbott. He was fostered firstly with Edmund MacTibbott of Castleaffy, in Burrishoole and, secondly, with Myles MacEvilly at Kinturk Castle, in the barony of Carra.

Tibbott was reared in a world that still adhered to traditional Gaelic practice and custom. The lifestyle and habitation of chieftains, like his father and foster-father, was suited to the outdoor nature of Gaelic life. 'They possess castles to which are joined halls sufficiently large and commodious formed and made of clay and mud. They are accustomed to take their meals in these halls. They have fixed strongholds and residences which are daily filled with a very great concourse of people.'[10] Outside the chieftain's stone fortress, dining hall and outbuildings clustered the cabins of his followers 'built of underwood, called wattle and covered with thatch and some with green sedge, of a barrel forme and without chimneys'.[11] An account of Gaelic dining customs is furnished by the chronicler Stanihurst:

> In winter they are used to dine before daybreak, in summer about seven o'clock. They dine splendidly and sumptuously ... and though city elegance is not displayed at the feasts, they have the tables most plentifully furnished with beef, bacon and other viands.... They consume as the all useful beverage a kind of fiery wine, drunk neat, which is commonly called Aqua Vitae by the heat of which the food is made more easy of digestion .... They buy a huge quantity of wines (especially Spanish wine) in the neighbouring towns. They recline at meals, couches being set up for the purpose. The first place at the head of the table is assigned to the lady of the house, who is clad in a gown reaching to the ankles which is often dyed saffron colour and is well sleeved ... a harper is present during dinner.[12]

Edmund MacTibbott's castle, in which Tibbott was fostered, was situated on an inlet of Clew Bay at the water's edge, some distance northwest of the present town of Westport. It was an imposing structure and the extensive ruins visible today testify to its substantial size. Within the family of his foster parents, Tibbott received all the affection, discipline and instruction bestowed by Edmund and his wife on their own children. His education placed much emphasis on military skills and he was trained in the use of javelin, bow and arrow, sword, dagger and dart, both on foot and on horseback.

The Gaelic method of horse riding tended to be without stirrups, often rendering the rider of little value as a fighting unit. Gaelic battle-dress consisted of a mail-shirt or a jacket of quilted leather, sufficient to withstand a sword thrust. It was worn over a leine or wide-sleeved shirt and tight 'trews' or trousers. Leaders and commanders in the field wore part armour in the form of helmets and breastplates of iron and shields made of wood or skin and an iron morion, which covered the head and the upper part of the face.

There were three main levels of fighting men in the army of a chieftain. The lightly armed cavalry usually comprised the ruling family members of the sept and their near relatives. The gallowglass, the heavy infantry of the Gaelic armies, were selected men of great stature and strength, armed with long swords and the famed battleaxe and employed on a mercenary basis. Thirdly, were the 'kerne' (*certharnach*), the light-foot of the Gaelic armies, much mentioned in the histories of 16th-century Ireland. Their weapons were the bow and arrow – made of ash or yew, the arrows with barbed heads – and the short sword. Towards the close of the 16th century, the kerne gradually adapted to the use of musket and caliver and were acknowledged by their English opponents as being 'good and ready shots'.

The Gaelic armies seldom fought to a predetermined military for-mation, but attacked the enemy with rapid and irregular forays on all sides, withdrawing and advancing when the opportunity presented itself and generally using the local terrain to better advantage than the English. Prior to the use of muskets and powder in the latter decades of the century, Gaelic weaponry remained rooted in its Celtic origins. The javelin, bow and arrow and dart were used to engage the enemy at a distance. The javelin was tied to the soldier's arm by a thong of con-siderable length, whirled rapidly above the head, flung at the enemy and recovered. It was cast with such strength to penetrate even the heaviest armour.

To succeed his father as chieftain of the Sept Ulick, Tibbott had firstly to be strong and sound of body. Any physical disability would automatically rule him out as a contender. He had to attain a proficiency in the use of arms, an understanding of military combat and show an ability to defend his sept and territory from incursion and attack. Reminiscent of the traditions of the native North American tribes, an initiation ceremony, usually in the form of a cattle-rustling expedition against a neighbour, allowed Tibbott demonstrate the combative ability he had acquired when he graduated from military training.

From contemporary observations, Tibbott became proficient in the use of arms, was a good military tactician, and an able and strong leader. The Gaelic poets refer to him as a 'warrior...of valiant feats' and 'emulator of the African lion'. The English refer to him 'as one of the chief rebels in Connaught' when he fought against them, and as 'a valorous knight' when he sided with them. Folklore, however, does hint at one moment of cowardice in his military life. During an assault on Kinturk, the castle of the MacEvilly chieftain, his formidable mother noticed that Tibbott had moved behind her in the heat of battle. 'An ag iaraidh dul i bholach ar mo thoin ata tu, an ait a dthainig as?' (Are you trying to hide behind my backside, the place you came from?) His mother's insult, it is said, had the desired effect and stung him into action.

There was, however, a double edge to Tibbott's military abilities. As well as a warrior, Tibbott became an accomplished mariner. In this career he had as his instructor one of the most able seafarers of the period, his mother Granuaile. By then established as a power, both by land and sea, Granuaile imparted the maritime tradition of her O'Malley background to her youngest son. She trained him, as she had been trained by her father, to survive in the dangerous and difficult environment. Tibbott took to the sea like the proverbial duck to water and his seafaring expertise was to add a vital, additional dimension to his power.

Seafaring was not an option for the faint-hearted in the 16th century. The sea, particularly along the hazardous west coast of Ireland, was a demanding mistress, allowing for few mistakes from those who chanced their lives to extract a living and survive her many moods. Rudimentary navigation, wooden-hulled vessels, rocky headlands, hidden reefs, shallows and sandbars, competed with squalls and swells for the mariner's life. The dangers by sea were augmented by the political and social disintegration that was beginning to occur on land, as English expansionism in Connaught came into conflict with local law and custom. The ensuing mayhem on land contributed to an increase in plundering activities by sea, as well as in the gradual incursion by English ships-of-war into the sea territory that was once the preserve of Tibbott's O'Malley relations.

Combined with his military and maritime attributes, Tibbott was a shrewd and wily operator, well clued into the vagaries and machinations of 16th-century politics. In this regard, he followed in his mother's, more than his father's, footsteps. In the constantly changing pattern of alliances and deals that mark the latter decades of the 16th century, his every action seemed a compromise, his real intent hidden and shrouded in subterfuge. He was like quicksilver. No one knew when they had him either as an enemy or as a friend. He weaves and bobs his way through the political mayhem with an audacity and cunning that leaves his contemporaries flummoxed. 'I know not of one day's service that Tibbott ne Long hath performed', the high priest of 16th-century intrigue, Sir George Carew, complained to Sir Robert Cecil, himself the arch Machiavellian exponent of the 16th century.

As Tibbott grew up the political situation in Ireland was becoming ever more fraught. In 1566, Sir Henry Sidney was appointed Lord Deputy with instructions from his queen to bring the dissident Irish chieftains and lords to heel. With greater determination than heretofore the chieftains were resisting the extension of English law where it affected the powers and privileges they enjoyed under Brehon law. Religion, too, was emerging as a divisive issue, reflecting developments in England and on the European mainland. In Ireland, where the old religion was only nominally practised in any event, it would take time before it emerged to cement individual revolts against the English system into a more cohesive opposition.

One attempt to use religion as a cloak for more secular motives did manifest itself in the first of the Desmond rebellions, fought primarily over obscure claims to lands in Munster by land-hungry Elizabethan adventurers. The rebellion, initiated for secular reasons, soon assumed a religious connotation. This provoked the Munster lords and chieftains to take 'sides in defence of their religion in the ideological struggle which then split Europe, the struggle of Catholic against Protestant – a contest heightened in 1570 by the excommunication of the Queen'.[13] Although the revolt, led by James Fitzmaurice Fitzgerald, was quickly subdued, for the first time, it had produced a banner for the 'use of religion as a catalyst to make a common cause of local grievances'.[14]

An important step towards neutralising the power of the local chieftains was introduced in Connaught and Munster in 1569 with the establishment of English presidencies and accompanying administrative and legal offices of state. In Connaught, Sir Edward Fitton was appointed president of the province and, with a retinue of officials, was given the task of extending English law into Gaelic-ruled areas. 'The institution of the presidencies did not immediately transform the south and west. The presidents were intrusive, their resources were limited and, dependent as they were on the support of the deputy and council, their fortunes were conditioned by the play of personalities.'[15] Yet by their very establishment, the English government was provided with a mechanism whence policies, plots and physical instruments, used to undermine the foundations and institutions of native Gaelic law, would emanate. Although the powers conferred on the president would meet a stiff challenge, and, at times, appear to cease functioning in the face of strong native opposition from individual chieftains, notably Tibbott's parents, the very institutional aspect of that power gave it the incentive to eventually succeed. It also provided the institution with an in-built ability to survive the challenge to its authority posed by a strong but individualistic society where such institutions were noticeably lacking.

The first of many Bourke rebellions against English expansionism in Connaught occurred in 1570. The revolt was loosely allied to the Desmond uprising in Munster. Governor Fitton and the Earl of Clanrickard laid siege to a Bourke castle at Shrule on the border of Mayo and Galway. The Lower MacWilliam, aided by Tibbott's father and by his relations, the O'Flahertys of Iar-Chonnacht, opposed them.

In the battle that ensued, both sides claimed victory, but later in the same year, the MacWilliam submitted to Fitton and agreed to pay a yearly rent of 200 marks to the Crown. His death, at the end of 1570, marks a milestone in the history of the Lower MacWilliam. During his reign, English law had gained a foothold for the first time in Mayo, hitherto a bastion of Gaelic law and custom.

For the next thirty years a turbulent struggle for power between the native lords and officials of the English crown took place. Most of the lesser chieftains viewed the encroaching influence of the English administration with a deep and well-founded suspicion. Henceforth, they were prepared to join in any enterprise that might ensure their sovereignty and status quo. On the other hand, some of the major chieftains, weary of centuries of dispute over succession, territorial rights and the general disorderly nature of the native system, and conscious too of the personal advantages with which the law of primogeniture would endow them, were desirous of a strong central form of government, which the Gaelic system seemed incapable of producing. Within each clan were septs or factions who rebelled on the pretext of resenting any change in their customs but who, in reality, were merely seeking to enhance their own positions as contenders for office and power.

The strength and influence of those rebels determined the actions of the chieftains in office who were often forced to join in a rebellion against their will. It was far easier to join the rebels and later gain a pardon at a small cost from an insecure English administration, grateful and willing to thus pardon, on cessation of hostilities than to actively resist the rebels and suffer the destruction of land and property.

Interference by the Crown in the native customs regarding succession was another cause of unrest. The English sought to appoint chieftains who were amenable to their policies, regardless of their eligibility by native law. Consequently the elected *tánaist* was less certain that he would automatically succeed to the chieftaincy by Gaelic law and, like Tibbott's father, was often obliged to resort to physical force to protect his rights.

❧ ❧ ❧

Shane MacOliverus Bourke became the MacWilliam in 1571. During his reign the English administration continued to assert itself in Mayo. As a result of a survey undertaken by English officials, Mayo was divided into ten baronies and the principal clans and chieftains of each barony were listed. Richard-an-Iarainn was recorded as chieftain of the barony of 'Burris'. The survey, though inaccurate on many accounts, was further proof of the Crown's determination to uncover, by means of such surveys, maps and reports, a hitherto hidden part of Gaelic Ireland, its social and political practices, its revenues and assets, and their potential for exploitation.

The subsequent arrival in Galway in 1576 of the Lord Deputy, Sir Henry Sidney, witnessed the voluntary submission of the Lower MacWilliam and many of the chieftains of Mayo.

On Sidney's subsequent visit to Galway in 1577, Granuaile, with her husband Richard in tow, also made the acquaintance of the English Lord Deputy. With her intuitive political savvy, Granuaile confronted the English with a show of strength, on the sound principle that if it became necessary to negotiate with them, she could expect to extract more. Sidney's account of their meeting is, in itself, a revelation.

> There came to me also a most famous feminine sea captain called Grany Imallye and offered her services unto me, wheresoever I would command her, with three galleys and 200 fighting men, either in Scotland or Ireland; she brought with her her husband for she was as well by sea as by land well more than Mrs Mate with him .... This was a notorious woman in all the coasts of Ireland.[16]

Thus was Tibbott's mother first written into the pages of English history as a figure of political importance and as the dominant partner in her marriage to his father. Granuaile's dramatic 'submission' to the English lord deputy was no more than a judicious gesture to enhance her husband's position as a future MacWilliam and a warning and demonstration of her power to the English should they seek to deny him. As he head-counted her army, numerically not much less than his own, and noted her sea-going fleet of galleys, well might Sidney be impressed.

While English law had not yet affected their remote kingdom, it was evident to Granuaile that 'as the power and influence of the English crown encroached more and more on the affairs of their country, that the English queen's representatives appeared to wield more power and influence than the highest ranking Gaelic chieftain. In order to survive politically, it was imperative to play along with the power of the day.'[17] Moreover, according to Gaelic law, Richard, as *tánaist*, was next in line to succeed to the MacWilliamship. However, because of the submission of the reigning MacWilliam and his undertaking to rule by the English law of primogeniture, it was less certain that Richard would now succeed to the title. Consequently, a submission in Galway, with a vague offer of assistance, but accompanied by a demonstration of power, was, perhaps, as good a way as any for Granuaile to make an impression on the English Lord Deputy.

That tenuous nature of Granuaile's 'submission' was revealed when, later in the same year, she resumed her piracy and plundering. This time, however, it was not to be with her usual success. Choosing the rich lands of the powerful Earl of Desmond from which to snatch her prey, she was captured in the ensuing confrontation and dragged before the aggrieved Earl. Desmond, lately released by Elizabeth from the Tower of London, was in no mood to countenance her incursion and threw her into his dungeons at Askeaton Castle, before having her moved to close confinement in Limerick goal.

Haughty, volatile, inflexible and ill, the Earl had problems of his own. Pressurised by elements in the English administration in Ireland, who saw the vast acres in Munster, over which Desmond held sway, as a means to their own fortune, he was being prodded and provoked into rebellion. Challenges to his leadership came from within his own family, while his client-lords throughout Munster demanded his protection from the incursions of the English into their territories. Over all these home-based problems hovered the international intrigue of the Counter-Reformation, which sought to use his problems with the English to further its influence.

Desmond desperately needed a diversion to buy time and keep the English at bay. Granuaile was an ideal sop. Her illegal activities by land

and sea were, by then, well-documented. When the English came knocking at the gates of Askeaton, Desmond produced his prisoner as evidence of his loyalty to Elizabeth. The President of Munster, Lord Justice Drury, was suitably impressed and had 'this woman, who hath impudently passed the part of womanhood...a chief commander and director of thieves and murderers...' [18] transferred for safe-keeping to Dublin Castle. Granuaile, however, survived her long imprisonment and was set free early in 1579. She returned to Mayo to restrain her headstrong husband from plotting with Desmond, for whom Granuaile had little sympathy. She was, however, too late.

By that time Desmond had thrown down the gauntlet to the English. He asked Richard-an-Iarainn and the MacWilliam to raise Mayo in support. MacWilliam declined but Richard, with the aid of the Clandonnells, O'Malleys, Clangibbons and septs of the Bourkes and O'Flaherties, set to and plundered the countryside right up to the walls of Galway city. To prevent him from linking up with Desmond, the Governor of Connaught, Sir Nicholas Malby, aided by the MacWilliam, took to the field against him. Malby attacked Donamona Castle, held by forces loyal to Richard, and put all the defenders to the sword. Driving Richard before him, Malby reached Ballyknock Castle near Cathair-na-Mart. There, as he recorded, 'Granny ni Maille and certain of her kinsmen came to me.'[19] Malby pursued Richard relentlessly to the edge of the ocean where, on 17 February 1580, he reached Burrishoole and established a garrison. Richard, in the meantime, as Malby recounted, 'considering that the Clandonnells forsook him and that he was narrowly persecuted by me and my companies on all parts of the country, not being able to keep the field nor make other resistance, abandoned the country and fled into the islands with his Scots and some gentlemen of his retinue'[20]. Qwing to a sudden storm, Malby was unable to pursue the fugitive among the islands of Clew Bay.

It was a dangerous time for Tibbott, then a youth of eleven years. Still in fosterage at Castleleaffy, with both his father and foster-father involved in the rebellion, and with the English army having over-run his father's estate, his life was in jeopardy. Hostage-taking as a method of bringing recalcitrant and rebellious chiefs to heel in 16th-century Ireland was common practice. His mother's meeting at Ballyknock Castle with the English governor was a tactic to divert English attention and ensure his safety. Taking no chances with the life of her son, Granuaile firstly removed him from Burrishoole before embarking on her meeting with Malby. That his father, the all-powerful overlord of the area, had been forced to flee for his life before the English within his own territory, was a lesson not lost on his son.

Under pressure from his wife, anxious to expedite Malby's departure from Clew Bay, Richard duly made a token submission and was pardoned. But mindful of Richard's ill-conceived alliance with the Desmond cause, Malby did not withdraw entirely from Umhall. Much to Granuaile's consternation, he left behind a garrison to monitor both Richard's and Granuaile's activities by land and by sea. Granuaile also feared that her husband's dalliance with Desmond could impact negatively on his aspiration (and hers) to reach the pinnacle of political power by becoming the MacWilliam of Mayo. She had not long to wait to find out.

In November 1580, the reigning MacWilliam died. By right of Brehon law, Richard, as his elected *tánaist*, expected to assume the title. His succession, however, was disputed by MacWilliam's brother, his nearest surviving heir, by right of English primogeniture. English and Brehon law thus became locked in a head-to-head confrontation as both sides prepared to fight for their rights. Most of the Bourke septs in Mayo aligned with Richard, the candidate by right of Brehon law. Granuaile brought in the gallowglass from Scotland and Ulster to overawe their opponent and his English supporters. The ruse worked. The English had little option but to deal.

Malby set out from Galway, more to placate Richard and his formidable wife than to try and subdue them, which was in any event beyond his military capability. They had mustered a substantial army of 700 mercenaries, 300 kerne and 20 horsemen, in addition to Granuaile's fleet and crews, and far out-numbered Malby's own army. But Malby also feared the additional influence and power that the MacWilliamship would confer on Granuaile and Richard. The title still retained its original privileges, power and land and, in such unpredictable and disloyal hands, could become the source of opposition to the tenuous English administration in Connaught. But English policy in Ireland was based mainly on expediency. Granuaile and Richard's show of strength won them the day and the coveted MacWilliamship.

Among Tibbott's papers in Westport House is, perhaps, one of the most remarkable manuscripts of the Elizabethan period: the Letters Patent, together with Articles of Indenture, conferring the MacWilliamship, a Gaelic title outlawed by Elizabeth, on his father Richard-an-Iarainn. In her letter patent, dated 16 April 1581, written in Latin, the Queen conferred 'upon our beloved subject Richard Bourke, alias Richard Inyeren Bourke, alias MacWilliam Eoghtar Bourke, that he be chief of his clans and seneschal of the feudal tenants and followers of our people and nation of his own and of his own and their lands and tenements in our province of Connacht in Ireland.'[21] In return, Richard is required to protect the lands and subjects entrusted to him, partake in English legal customs and to fulfil the more specific obligations of the indentures. The indentures detail the exact duties required of Richard, whom they describe as having 'assumed the title and name of MacWilliam Eighter Burke in Eighter Connaght ... without permission from her Majestie'.[22] They bind him to ensure the introduction and practice of English law within his jurisdiction, to obey the Queen's representatives in the country and to pay 'each year 50 cows or fat martas [bullocks] or in place thereof 250 marks legal money of England at the Michaelmas term each year' as well as provide food and lodging for 200 soldiers for up to forty-two days each year as appears expedient'. He also agreed not to 'suffer any Scotts or other rebels or enemies of her Majestie or help in any way any prescribed or notorious malefactors within the limits of his authority and government'.

Two copies of each document were drawn up. The one given to

Richard is in the Westport House manuscript collection and, as was recorded, the second, 'in the possession of the Lord Deputy and the council, the aforesaid Richard has appended his seal and signature'.[23]

The Letters Patent and indentures are significant historical documents. They confer and authenticate by English law a title that is Gaelic in origin and in form, together with the privileges appertaining to the title by right of Brehon law. While the wording of the document reflects the feudal customs of its authors, Gaelic-sounding clauses like 'chief of his clan', 'seneschal ... of his own clan and of his own and their lands', 'that he may tax, exact and levy', 'that he shall ... have ... profits and commodities which he the said Richard has by right possession in the province of Connaught', testify to the Gaelic nature of the office being conferred. That the title had been abolished some years previously by the very power that now conferred it on Richard mattered little if, by this reversal, the Crown's interests in Connaught were enhanced and recipient's loyalty retained.

The MacWilliamship was well worth the effort that Tibbott's parents had expended in acquiring it. By right of his position as the MacWilliam, Richard acquired the extensive territories pertaining to the title, *viz* Ballinrobe Castle with 1,000 acres, Lough Mask Castle with 3,000 acres, Kinlough (near Shrule) with 2,500 acres, together with the demesne lands which were scattered over the baronies of Kilmaine, Carra and Tirawley. In addition, he received the traditional privileges and tributes, known as 'cuttings and spendings', due the MacWilliam from the lesser chieftains in Mayo and alluded to in the English indentures. In an attempt to de-gaelicise the title, Richard was knighted by the English Lord Deputy in September 1581. With the assistance of his formidable wife, Richard had achieved the improbable, succeeding to the MacWilliamship by right of both Gaelic tanistry and by English law.

By his father's accession to the MacWilliamship, Tibbott's own right as a future contender for the title by Gaelic law was enhanced. But English interference in the procedure governing the appointment to the office was a forewarning to him, and to others with similar aspirations, that right by Gaelic tanistry alone was no longer a guarantee of succession. Two methods now emerged by which a title such as the MacWilliamship could, in future, be secured. One was by a show of military strength, as demonstrated by his parents; the other by aligning with the power, native or foreign, which seemed most likely to emerge the eventual victor in the final confrontation between the two opposing systems.

On his accession to the MacWilliamship, Richard removed his household from Burrishoole inland to Lough Mask Castle, the principal seat of the MacWilliam. The castle was situated on the eastern shore of the lake. Tibbott, now thirteen years old, was placed in fosterage with a tributory chieftain, Myles MacEvilly, at Kinturk Castle, in the barony of Carra, an event that was to have amajor impact on his future prosperity.

The Barony of Carra was a well-defined territory from earliest times. After the 4th century, it was occupied by Hy Fiachrach clans. By the 13th century, it was held by the O'Connors, who were ejected by Richard de Burgo around 1236. Adam de Staunton, a Norman baron with lands in Moone, County Kildare and Lota, County Cork, had accompanied de Burgo to Mayo. In 1237, de Burgo subsequently granted him the cantred of Carra for his loyal service. While de Staunton did not actually reside on his new property, he built a castle, Castlecarra, to control the territory and installed a constable there. He re-granted sub-fiefs to his relations and to other Norman knights and founded a small town there. Only the name, Burriscarra, survives today.

When the chief lord of Carra, Adam de Staunton, died, he was succeeded by his son, Philip. Philip's son and heir, Adam, died in 1300 without a male heir and the Carra estate was divided between his five daughters. Eventually, however, the entire estate came to the eldest daughter, Nesta, who had married Fromand Le Brun. They assigned the chief fief to John Bermingham, the Earl of Louth, from whom it passed to Peter, Baron Trimbleston, the heir of Nesta and Le Brun. The

De Burgos themselves had also attained a footing in Carra around Bellabourke.

A minor branch of the de Stauntons, said to be descended from a Sir Bernard de Staunton, subsequently established themselves in Carra and built Kinturk Castle (their original fee) as well as Manulla and Kilboynell Castles. On the division of Connaught between the two MacWilliams in 1340, this branch later became gaelicised and changed its name to Mac-an-Mhilidh (the son of the knight), which in turn became anglicised as MacEvilly. Little is heard about the MacEvillys until 1574, when in the Division of Connaught, in the barony of Carra, Myles MacEvilly is listed as holding Kinturk, Castlecarra and Kilboynell Castles, while Walter MacEvilly is in possession of Manulla.

Tradition states that Tibbott's connection with the MacEvillys began when his mother, Granuaile, evicted Myles MacEvilly from Kinturk and exacted a yearly fine of 'a bag of meal, a fat pig and an ox' from each family in the district. However, in this instance, perhaps fact is stranger than fiction. Preserved among the manuscripts in Westport House is a deed dated 20 May 1582 and signed by 'Meyle McBreyone alias McEville chiefe of his name'. It confers on Richard-an-Iarainn, on behalf of his son Tibbott, the greater part of the MacEvilly inheritance in the barony of Carra. The deed states

> I (Myles) doe give graunt barggaine sell enfoeffe and confirme unto the said Sir Richrd Bourk alias McWilliam knight and his heires to the use and behoffe of my foster sonn Thibbott Bourk and the heires of his body lawfully begotten or to be begotten to the said Tybbott. The castle and Bawne and ten quarters of land to me belonginge of and in Kintourke, viz. the half towne of Kinturk Eighter and Kinturk Oughter, the four quarters of Ballycloy and the four quarters of Ballybonykone with the appurtenances. The castle Bawne and towne and eight quarters of land of Castlecarry and the four quarters of land of Ballykally. The castle towne and barbickan and foure quarters of lande of Moynulla … together with all the messuages buildings orchards gardynes moores meddowes feedinge pastures woodes and underwoods watter courses fishinges emollements and other heredi-ataments.

All this was conferred on Richard, in trust for Tibbott, 'for and in consideration of a certaine some of money … and also for other good causes and consideration … be the consent of my sones and cousins'.[24]

The 1582 deed, while not granting Tibbott immediate ownership of the MacEvilly properties, served as the foundation upon which Tibbott would later lay claim to the properties and lands listed in the deed from Myles's descendants. But the fact that the chieftain of the MacEvilly clan would consider endowing his ancestral inheritance, albeit in consideration of a 'some of money', to a foster son and with the expressed consent of his natural sons and heirs, seems extraordinary. While fosterage in Gaelic Ireland commanded extreme degrees of affinity, friendship and indebtedness, the voluntary conferring to an outsider of clan property is rare. The fear of being dispossessed by force, the need for protection from the English, or relief from monetary pressures, may have been contributory factors in this unique case.

Secure in his position as the MacWilliam, Richard continued his overlordship of Mayo according to his own rules, disregarding the conditions of the indentures he had made with Elizabeth I – except when they suited his own purposes. In 1582 he became embroiled in another dispute with the former contender to the title, Richard MacOliverus, who had refused to pay him rent. Whether from a sense of duty as befitted a recently knighted lord, or revenge on a former opponent, Richard 'entered their country and slew a son of Richard MacOliverus and the son of Edmond Bourke of Castle Barry and twenty more'.[25]

In 1583, however, both Richard and Granuaile were themselves reluctant to pay rent due to the Crown, as specified in the indentures, amounting to £600. They threatened Sir Theobald Dillon, who was sent to collect the arrears. Dillon complained to Court that 'they would have my lyfe for comying soo farr into their countrie and specialie his wife wold fyght with me before she was half a myle nier me'.[26]

Richard-an-Iarainn held office for less than three years and died at Easter 1583. The Four Masters record his death and describe him as 'a plundering, warlike, unquiet, rebellious man'.[27] His former opponent, Richard MacOliverus, succeeded to the title and was knighted in 1583. This succession was hotly disputed by Richard's sept, who contended that, by Gaelic law, the next MacWilliam should be chosen from among their members. Malby was forced to lead a large army and raid Umhall Uachtarach and Umhall Íochtarach. He 'took a countless number of cattle spoils ... and also burned and totally destroyed Cathair-na-Mart'[28] before opposition to the appointment abated. This quarrel between the sept of Ulick, to which Tibbott belonged, and the Bourkes of Erris, continued to the close of the century. Ten years later the dispute was to become embroiled in the wider conflict between the leaders of the Gaelic Confederacy and the English Crown and was to lead to fragmentation of loyalties among the various septs of the Mayo Bourkes.

At Richard's death, Tibbott, a young man of sixteen years, left behind the protection of fosterage and entered into his inheritance in Burrishoole. According to her own testimony, his mother 'gathered together all her own followers and with 1,000 head of cows and mares departed and became a dweller in Carrickahowley in Borosowle'.[29] This implies that Tibbott and his stepbrothers inherited Burrishoole and Ballyvechin Castles and that, before it could be withheld from her, Granuaile seized the smaller but strategic castle of Carrickahowley, in lieu of the 'thirds' or portion of her marriage dowry to Tibbott's father.

CHAPTER FOUR

Rebel in Arms
1583-1593

AFTER RICHARD-AN-IARAINN'S death and the instal-
lation of Richard MacOliverus as the MacWilliam, peace
descended on the region. John Browne of the Neale, the first
Englishman to settle in Mayo, was able to write in November 1583,
that 'Connaught standeth on good terms and the people live and keep
their goods in more safety and travel with less fear and in less danger
than in any other part of Ireland'.[1] But it was an uneasy peace in which
native and newcomer drew breath to take stock of the other.

In 1584, Sir John Perrot succeeded Lord Grey de Wilton as Lord
Deputy. On the death of Sir Nicholas Malby, Sir Richard Bingham was
appointed Governor of Connaught in his place. The arrival of these
two English administrators is an important milestone in the Tudor re-
conquest of Connaught. While diametrically opposed to each other,
both personally and politically, the policies they pursued – a policy of
conciliation by Perrot, a policy of the sword by Bingham – prepared
the way for the eventual reconquest of the province at the end of the
century.

The English had learned by experience in Munster the high price to
be paid for the subjugation of Gaelic power by force. The Desmond
rebellion had been ruthlessly crushed leaving, as the poet Spenser chron-
icled, 'a most populous and plentiful country suddenly void of man or
beast'. Gaelic resistance lay in shreds and the fertile lands of the province
lay unprotected and open to the hungry eyes of the English colonists

who, before the close of the century, would be its new owners. But the reduction of Munster had been accomplished at a considerable cost to the English state coffers. Elizabeth I did not want to repeat the same experience in Connaught and was not insensible to the advantages of inducing, rather than coercing, the Gaelic chieftains there to adopt English law and customs. Many of the Gaelic chieftains, themselves were growing weary of the desultory conflicts, both amongst one another and against the English. In order to establish legal claim to their possessions, many were prepared to forego their independence and seek title to their position and estates through the English law of primogeniture.

During 1584 and 1585, Perrot prepared to facilitate the chieftains who wished to secure English title to their lands, pay rent to the Crown and adopt English law, and to pressurise those who did not. A detailed survey of the lands of the province and their owners, which was to become known as the Composition of Connaught, was undertaken. The Composition was Perrot's attempt to subdue the province by a quasilegal and inexpensive method rather than initiate a prolonged and expensive military campaign. The Composition sought not only the continuance of Henry VIII's 'surrender and re-grant' policy, but also the extension of the Crown's jurisdiction into other aspects of native life hitherto governed by Gaelic laws. It provided for the abolition of the custom knows as 'cess', whereby the English administration in the province cessed or quartered troops on the chieftains. The 'cuttings and spendings' – the Gaelic custom by which the chieftains exacted payments and services and quartered themselves and their retinues on their client chieftains – was to be abolished. In its place, a rent of ten English shillings (or one Irish mark) was introduced upon every quarter (120 acres) of arable land. Certain lands were to be allowed rent-free to the principal lords and chieftains but their positions as overlords were to be abolished and each chieftain was to be responsible for his own sept only. The English law of primogeniture was to replace the native election and tanistry customs.

Generally the Composition proved beneficial to the majority of people in the province, particularly the tributary chiefs, relieved from the customary rights of their overlord. The Composition, however, heralded the death-knell for the Brehon code, its laws and customs rapidly becoming ineffective in the face of the incoming English legal system. Through the collection of the composition rents, the Gaelic chieftains, whether freely or forcibly, began to participate in English administrative practices. The introduction of the English legal system, with its sheriffs, courts and sessions, resulted in the gradual replacement of the old Brehon courts.

For the Bourkes of Mayo, the Composition effectively ended the MacWilliam title. While MacWilliams continued to be elected, contrary to the provisions of the Composition, by disaffected factions to the close of the century, the title would never again command the same power, privilege or allegiance it had in the past. To the holder of the office by English law, it should have brought security of title and tenure and the knowledge that the title would be inherited by primogeniture. To those denied access to the title by the Gaelic custom of election and tanistry, it would continue, for some time yet, to provide a focal point for rebellion against the new regime.

The Composition was signed on behalf of Tibbott and his stepbrother Edmund by Edmund Bourke of Castlebar, chief of the sept of Ulick and *tánaist* to the MacWilliam title. It was signed also by their uncle William Bourke of Belcarra, nicknamed the Blind Abbot and by their ally, O'Malley, chief of Umhall. It is open to question how familiar these chieftains were with the implications of the indentures they signed, and how sincere were their intentions were to abide by the provisions of the Composition. Writing in the 19th century, Sir Owen O'Malley stated that it was most likely that those who signed the Composition of Connaught would 'have done so without any intention of observing its terms further than was either unavoidable or beneficial to themselves, and that both they and their adherents and clansmen should not have abandoned in material respects the rights and obligations traditionally due from and to each other'.[2] What is clear from the contemporary documents relating to Tibbott Bourke is that the old Brehon code of clientship and dependency continued to co-exist with English practices into the early decades of the 17th century and that Tibbott took advantage of both.

The Composition resurrected the shadowy claim of the Earls of Ormond, which had originated in the Anglo-Norman conquest, to lands in Umhall Íochtarach in the Barony of Burrishoole, then held by Tibbott and his stepbrothers. These lands were denoted as 'Achill, consisting of 4 quarters, Tiranoir (Tír-an-Áir) and Burishowle, consisting of 12 quarters. Also Ballyvighan (Newport) consisting of 6 quarters whereof belongeth to the Archbishopric of Tuam, 2 quaraters.'[3] If successful, the claim would reduce Tibbott and his family to the position of mere tenants. The Composition, however, was destined to never be fully ratified but nonetheless its provisions were later to affect Tibbott in a way that he, perhaps, never imagined.

Tibbott was taken hostage during the summer of 1584 by the new governor, Sir Richard Bingham, as a deterrent to his mother and stepbrothers from rebelling against the provisions of the Composition. Since her husband's death, contrary to her claim of 'leading a poor farmer's life' Granuaile was actively operating her fleet of galleys on missions of both trade and piracy along the coastline, undaunted by the increasing presence of the English administration. In an effort to limit her activities and influence, Bingham considered that the confinement of her son might be the best method to contain the mother. Tibbott, a youth of seventeen years, was taken by George Bingham, the governor's brother and sheriff of County Sligo, to reside under constraint at Ballymote Castle.

Sir George Bingham was a son of Robert Bingham of Melcombe Bingham, Dorset in England. He had married Cicely Martin of Dorset in 1569 and, at the time of his appointment to Sligo, they had two sons, Henry and John, about the same age as Tibbott. That Tibbott was treated well in the Bingham household is not unlikely. It was expressed English policy at the time that the sons of the Gaelic nobility taken as hostage and placed in the homes of high-ranking English officials should be well cared for. Furthermore, it was the expressed wish of the Queen that they were to be educated and dressed according to English custom.

During his time as a hostage, Tibbott learned to read and write English – a fact referred to by Sir Richard Bingham, who reported to the English court that 'he [Tibbott] both speakith and writith English being brought up a while in my brother George's howse'[4] and particularly commented upon later by Queen Elizabeth. His knowledge of English is also evident from his own letters and despatches, which are preserved in the Elizabethan State Papers. While his confinement as a hostage was undoubtedly difficult, it also had its advantages. Being conversant in English stood Tibbott in good stead later when faced with the challenges posed as the old Gaelic customs were replaced by the English legal system. To be able to communicate, understand and negotiate within the new political and legal framework gave him many benefits over his neighbours, of which he took full advantage.

It was during his confinement in the Bingham household that Tibbott met and married Maeve O'Connor Sligo, niece of Sir Donal O'Connor Sligo, chieftain of Carbury. There is no definitive evidence to show whether this was an arranged match, as was the custom among the Gaelic aristocracy, or whether love determined the marriage. That it was a match arranged in the usual way by the parents or guardians of the couple is unlikely, given the circumstances of Tibbott's confinement. The arrangement was most likely made by George Bingham, who may have considered that a match involving the then loyal house of O'Connor Sligo and a scion of the rebellious Mayo Bourkes might have the desired effect and maintain Tibbott in loyalty after his release. Whatever the circumstances, Tibbott's marriage to Maeve O'Connor Sligo endured and survived many personal and political tribulations in the succeeding decades until his death.

In the summer of 1585, Bingham held the first sessions in County Mayo at the castle of Donamona, near Castlebar, and subsequently commenced a campaign of retaliation against all absenting clans, especially against the Bourkes of Carra. They refused to conform to the Composition, because its provisions meant a loss of position and supremacy over their tributary septs. While Perrot may have been the architect of the Composition, the more difficult task of its actual implementation was left to Bingham.

History has tended to depict Sir Richard Bingham as a villain, the 'Flail of Connaught', executioner of innocent children, the epitome of cruelty. The methods he employed to subdue the Connaught clans, especially Tibbott and his extended family, tend to concur with this picture. Execution by martial law, even of the very young and the elderly, torture, scorched-earth warfare and hostage-taking, as in Tibbott's case, are attributed to Bingham's personal cruelty and depravity. In reality they were long-established tools of conquest, and Bingham carried out his orders to the letter. Bingham was the wrong man in the wrong place at the wrong time. While a proven military campaigner, his singular failing was his inflexibility and his inability to adapt his orders to the reality of Gaelic Ireland. His rigid adherence to orders extended to his thoroughness as an administrator and his relative honesty in his office (at a time when fiscal abuses by English administrators abounded in the Irish service) ensured the ill will of his fellow administrators. Tibbott's mother, Granuaile, was to take full advantage of this situation.

To demonstrate their objection to both Bingham's style of governorship as well as to the Composition, the Bourkes fortified themselves in Hag's Castle in Lough Mask. They were besieged by Bingham, who was forced to abandon the siege owing to a 'sodayne rysinge of wind and fowle weather'. The Bourkes escaped and fled into the cover of the nearby Partry mountains. The revolt of the Bourkes appeared to be of little significance, their seizure of Hag's Castle no more than an isolated incident until late 1586, on the death of the MacWilliam. Their actions suddenly assumed a wider political importance when their chief, Edmund of Castle Barry, lay claim to the MacWilliamship by right of Gaelic law. Described by one English official as 'a most badd member of the state and his wife as badd as himself', Edmund was an old man of some eighty years. Despite his age, he considered the MacWilliamship to be the Holy Grail and there was much status and wealth at stake. Too old to lead the campaign, his cause was pursued on his behalf by his sons.

In June 1586 the Lord Deputy decided that the bulk of the MacWilliam lands and property was to be given, by right of primogeniture, to the late MacWilliam's son, William Bourke, while Edmund, the successor by native law, was to receive a small portion only. The decision provoked anger among the septs of the Bourkes who maintained that William 'was young and had no claim to a preference'.[5] The English, however, considered him to be more pliable to their policies in Mayo. The Bourkes' anger gave vent to outright rebellion. They were joined by their traditional allies – the O'Malleys, the Joyces, Clan Gibbons, Clan Philpin and many of the Clandonnells. Richard Bourke of Corraun, known as the Devil's Hook, who was married to Tibbott's half-sister, Margaret O'Flaherty, sailed north to Ulster to recruit additional gallowglass.

Tibbott was released from the custody of George Bingham in early 1587. Though indoctrinated in English manners and customs during his confinement, he promptly reverted to type on his release and together with his sept and his stepbrother Edmund Bourke, joined the rebellion. He was subsequently referred to by Bingham in a letter to the Queen's private secretary, Walsingham, as one of the 'chief rebels in Connaught'.

In July Sir Richard Bingham assembled a large force at Ballinrobe to confront the Bourkes who immediately sued for a truce. The Protestant Archbishop of Tuam and the Earl of Clanrickard delivered the Governor's terms to the Bourkes, who rejected them, insisting on the inauguration of Edmund Bourke as the new MacWilliam. In response, Bingham ordered that the hostages who had been given as pledges by the Bourke leaders were to be hanged. The hostages, some mere boys – among them Tibbott's first cousin, Ulick, the son of William Bourke, the Blind Abbot – were then in the custody of the sheriff, John Browne.

Subsequently, Bingham captured and imprisoned Moyler and Tibbott Reagh Bourke, also first cousins of Tibbott, in Roscommon Castle, on suspicion that 'they practiced to draw in Scotts'. Later, Bingham had them hanged by martial law on the grounds 'that they practiced by their letters out of prison ... to cause theire friends to rebel in hope thereby to ensure their libertie'.[6] According to Bingham's later testimony, another hostage, Richard Roe Bourke, was 'well and worthelie executed likewise for he pretending to do service laide plot indeed to bring in Scotts and cause a general rebellion in that county [Mayo] having manned his castle for the same purpose'.[7] Bingham now moved against the Bourke leaders and captured their castles at Newbrook and Togher, and at the end of July, the strategic castle of Donamona. The Bourke confederacy fell into disarray and by August they submitted. Notwithstanding the submission, Bingham seized the aged Edmund of Castle Barry, the contender for the MacWilliamship, and hanged him on a charge of treason. Since his conviction was by the common law of England, Bingham deemed that his estates were thereby forfeit to the Crown. They were subsequently granted to Bingham's relations.

Tibbott's mother did not escape Bingham's fury. Bingham's brother, Captain John Bingham, entered Granuaile's territory in search of booty, particularly cattle, a commodity with which she was well-endowed at the time. Aware of Granuaile's reputation and that she was considered by successive administrations as being 'nurse to all the rebellions in Connaught for 40 years', Bingham captured and arrested her. Granuaile later testified that 'she was apprehended and tied with a rope, both she and her followers at that instant were spoiled of their said cattle and of all that ever they had besides the same, and brought to Sir Richard, who caused a new pair of gallows to be made for her last funeral where she thought to end her days and she was let at liberty upon the hostage of one Richard Burke otherwise called the Devil's Hook'.[8]

Captain Bingham next moved against Tibbott's half-brother, Owen O'Flaherty, Granuaile's eldest son by her first marriage. Although married to Katherine Bourke, daughter of Edmund of Castle Barry, Owen had not participated in the recent rebellion. Booty appeared to be the motivation for Bingham's incursion into O'Flaherty's territory of Iar-Chonnacht. Owen was duly arrested, his cattle and horse herds confiscated and, while in the custody of Bingham, he was stabbed to death.

Shortly after her son's murder, in fear for her own life, Granuaile fled north with her galleys to seek protection from O'Neill and O'Donnell in Ulster, where English power had yet to become established. However, the fact that her galleys were damaged by a storm on their way north and a force of a thousand gallowglass crossed by foot from Ulster into Mayo shortly after her departure, gives some credence to Bingham's accusation that her journey to Ulster was for reasons other than to seek protection. After weeks of skirmishing, Bingham finally routed the gallowglass across the River Moy at Ardnaree. Peace finally descended on Connaught and, to the relief of the Bourkes, Bingham was transferred for military service to Flanders. His brother, George, Tibbott's former custodian, was appointed deputy governor in his place.

In May 1587, Granuaile journeyed to Dublin where she obtained a meeting with Bingham's implacable enemy, the Lord Deputy, Sir John Perrot. She sought and was granted the queen's pardon for herself, Tibbott, her daughter, Margaret O'Flaherty and for her surviving son by her first marriage, Murrough O'Flaherty of Bunowen. As Tibbott's wily mother had surmised, Perrot proved more than receptive to her case and to her complaints against Bingham. Perrot often tended to find common cause with the Gaelic lords and chieftains more than with his fellow-administrators, especially Sir Richard Bingham. He frequently petitioned the Queen to be relieved of his duties in Ireland on the grounds that 'the perverseness of her subjects in Ireland of the English race had rendered intolerable. I can please your Majesty's Irish subjects better than the English'[9] – as he did on this occasion with Granuaile, one of Bingham's most determined opponents. Shortly after this event, Perrot was recalled to England.

In September 1588 the 'invincible' Spanish Armada, limping home-wards after its ill-fated attempt to invade England, was driven by cross currents and fierce winds along the west coast of Ireland. An estimated twenty-six ships crashed onto the Irish coastline and were wrecked on the rocky headlands. A mixed fate awaited the Spanish survivors who managed to clamber ashore.

Exaggerated reports had reached the English administration in Dublin of great contingents of Spanish soldiers holed-up in coastal areas of the west of Ireland. Fearful that the Spanish castaways would make common cause with the local chieftains, Sir William Fitzwilliam, the newly-appointed lord deputy, issued a proclamation making it a crime, punishable by death and confiscation of property, to harbour or aid the Spanish. The Spanish wrecks were also rumoured to contain untold treasure, the possession of which appealed alike to both Irish chief and English administrator.

Sir Richard Bingham was hurriedly returned as Governor of Connaught and took immediate action. He ordered his captains in the field to dislodge and kill the Spanish survivors to deter any collusion between them and the Irish. Some five ships were wrecked on Mayo's jagged coastline, two of which foundered in Clew Bay. The Spanish survivors received a mixed reception. It was reported to London that the O'Malleys on Clare Island had killed one hundred survivors from the wreck of the converted merchantman *El Gran Grin*. There is, however, no local tradition of such a massacre taking place on the island and official reports must be viewed in the context of exaggerated claims made by English officials and soldiers anxious to curry favour with their superiors. In addition, three officers from the *El Gran Grin* were later listed as being in Bingham's custody in Galway. That some survivors received succour from Tibbott and his O'Malley and Bourke relations along the coasts of Clew Bay and north Mayo is more certain. The harbouring by Tibbott and his relations of the Spanish castaways, combined with the animosity that arose between the sheriff of Mayo, John Browne and the Bourkes, sparked the next rebellion in 1589.

In January 1589 Bingham commissioned John Browne to raise levies and to prosecute the Bourkes and their confederates. The commission subsequently became the centre of a series of charges brought against Bingham by the Bourkes later that year. The English Lord Deputy, Sir William Fitzwilliam, as well as the Bourkes, blamed the revolt in Mayo 'on the bloody and wicked commission to Browne'.[10] The legality of the commission was certainly questionable since it bore only one authorising signature, that of Bingham, instead of the two legally required. Bingham's answer was that the only English councillor resident in Connaught at the time was Justice Dillon, who, through illness, was unable to sign the commission documents. Bingham also contended that the commission was valid because of the power vested in him in wartime, which permitted him to grant extraordinary commissions when the occasion demanded.

On the strength of the commission, the sheriff, John Browne, entered Tibbott's territory on 7 February and reached Carrickahowley Castle with an army of 250 soldiers. The Bourkes blocked his advance and ordered him off their lands. But Browne persisted and foolhardily sent the main body of his troops onwards into Erris. He and a smaller escort of twenty-five soldiers were subsequently attacked and slain by the Devil's Hook. Browne's implication in the murder of the Bourke hostages in his custody was undoubtedly an added spur to the attack.

The killing of the sheriff heralded the start of a wider rebellion in Mayo. The Bourkes maintained that they had been forced to rebel owing to the excesses of Bingham's government in Connaught 'and excuse themselves of everything laid to their charge before the tyme and instant of their killing of John Browne'.[11] Moreover, they claimed that John Browne was killed because he 'took 30 cows or thereabouts from Walter McEdmund Bourke of Castlebar and did after the taking thereof so vehemently persecute the sd Walter and 4 of his brethren that he made forsake the realm and as yet it is not known where they are'.[12] Bingham, on the other hand, claimed that the real cause of the rebellion was that the shipwrecked 'Spaniards had as intention to remayne in the county of Mayo and that the inhabitants of the same were agreed to join with them'[13] and, by these actions, he maintained, they had broken any previous protection given to them.

The Browne incident was the signal for those chiefs who had previously stood aloof to join the rebellion. The Blind Abbot, the Bourkes of Tirawley, the Clangibbons and the Clandonnells combined with other septs already in action. Sir Mourrough-ne-Doe O'Flaherty, once an upholder of the Crown in Iar-Chonnacht, crossed Lough Corrib with 500 men and joined the Bourkes, despite the fact that his son was a hostage and was subsequently executed by Bingham. The combined force plundered Kilmaine and Claremorris taking substantial booty.

The English administration in Dublin grew alarmed as the rebellion continued to spread. Garrett Comerford was sent by the Lord

Deputy to initiate a cessation and to work out a peace formula. Sir Murrough-ne-Doe and the Blind Abbot met with Comerford. They blamed the uprising on the cruel and corrupt dealings of English officials in Connaught. However, any peace formula would, they maintained, have a price. The price was the reinstating of the MacWilliamship, this time with, Tibbotts uncle, the Blind Abbot, as the nominated candidate. Comerford insisted that the title had been abolished by English law and would not be revived by the Crown, whereupon the confederates left the conference, vowing that there would be no peace without a MacWilliam. Comerford reported back to his superiors that 'these people will never be obedient subjects until they be cut off. For daily they are making of Gallowglass axes and other weapons and yet have they great store of shot and powder and munition of the Spaniards and are rich by their means.'[14]

In active rebellion with his kinsmen, Tibbott was named as one of the principal rebel leaders by Bingham in his despatches to England. He had settled in his father's castle of Burrishoole with his wife and two sons – Myles, named after his munificent foster-father, Myles MacEvilly, and Theobald, a traditional Bourke name. Nearby, in Carraigahowley, his mother, Granuaile, despite her advancing years, continued at every opportunity to thwart her avowed enemy Bingham by land and sea.

In a poem by the 16th-century poet, Mathgamhain Ó hUiginn, preserved in the Royal Irish Academy, Tibbott is referred to as a brave warrior as well as something of a ladies' man. Describing him as ruddy-faced and fair-haired, Ó hUiginn lauds the attributes of the twenty-year-old chieftain:

> Tiboid a burc of the valiant feats
> Of the hawklike blue eye
> He is the warrior whose curving neck
> With ringleted golden-yellow hair
> Is secretly loved by girls in every region.

While the famous poet, Eochaidh Ó hEoghusa, praises his military prowess and bravery in the lines:

> Tiboid, Tower of Achill
> Salmon of Clar Gara
> Emulator of the African lion.

Tibbott would need to possess all the above-mentioned attributes and more if he were to realise his ambition to succeed his father as the MacWilliam. By 1589 only one avenue presented itself: to resist the power that sought to abolish the title and the political and social structures that supported it – to rebel against English expansionism in Connaught. By actively partaking in the rebellion, Tibbott was also giving notice, in the age-old custom of his ancestors, of his prowess as a future contender. If, however, an alternative way to the title and, more pertinently, to the prestige and wealth it represented, presented itself in the future, such an option could not be ignored by a contender as ambitious as Tibbott.

Alarmed at the ever-widening Bourke confederacy, the English Council in Dublin ordered Bingham to desist from further confrontation. By April a tentative truce was concluded and negotiations opened between both sides at Newcastle, County Galway, the Bourkes having refused to enter Galway city. In addition to their demands for the restoration of the MacWilliam title, the Bourkes now added another – the removal of Richard Bingham as Governor of Connaught. They were supported in this by a conspiracy among Bingham's own colleagues in Dublin to have him removed from office. The Bourkes knew that they were negotiating from a position of strength and extended their rebellion into Roscommon and Sligo.

Alarmed at the deteriorating situation and the increasing cost to the state coffers, the Queen ordered Fitzwilliam to adopt a more temperate course with the rebels in an attempt to woo them to peace. The

Lord Deputy reached Athlone on 7 June. Fitzwilliam, whose dislike of Bingham was matched only by the Bourkes, ordered the governor to remain in Athlone and forbade Bingham to accompany him into Connaught, on the pretext that Bingham's very presence in Mayo would incite the Bourkes further. However, Sir Nicholas White, the master of rolls, who seemed to have acted impartially during the many conspiracies directed against Bingham, was of the opinion that the rebellion would be long over if Bingham had not been hamstrung by the jealousy and ill will of his fellow administrators, and if he had been given a freer rein against the Bourkes.

Fitzwilliam subsequently travelled to Galway and obtained a cessation and even a submission – albeit a token one – from some of the rebel leaders at a meeting in St. Nicholas's Cathedral. On 12 June, the Bourkes submitted a 'Book of Complaints' against Bingham. After a few months' delay, the complaints were eventually examined by the Council in Dublin on 8 November 1589.

Many charges were brought against Bingham, including breaches of the Composition, quartering his soldiers and servants on the people, encroachment by his officials on the lands and livings of the chieftains, and the seizing of cattle by officials in Bingham's administration. Specific charges of murder and cruelty were cited against him personally. These included the executions of Tibbott's cousins, Richard Óg Bourke, Moyler and Tibbott, the sons of Walter Fada; the hanging of the old chieftain, Edmund Bourke of Castle Barry; and the execution of the hostages, Ulick Bourke, son of the Blind Abbot, Richard Bourke, son of Shane McMoyler, and William Bourke, son of Moyler Oge. The Bourkes further accused Bingham of oppression, extortion and imprisonment while they were under protection. Notwithstanding these alleged cruelties and injustices perpetrated by Bingham, the Bourkes maintained that they would have desisted from rebellion but for the commission given by Bingham to John Browne 'to prosecute them with fire and sword while they were in Her Majesty's protection'.[15]

Bingham denied the allegations, insisting that he had never broken the Composition and that it was Sir John Perrot and, more recently, Sir William Fitzwilliam, who had levied cattle off the people without payment on their respective journeys through Connaught. Bingham claimed that when he required provisions for his troops and household he paid for them, sometimes in cash but more frequently by redeemable bills payable out of Crown revenues. However, since these bills were redeemable only on application to Bingham, it is likely that many of the chieftains may have preferred to forego payment altogether rather than present themselves before the much-feared Governor and risk imprisonment.

Regarding the execution of the Bourke hostages, Bingham justified it on the grounds that, all were 'by ordinaire triall and course of law condemned and accordingly executed'[16] for their rebellious actions and for hiring Scots mercenaries. He justified his commission to John Browne on the basis that 'Browne had his direction to prosequete those who were in action' and that Bingham 'hath all the process of matter yet to show sufficient enough to justifie what was don'.[17] He also maintained that he had commissioned John Browne against the Bourkes on the grounds that by harbouring Spanish soldiers, survivors of the Armada, they had automatically breached any former protection granted to them by the Crown.

No witness appeared before the Council to substantiate the Bourkes' claim, either through fear or lack of evidence. Bingham's own witnesses were examined in November and on 4 December he was formally acquitted, ordered back to Connaught but forbidden to actively oppose the Bourkes. The articles of the Bourkes' submission were appropriately contrite in tone and even contained a promise that they would 'forthwith deliver to the Lord Deputy such Spaniards, Portugalls and other foreigners of the Spanish fleet as are now amongst them'.[18] But their submission was no more than a ploy. No hostages were given by the rebel leaders. On the other hand, the Bourkes prevailed on the Lord Deputy to withdraw all English troops from their territories and to curtail the activities of Bingham, whom they acknowledged as their greatest threat. The English were in no position to argue.

While the clan elders haggled with FitzWilliam in Galway, Tibbott sailed to Scotland with his mother's fleet to hire additional mercenaries. He arrived back with five hundred gallowglass. Bingham reported him to the Privy Council in England: '7 gallies bee arrived in Erris with Scottes ... having for their guyde and conductor, one of Grany O'Malleys sons ...'[19] Suitably reinforced, all the septs of the Bourkes of Mayo gathered at the traditional inaugural site near Kilmaine, where they elected Tibbott's uncle, the Blind Abbot, as the MacWilliam. They then recaptured the Lough Mask Castle, the principal residence of the MacWilliam, and plundered the countryside from the Neale to Shrule.

The Queen ordered FitzWilliam to determine whether or not Bingham was guilty of the charges brought against him both by the Bourkes and by his own colleagues. After a further investigation, he was cleared of all charges. In January 1590 he was given free rein to prosecute the Bourkes as he thought fit and he set to with determination.

Aided by the earls of Clanrickard and Thomond, Bingham advanced into Mayo with 809 foot soldiers and 228 kerne. The Bourke forces were reckoned at 1,000. From Castle Barry he marched through the mountain pass of Barnagee into Tirawley, a remarkable feat of endurance given the terrain and the time of year. Passing through the mountain fastness and marshlands, Bingham's forces were shadowed by a party of horsemen led by the Blind Abbot, Tibbott and his half-brother, Edmund Bourke. The Bourkes made a sudden attack on a section of the Earl of Thomond's forces. In the ensuing skirmish the Blind Abbot's foot was cut off from the ankle. The Bourkes withdrew and ferried their injured leader across Lough Conn to a small island where his foot was amputated, thereby ending his hopes of retaining the MacWilliamship. Gaelic law, as Bingham later related to Walsingham, 'reckon him now as a dead man'.

With the pivotal figure in the rebellion removed, the Bourke confederacy slowly began to disintegrate. Bingham pressed home his advantage. He harried the Bourke forces, which in turn burned their houses and crops as they fled before him. Bingham pursued them relentlessly, gathering any livestock left behind, and by the time he reached Erris, had amassed a herd of 2,000 cattle. He then divided his forces and plundered south and north of Erris. The opposition crumbled. The Clandonnells, the standing army of the Bourkes, were the first to submit and were quickly followed by the leaders of the other allied septs. On 22 February 1590, Edmund Bourke sent messengers to sue for peace on behalf of himself and his sept. By March, the rebellion had been quelled. The Bourkes paid over the Composition rent, while Bingham rebuilt the English garrisons at Cong, Kilmaine and Ballinaloob.

With the removal of the Blind Abbot as leader of the Mayo Bourkes and the deaths of Walter ne Mully and Walter Kittagh, chief of the Tirawley Bourkes, during 1591, Edmund and Tibbott emerged as senior chiefs in the Bourke hierarchy. While the MacWilliam title may have been proscribed by the Crown, the duration of its proscription was dependent on the strength of the English administration in Connaught to enforce it. No definite pattern had yet been defined in the struggle between the Gaelic and English worlds in Connaught and the ultimate outcome of the struggle was still far from certain. Even with Bingham triumphant in his latest victory, further unrest was already brewing.

In spring 1592, Tibbott and Edmund were approached by Bishops Hely and O'Boyle to raise Mayo against the English as a decoy for the start of a wider rebellion. This time, the young chieftain of Tirconaill, Hugh O'Donnell, lately escaped from captivity in Dublin Castle, held out the promise of Spanish aid.

Tibbott, however, reacted cautiously. Cut off as he was from the eastern and southern septs of the Bourkes by the strong English garrison at Castle Barry, co-ordinated action was rendered more difficult than in previous times. However, on the request of the Clandonnells to rescue one of their leaders imprisoned in Cloonagashel Castle by Bingham, Tibbott and Edmund, on the pretext of a rescue mission, initiated a rising in support of O'Donnell and his foreign allies. At midnight on 30 June, as Bingham reported, 'Tibbott Ne Long, with the Burkes and Clandonnells, gave an attempt to Cloniscashell, thinking to have surprised the Governor and Council holding a session there'.[20] The garrison repulsed the attack. The Spanish aid promised did not materialise. Tibbott held out against Bingham until he heard that

O'Donnell himself had submitted. Left high and dry by the Ulster chieftain, there was little else he could do.

In retaliation, Bingham entered Tibbott's territory of Burrishoole and English warships penetrated Clew Bay for the first time, much to Granuaile's fury. Further resistance was futile and at Aghagower, as Bingham reported, 'Tibbott Burke Mac Richard-an-Iarainn came into us and agreed into 'all things for the Bourkes, O'Malleys and Clangibbons to be received into her Majesty's mercy and protection laying on his foster-father Edmund MacTibbott and one Tibbott MacGibbon to remain as pledges, till the other pledges for several septs should be brought in and the other conditions be performed.'[21] It is apparent from Bingham's statement that Tibbott had now emerged as the principal chieftain in the area. In an attempt to lessen Tibbott's influence over the other clans and septs on whose behalf he negotiated, Bingham ordered that each clan leader would in future be responsible for his own conduct and submit individual hostages. Bingham further fined Tibbott the sum of 1,500 mark to pay for the cost of quelling the revolt. Triumphantly Bingham recorded how Tibbott and his half-brother Edmund were now 'men of no possession or to have of any goods so much as half a dozen cows apiece'.[22] Bingham's conditions were presented to Tibbott and Edmund at Cathair-na-Mart in September and, after due consideration, were accepted and signed by them at Aghagower later that month. Official pardons were subsequently issued to them and their confederates in March.

Bingham's actions sought to eliminate the influence Tibbott enjoyed by right of the Gaelic custom of *célsine* over various Bourke septs and neighbouring clans. As an ambitious chieftain, with a hunger for power, Tibbott would continue to resist Bingham's designs. Initially he met with little success, until the changing political situation showed him that his path to power could well be to ally with the enemy that now sought to eliminate him.

CHAPTER FIVE

The Hare and the Hounds
1593-1597

R ESTRICTED BY THE CONDITIONS of his deal with
Bingham and impoverished by the recent rebellions, Tibbott
had no alternative but to play a waiting game. There was little
he could do personally to affect any improvement in his reduced circumstances. Like the myriad of his fellow chieftains elsewhere in the
country, his future depended on the actions and aspirations of others
more powerful than himself. His survival depended on what he had to
offer the opposing factions in terms of local influence and military
power and how much leverage such advantages afforded him to enable
him to secure the best deal for himself. There was little room for anything more idealistic. By 1593, survival had become the single motivation in Gaelic Ireland.

Hugh O'Donnell convened a confederation of northern chiefs in May.
The confederation sent an envoy was sent by the confederation to the
court of King Philip of Spain to determine the role Gaelic Ireland
might play in the conflict between England and Spain. In Ulster, the
English-educated Hugh O'Neill, 2nd Earl of Tyrone, also played a
waiting game. For the present, a display of loyalty to the English
Crown was his preferred option. Yet rumours of intrigue between him
and O'Donnell had reached the English court and cast doubt on his

frequent protestations of loyalty. For O'Neill in Ulster, as for Tibbott Bourke in Mayo, personal advancement was the motivation and the way to achieving it was still far from clear.

During 1593 the build-up of Gaelic resentment in Ulster against increasing English incursions into the province gradually intensified. The massacre of the Scots on Rathlin Island, the slaying of Brian MacPhelim of Clandeboy, the kidnapping of Hugh O'Donnell and his incarceration in Dublin Castle, and the execution of MacMahon and Brian O'Rourke fuelled resentment and resistance. The colonisation of Munster and Bingham's more recent subjugation of Connaught were ample proof, if proof was needed, as to the outcome for Ulster should the English overrun it. The opening salvo in the confrontation was fired when Hugh Maguire, chief of Fermanagh and son-in-law of the Earl of Tyrone, to protect his territory from an attempted English incursion. Assistance was forthcoming, openly from O'Donnell and covertly from the Earl of Tyrone, and so the seeds that would grow into a long and bitter war for control of Ulster were planted.

With the rest of the country Mayo waited for the storm to break. As well as subduing the Bourkes, Bingham had struck hard at the way of life of other clans such as the O'Malleys and O'Flaherties. By penetrating their hitherto impregnable sea domain, he had effectively reduced the independence and power that their maritime capabilities had given them. The seaside and island fortresses of O'Malley and O'Flaherty chieftains, for centuries protected by a screen of sea, island and a treacherous coastline, now lay exposed. The Mayo countryside had been reduced to a blackened heath, denuded of produce. Powerless and dispirited, the surviving chieftains hardly knew which way to turn for salvation from their terrible predicament.

For the first time an option in the form of a Gaelic confederacy emerged as a possible way of restoring their status. Reduced in circumstances and rendered virtually powerless in Mayo, Tibbott had learned the bitter lesson that opposition by individual clans was a wasteful and useless exercise. However, an alliance with a greater power, a confederacy of more powerful chiefs, was one way he might recoup his losses, the limit to which his aspiration extended at this time.

Tibbott initially contacted Brian Oge O'Rourke, chief of Breifne and ally of O'Donnell, by letter, written in Irish. He proposed that if O'Rourke would 'raise stirres in the Breny [Brefny] and to hold out but two monthes, that he would undertake that the banished Rebels, the Devil's Hook and the rest should returne to Mayo againe and with his help make warres there'.[1] He also promised to raise 1,500 Scots and that, together with the forces of the Earl of Tyrone, O'Connell, Maguire and O'Rourke, they could become such a formidable force 'that there is no Irish lord in Ireland but will join with them and take their parts'.[2]

The letter was intercepted by George Bingham, who forwarded it to his brother. The Governor seized Tibbott and imprisoned him in Athlone Castle. Despite insufficient evidence to bring him to trial, Bingham was determined that, having procured Tibbott's imprisonment, he should remain behind bars on the premise that, as he wrote, he 'could do no less than restrayne him of libertye, not hastening him to any tryall unless further matter had appeared then yet is known to me and nevertheless I hold him hereby touched in the highest degree'.[3]

Tibbott was confined in Athlone Castle, the principal fortress of the English military presence in Connaught and much favoured by Sir Richard Bingham as his operational headquarters. He faced the charge of treason, which carried the sentence of death by hanging. Confined in a dank cell, he suffered deprivation and torture as his gaolers sought to extract a confession and information on the activities and plans of his fellow conspirators. Tibbott later wrote of the treatment he had endured during his imprisonment, stating that 'he could not stand upon his legges through that durance and misery he suffered there'.[4]

The gallows would most probably have been his end if his indomitable mother had not decided on a remarkable course of action. Bingham's latest move against her son, and the imprisonment of her stepbrother, Donal-na-Píopa O'Malley, on suspicion of murder, together with the treatment she and her extended family had been subjected to by Bingham, determined Granuaile to place her case personally before the Queen of England. She sailed to London and, through the influence of Thomas, Earl of Ormond, was granted an audience with the Queen at the beginning of September 1593. Granuaile succeeded admirably in her quest. Despite Bingham's protests, she obtained the release of her son and stepbrother and also extracted the Queen's blessing to return to her former lifestyle of 'maintenance by land and sea', much to Bingham's fury. On her return to Connaught, Granuaile confronted Bingham with the Queen's letter. Reluctantly he released Tibbott from Athlone Castle in November.

An incident occurred on Tibbott's release that was to shape Tibbott's future political direction. Richard Bourke, the Devil's Hook's son, who had been in action with Maguire against the English in Ulster, returned to Mayo. Hugh O'Donnell sent him with 300 followers to plunder north Mayo as a decoy to divert Bingham, who on his way to attack Maguire in Fermanagh. Bingham despatched a force from his main army against Richard and killed sixty of his followers. Richard not only suffered Bingham's vengeance but was also attacked by the Bourkes of Tirawley, who objected to their lands and livestock being exploited and sacrificed in support of O'Donnell's strategies in Ulster. Aided by the Bourkes of Erris, Richard was forced to seek sanctuary on the lonely island of Iniskea. Bingham's troops followed him there and after a bloody battle forced Richard and a few of his followers to flee by boat to Ulster.

Bingham forced Tibbott and Granuaile to participate in the incident, albeit against their own kinsmen. As Granuaile would later complain to Court, on Tibbott's release from custody in Athlone, contrary to the provisions of the Composition and the provisions of the Queen's letter, Bingham forced 'her sons, coisens and followers of the Mailles with a number of galleys ... fournished with menn and victuelles at their own charges, accompanied with Capten Strittes and his band of soldiers to repair to the sease, where in certainie Illandes eighteen of the chiefest of the Bourkes ... being proclaimed traitors',[5] were defeated.

This was the start of the divide and rule policy that the English ruthlessly pursued in Ireland to the close of the century. The previous Bourke rebellions had witnessed the various Bourke septs allied in opposition to the English. Now, with the undermining of Gaelic law, especially in regard to rights of succession and land tenure and its substitution by English law, Gaelic opposition became fragmented in Mayo as elsewhere. Each sept of each clan, each leader of each sept, with aspirations to power, whether lawfully or unlawfully held, sought to further his ambition by whatever system, English or Gaelic, that seemed most likely to fulfil his ambition. Added to this, the economic state of Mayo was only slowly recovering from the effects of the previous rebellion. Provision of the basic necessities of life, food and shelter, hung by a thread. The plunder of lands, already depleted of cattle and crops, was bound to be violently resisted at local level, regardless of whomsoever or whatever cause the plunderers served.

Richard Bourke's mission into Mayo on behalf of O'Donnell had brought swift retaliation from the local sept whose lands he had plundered. On the other hand, he was opposed by the English as a rebel and law-breaker. It was, perhaps, inevitable that both his antagonists would eventually unite.

As the anglicisation process continued to make inroads into every aspect of native law and custom, the chance of Tibbott succeeding to the MacWilliamship by Gaelic right receded. An alternative route to the power and status the title represented, however, was beginning to become apparent. With the principal exception of Sir Richard Bingham, Tibbott and Granuaile had generally received a fair hearing from the English administrators in Ireland. His mother had been received at Court and continued to have the ear of Lord Burghley, the highest-ranking official in the Queen's government. Both were attuned to the wider political machinations. Unlike their land-bound neighbours, their maritime freedom gave them access to other countries and cultures and a view of the wider world outside Ireland. In her visit to London for her meeting with Elizabeth, Granuaile had witnessed at first-hand the power and wealth that drove the English conquest of Ireland. Gaelic opposition to it had been disorganised and fragmented. Even a powerful overlord like the Earl of Desmond had been overthrown by the English conquerors. Gaelic opposition lacked cohesion. Most of all, it lacked a single leader who could absorb the individualistic aspirations of the Bourkes and other clan leaders and mould them into a force which marched behind a banner that represented a common cause and ideology. By 1593 that leader and that ideology had failed to emerge.

Consequently and, perhaps, in a show of good faith for the promises made by his mother at Court, Tibbott joined forces with the English administration soon after his release from prison and assisted them in quelling some minor disturbances within the province. He was required to hand over his eldest son, nine-year-old Miles, as a pledge of his loyalty and as a deterrent from involvement in further rebellion against the Crown. However, his service to the English also gave him the opportunity to establish personal supremacy over the Bourke septs. When an English official commends 'young Tybalte Burke' to the Government for his services 'whereby are cut off the relics of the principal heads of the sept of the Burkes in Mayo',[6] he perhaps unwittingly reveals the real reason for Tibbott's 'loyal' actions – the removal of likely competitors. Tibbott's subsequent actions against the Bourkes of Erris, when he killed John Bourke MacMeiller and, as he wrote, 'sixtin of his sonnes and cozens, so that there are no more left alive this day of all that trayterous crewe....'[7] further demonstrated his determination to eliminate all likely competitors, as well taking the opportunity to settle old tribal scores.

The build-up towards the final showdown between Gaelic Ireland and Elizabethan England commenced by 1594. In February, English forces under John Dowdall and George Bingham attacked the island castle of Enniskillen. After a barrage of shot from the falcons and robinets, the eight-foot-thick walls of the fortress were finally breached. The close work of the crowbars and scaling ladders ended the spirited defence of the garrison who were summarily put to the sword. With the capitulation of Enniskillen, the English had a circle of garrisoned forts at Carrickfergus, Newry, the Blackwater, Monaghan and Sligo, which effectively isolated Ulster from the rest of the country. Yet, while these forts had been established with relative ease, the real test of maintaining them had yet to be proved.

The incident finally spurred the principal Ulster chieftains into the formation of a confederacy to halt the English advance. While maintaining his outward show of loyalty to Elizabeth, O'Neill secretly conspired with O'Donnell. Authorised by the English to maintain an armed 'peace-keeping' force within his territory, O'Neill took advantage of this liberty and set about building an efficient and modern standing army. He bought arms and equipment from western Scotland and Spain and mercenary troops to supplement his own army. The English heard rumours of these manoeuvres, yet had little option but to believe O'Neill's denial. The significance of O'Neill's army, the first of its kind in Gaelic Ireland, was noted later by an English observer, who stated: 'why the fire of rebellion increased to a devouring flame, was the entertaining and arming of Irishmen .... It furnished the enemy with trained men and filled our bands with such falsehearted soldiers as some doubted whether we had not better have enemies than friends.'[8]

On the surface Connaught appeared peaceful at the beginning of 1595 but this was a mere illusion. Underneath bubbled the shifting allegiances of the chieftains as they shaped up for forthcoming conflict. Bingham maintained a firm grip on the province and allowed Tibbott little leeway to renege on his commitment. Consequently Tibbott became a target for the chieftains affiliated to O'Donnell 'and procured to himself both enemies and danger among the confederates and allies of the said traitors'.[9] His standing in Connaught reached its nadir. Combined with this, his newly-found English allies had hardly repaid his service and allegiance. On the contrary, ever suspicious of his loyalty and contrary to the provisions of the Composition, Bingham cessed a company of soldiers on his lands and on his ships to deter him from intrigue with the Ulster chieftains.

This added burden, combined with the ruinous and wasted state of his territory, forced Tibbott and his mother, as they stated, 'being not hable to sustain the burthenn [burden] of that cesse and to pay the said rent, to abandon and leave the country and to withdraw themselves into the province of Munster, where they do remain in great distress'.[10] Tibbott-ne-Long and Granuaile sought assistance from the Earl of Ormond, Granuaile's go-between in her meeting with the Queen in

1593. Ormond received them cordially at his newly-constructed Elizabethan manor house at Carrick-on-Suir and agreed to help.

On 12 April, Granuaile took two petitions to Lord Burghley in London, together with Ormond's introductory note. One was on behalf of Tibbott, the other on behalf of herself and her dependent relatives. In his petition, Tibbott offered to surrender his lands in Mayo and to hold them of the Crown and offered the same on behalf of his 'cousin Milles Staunton of Kinturk Castle'. He asked the Queen 'to grant him a yearly pension such as Her Highness shall think good for inhabling him to serve hereafter'.[11] A schedule relating to the surrender of their lands in Iar-Chonnacht on behalf of Granuaile's other son, Murrough O'Flaherty, and her grandson, Donal, son of the murdered Owen, was also attached to the petition.

In a meeting with Burghley, Granuaile related the details of Bingham's hard dealing of herself and her family since her previous visit to Court. The situation in Ulster was steadily worsening and Burghley listened with more than a little interest. The results of Granuaile's perseverance manifested itself when in August 1595 the Queen ordered her Council to investigate the lands to be granted to Tibbott, Morrough O'Flaherty, O'Malley and MacEvilly, with the intention of securing them in their title. Granuaile's attempt to get Bingham removed from office was destined to wait a little longer but not before he struck one final time against her family.

In Ulster the Earl of Tyrone finally shed all semblance of loyalty to the Crown and sent his brother, Art, to attack and capture the fort on the Blackwater which Tyrone had earlier assisted the English to establish. The attack was an open act of war and had immediate consequences. On 3 January 1595, Sligo Castle was captured from the English and offered to O'Donnell. The castle was essential to the defence of Connaught and had been garrisoned by Captain George Bingham with a company of soldiers in which Ulick Burke, son of the Earl of Clanrickard, served as ensign. Ulick was secretly in collusion with

O'Donnell. He mutinied, killed George Bingham and seven of his soldiers, imprisoned the remainder of the occupants and delivered the castle to O'Donnell. With Sligo Castle protecting his route to and from Connaught, O'Donnell increased his raids into the province in an attempt to force the chieftains to align with him.

Owing to lack of soldiers and supplies, the English were unable to contain O'Donnell's predatory incursions and incapable of protecting chieftains, like Tibbott, with whom they had treaties. As Sir Geoffrey Fenton reported to the Privy Council, the Connaught chieftains 'through the fear the people had of Sir Richard Bingham, their necessity drives them to depend upon O'Donnell whom they hate for his pride and ambition and are weary of the burdens he daily lays upon them'.[12] By August, 700 insurgents from the baronies of the Owles, Carra and Gallen were out in Tirawley in support of O'Donnell.

The revolt was gradually becoming part of the wider confederacy spear-headed by O'Neill. Sectional and personal interests were, for the first time, gradually sidelined. O'Neill and O'Donnell, in their dispatches, now represented their cause as an 'Irish' one, and claimed they spoke on behalf of 'the whole Irish nobility'. They sought to make their confederacy part of the greater international conflict between Catholic Spain and Protestant England, by offering the 'crown of Ireland' to Philip of Spain if 'he would deliver them from their English oppressors'.[13]

In August, Tibbott's half-brother Edmund Bourke, incarcerated by Bingham in Galway, attempted to escape. He was recaptured and Bingham had him hanged without trial. Tibbott had a close relationship with his older half-brother and bitterly resented Bingham's act. To take advantage of the situation, O'Donnell sent envoys to persuade Tibbott to join the growing alliance against the English. But still Tibbott held back, not certain of how the pendulum would swing and still suspicious of O'Donnell's real intent.

As the English grip on Connaught faltered, further complaints against the harsh methods adopted by Bingham continued to be lodged both in Dublin and England. The Queen wrote of her displeasure to the Lord Deputy. 'It troubles us to find such slackness in the trial of the enormities complained of in Bingham's Government, for the people must needs think our heart alienated from doing them justice.'[14] Consequently, the Lord Deputy travelled to Connaught in November 1595 and relieved Bingham of active duty. He appointed commissioners in Bingham's place to oversee the security of the province in the face of the widening crises.

On the death of his half-brother, Edmund, Tibbott emerged as the principal leader of the Bourke septs of Mayo. Both sides sought his allegience, as well as his sea power. The English were first into the fray. With Bingham, the major-stumbling block, out of the way, the Lord Deputy secretly sent one of the Connaught commissioners, Anthony Brabazon, to ask the Mayo chieftain to meet him in Galway. O'Donnell too sent messengers into Mayo to seek a meeting. Tibbott could now afford to stall, see how the wind was blowing and get the best deal he could by playing both sides against the other.

In a polite, if audacious, manner, he wrote to Brabazon, excusing his inability to attend a meeting with the Lord Deputy, because of a similar request he had received from O'Donnell,

> promising us by all meanes as you shall perceave by the contentes of theis letter wch I send you here inclosed, to meete him in Tyrawly...and cannot delay anie further for satisfying of his pleasure, but upon the perusing of his letters, begin or journey towards him. Wherefore seeing we cannot remedie our abasence from my L[ord] at this instant, we think good to certefie his L[ordship] thereof and to send in unto my L[ord] our griefes in hope that his L[ordship] would pittie our poore estate and see the same redressed. Thus leaving to trouble you more we betake you to God from Kilmeane this present Monday 1595
>
> > your friend to use
> > Theobald Boorke.[15]

To ensure that the English were under no doubt that he was in as much demand by the other side, he enclosed O'Donnell's letter.

With the English left stalled on the sidelines, Tibbott set out to ascertain O'Donnell's intent. They met in Tirawley and O'Donnell outlined his proposal. He would re-establish the MacWilliamship, the title outlawed by the English, and promised that the chieftain elected would be nominated by the Bourkes themselves. The seductive prize was once again in the offing and, like every Bourke chieftain before him since its inception, Tibbott found its allure too potent to resist.

In late December 1595, Tibbott and his relatives, together with every Bourke sept in Mayo, travelled south to Kilmaine for the election of the new MacWilliam at the Rath of Rausakeera, the inaugural place of their ancestors. They were accompanied by the O'Malleys, MacJordans, MacCostellos and the Clandonnells, the traditional tributary clans of the MacWilliam and their respective followers. O'Donnell arrived with his army, accompanied by the chieftains of his tributary clans.

On the elevated, grassy mound, with its ritualistic connections stretching back a millennium, this vast concourse of people made open camp, on the great limestone plain of south Mayo. Chiefs on horseback, accompanied by members of their families, their client lords, their armies of kerne and gallowglass, the clan brehons, whose knowledge of the procedures to be enacted had been inherited from generation to generation, the clan *fili*, whose verse extolled the attributes of each candidates, musicians with pipes and harps to entertain the throng, the nimble-fingered carrows [professional gamblers] to relieve them of their money – all were drawn like ants to an anthill from every part of Mayo. The mid-winter gathering represented one last mass demonstration, before its downfall, of one of the last elections by right of the ancient Brehon law of tanistry, to be recorded.

There was one major difference, however, in this inauguration at Rausakeera from the many that had been held before. An outsider, in the person of the O'Donnell chief of Tirconaill, had made himself master of ceremonies. As the Annals recorded, contrary to custom, O'Donnell took control of the proceedings. He firstly ordered Shane Oge O'Doherty to form

4 lines of troops back to back around the liss and the chiefs all about. Eighteen hundred of his soldiers and hirelings and mercenaries round the royal rath were the first body. O'Dogherty himself and Tadhg Oge O'Boyle with the infantry of Tyreconnell outside them; the men of Connaught with their party outside all. O'Donnell himself with the chiefs and nobles in a close circle on the summit of the rath and no one of the nobles or gentlemen was allowed to go into the presence in the rath but whomsoever he commended to be called to him.[16]

Tibbott and the other chiefs of the Bourke septs protested at their physical exclusion from the traditional election process but to no avail. O'Donnell and his army were the more powerful and strength was to prevail both in the election process and in the result.

The contenders for the title were, in order of seniority, William Bourke of Shrule, the senior Bourke; Richard, son of the Devil's Hook; Oliver, son of John, son of Oliver of Tirawley; Tibbott, son of Richard-an-Iarainn; Edmund, son of Thomas of Cong; John, son of Richard, son of Shane-an-Termainn; and Theobald, son of Walter Ciotach. Reneging on his promise and contrary to Gaelic law, O'Donnell selected his protégé, Theobald, son of Walter Ciotach of Tirawley, the least eligible of the candidates, as the new MacWilliam, though, as the Four Masters recorded, 'there were others of the tribe older in years and better qualified than he'.[17] The fact that the territory of the new MacWilliam bordered O'Donnell's territory, and would serve to protect his access into Connaught, was O'Donnell's motivation.

The Bourkes received the result with uproar. The meeting broke up in great disorder. Bitter and disappointed, Tibbott and the other Bourke contingents departed from Rausakeera to make their way home, hopes of their voluntary allegiance with the Ulster confederates in the forthcoming war against the English dashed. 'Hitherto the old customs were the alternative to the Queen's government. Now, the choice was between the Queen's government and the old customs, subject to the very heavy burden of O'Donnell's domination.'[18] The all-powerful title of MacWilliam had, in effect, been rendered useless.

The rest of the Bourke refused to acknowledge O'Donnell's puppet

as the MacWilliam and the Ulster chieftain was forced to shore up his
protégé. By April O'Donnell's army in Connaught was 3,640 foot and
392 horse soldiers, seriously outnumbering the English, who could
muster no more than 600. The blatant weakness of the English administration and its lack of support left Tibbott exposed to pressure from
O'Donnell. He outlined this dilemma in June 1596 in a letter to
Brabazon, who acted as a go-between with the English administration
in Dublin. He needed the English to honour their promise of military
support if he were to resist O'Donnell's incursions into Mayo. He
wrote to Brabazon:

> Wee will prepare our complaints and other aggrievancies and will be
> provided with provisions and other necessaries wch cannot be done
> before that time. Further for in as much as Galloway men to not fur-
> nishe us with anie commodities wee desire your Honor to direct your
> warrant unto the Mayor to th' end that wee maye be furnished with
> such things as ys expedient excepting munition for warres and will all
> to send provicon for thse as well repaire for soch things in Gallowaye.
> Thus desiring your Honor do not faile herein. I bide you hartey far-
> rwell. From camp the VIIIth of June 1596.
> Signed Theobald Boorke

At the same time, and unable to stop O'Donnell over-running
Connaught, the English asked Tibbott to set up a meeting with the
Ulster chieftain. Tibbott in reply agreed:

> Wee have received your last letter and for the meeteing it is impos-
> sible to be answeared as speedily as you will but wee will hasten with
> as moch expedicon as wee maye over as wee have written above, and
> our meeteing wee will have in anie Castle or Athloan for wee will not
> have it to be neerar except you have some inward meaning of which
> wee cannot be satisfied of
>
> Theobald Boorke [19]

Subsequently O'Donnell, accompanied by his MacWilliam, met with
the English, lead by Warham St Leger and Brabazon, at Ballinrobe.

O'Donnell demanded the return of the seigniorial lands and privileges of the MacWilliamship, a prize already in Tibbott's sights, by right of the English law of primogeniture, as heir to his father. The English refused and the meeting broke up. The meeting was, in any event, merely a delaying tactic by O'Donnell who, confident in his power, saw little reason to come to terms. Hopes of Spanish aid were growing daily, and already weapons and supplies had been sent to Ulster by the King of Spain.

Left high and dry by the English and without protection, Tibbott had little alternative but to play for time also. When O'Donnell returned to Mayo, Tibbott, either forcibly or voluntarily, returned with him to Tirconaill; suspicions abounded in the English administration that it was the latter. In a dispatch to the Lord Deputy, Sir Geoffrey Fenton noted that Mayo had been left unprotected and open to O'Donnell, 'now that Tibbott ne Longe is already in their hands'.[20] Tibbott's duplicity is reflected in Fenton's statement which could be interpreted either way: that he was in collusion with O'Donnell or that he had been imprisoned by him, as Tibbott later claimed he had been. Whichever was the case, Tibbott was back in Mayo by December; whether he escaped or was set free by O'Donnell is uncertain.

In January 1597, Sir Conyers Clifford was appointed to succeed Richard Bingham as Governor of Connaught. His arrival marked a decisive turning point in Tibbott's shifting strategy. Clifford's conciliatory style of government differed from the uncompromising harshness of Bingham. More importantly, he was accompanied by a substantial army. The chieftains who had hitherto been at O'Donnell's mercy or who, like Tibbott, wavered in their allegiance, now had a choice.

Tibbott's brother-in-law, Sir Donough O'Connor, chieftain of Sligo, was the first to acknowledge his allegiance to and personal friendship with Clifford, with whom he had become acquainted at the English court. He was on hand to greet him on his arrival in Connaught in February. O'Connor Sligo's loyalty was rewarded and

English interests enhanced when Clifford recaptured Sligo Castle from O'Donnell and reinstalled O'Connor Sligo there with a garrison.

At the end of December, Tibbott returned from Tirconaill to a Mayo decimated by famine-like conditions, the result of O'Donnell's predatory incursions. When O'Connor Sligo offered to 'establish friendship and concord between his brother-in-law, Theobald-ne-Long … and Sir Conors Clifford',[21] Tibbott agreed to meet the new governor. The Lord Deputy, Sir William Russell, was anxious to cement the initial meeting into something more permanent in order to direct Tibbott's ambitions and his loyalty away from O'Donnell. Russell considered Tibbott 'a Burke better descended than MacWilliam and near as strong as he in the followers of the country'.[22] He advised his successor, Lord Burgh, 'that it will be a good purpose for Her Majesty's service if he [Tibbott] might be separated from MacWilliam, for that by his practice and example to leave him, it is like that sundry other septs would fall from him'.[23] Tibbott needed little persuasion to oppose O'Donnell's MacWilliam, if only to prevent him from getting his hands on the coveted seigniorial lands of the MacWilliamship. If opposition to MacWilliam meant opposition also to the source of his power, then Tibbott would, of necessity, also oppose O'Donnell. It was perhaps inevitable that the English, with their disposition to divide and conquer, would use the coveted MacWilliam lands in their bid to secure Tibbott's allegiance. But before Tibbott was prepared to sign on the dotted line, his potential allies had first to prove their *bona fides.* This was an opportunity to secure his future and, knowing he held the trump card, Tibbott held out for as much as he could get.

To demonstrate the Crown's goodwill, Clifford, with Tibbott and O'Connor Sligo, firstly marched into Tirawley 'and expelled and banished MacWilliam from his patrimony back to O'Donnell. They despoiled and totally plundered all those who remained in confederation and friendship with him in the territory. The country generally on this occasion adhered to Theobald ne Long and the Governor.'[24]

However welcome Clifford's action against O'Donnell's MacWilliam, Tibbott realised that English intervention in Mayo was motivated by considerations other than promoting his ambitions.

When Clifford sought a declaration of his allegiance, Tibbott still held back. Without opposition in Mayo, his bargaining power had soared and from this strong negotiating position, Tibbott put a price on his allegiance.

At Lehinch, near Kilmaine, on 25 April 1597, Tibbott presented Clifford with a list of fourteen demands. Clifford forwarded them to the Privy Council for its consideration. In return for his valuable services, Tibbott demanded the extensive lands of the MacWilliamship and 'in lieu of the name MacWilliam to have some title to be bestowed upon him according to the worthiness of his service'.[25] The seigniorial lands of the MacWilliam around Lough Mask were conditionally granted to him, subject to the Composition rent, while consideration of a suitable title was also promised by the Privy Council. His demand for the lands of former rebels, seized by Bingham and given to English arrivals in the county, to be returned to the rightful owners or their heirs, was denied. He asked for the Queen's letters of protection on behalf of himself, his mother, his stepbrother, Morrough O'Flaherty, and his uncle Donal-na-Píopa, and this was granted. He received all the lands forfeited in past rebellions by members of his own sept, except for the lands and castle of Castle Barry, already in the hands of the relations of Sir Richard Bingham. He was granted a company of 100 soldiers 'in his own charge and leading'.[26] His demand to 'have free licence and authoritie to protect all such within the county of Mayo as make sute for the same and that none elsse may do the same without his advice'[27] was mitigated by the Privy Council since it would have conferred him, in effect, with even more power than he would have had as the MacWilliam. He also obtained protection and a pension for Richard Bourke, the Devil's Hook's son, and for others of his family and followers. His demand for a portion of the MacWilliam's personal estate, 'as was by the Lord General's last parlay agreed upon',[28] was also granted.

While the Privy Council deliberated, Tibbott continued with his personal vendetta against O'Donnell's MacWilliam and, as was reported to Clifford, he drove MacWilliam 'to such strait and exigent meanes that he cannot well tell on what elbow to lean'.[29] Fearful that O'Donnell, in view of Tibbott's success, would attempt to woo him to his side, Clifford urged the Privy Council to accede quickly to his demands. By obtaining Tibbott's loyalty, he wrote, they would thereby 'acquire the man not only to pull down O'Donnell's MacWilliam but also to render all those unruly Burkes and hold them in reformation'.[30]

Before conceding to his demands, the Privy Council instructed Tibbott to pay the Composition rents due on his lands, as well as the outstanding arrears. Moreover, they demanded 'that he perform the duties and obligations to the Crown required of him by the Composition, that he seek pardon for his past offences against the Crown and give pledges for his continuing good conduct and loyalty, as the said Sir Conyers Clifford shall demand, name and chose at his own liking. And the said pledges to remain in safe keapying as long as by the State it shall be so thought requisite.'[31]

Accompanied by his cousin, Richard Bourke, the Devil's Hook's son and others, Tibbott formally signed the covenant with Clifford at Castle Barry. He received a formal pardon on 18 June and prepared to submit his hostage. Clifford insisted that the hostage should be his eldest son, Miles, who had been freed after Bingham's departure. Tibbott duly delivered his son to Clifford's custody at Castle Barry, together with the pledges of the other principal chieftains of Mayo. They are listed in the State Papers:

1. Moyler, (Miles) Burke, Tybott ne Long's als Boorke his sonne as pledge for him selfe and the Sept of Ulick Booke (saving the Devill's Hook).
2. Davy Boorke. The Devill's Hook's sonne as pledge for him selfe and his followers only.
3. Edmond O Mayle. O'Mayle his sonne as pledge for him selfe and his followers only.
4. Goree McDonnall Mac An Abb the chief of the Clandonnell, his sonne as pledge for him selfe, his sonne and followers.
5. Walter McDonnell. For the sept of Rury og Mac Donnell as pledge for him selfe and his followers.
6. Hugy boy McDonnell. Mulmurray Mc Ronal Mc Donnel his sonne as pledge for him selfe and his brothers.

7. Willm Boorke, Davy Mc Moyler Mc Walter fadda his brother for him selfe and his followers.
8. Walter Boorke Davy Daneght als Boorke his sonne, for him selfe and his followers.
9. Brien Mc Thomas Reaugh, Mac Jordan his pledge.
10. Walter Mac Jordan Thomas ne Cogill mac Jordan his sonne as pledge for him selfe and his followers.
11. Colla Mac Donaell. For the Clandonnells of Castylee and the Sleight Markys Wualteer mac Ferry his sonne as pledge.
12. Shane Boy Als the Clan Jordans of Catyloe.
13. Mac Walter and Rycard Boy's sonn. Walter mac Moyler his sonne and Rycard By mac Shane mac Moyler his sonne, as pledge for him selfe and his followers.

13 Pledges[32]

On 28 June, the Privy Council recorded its satisfaction at the outcome of Clifford's negotiations with Tibbott and stated 'that Her Majesty is so well satisfied that she has expressly commanded them to give Sir Conyers as great thanks as they can in words'.[33] Elizabeth further directed that the pledges in confinement were to be treated well.

Tibbott now assumed the power and influence that, in effect, had once been the prerogative of the MacWilliam. He had set a high value on his worth and the English government had been willing to pay. O'Donnell's mistake was that he had promoted the wrong contender for the MacWilliamship and had thereby alienated Tibbott, not merely from him, but from the cause of the Ulster Confederacy. But as the century drew to a close, and as the ebb and flow of the battle for supremacy in Ireland raged between the Gaelic confederacy and the Crown, Tibbott's loyalty continued to fluctuate and his tenuous allegiance to the English continued suspect.

Tibbott took up residence initially in Belcarra Castle, the former residence of his uncle, the Blind Abbot, and entered into possession of the extensive lands that had been granted to him around Lough Mask. He was now thirty years old and in a relatively short time had attained a position of power in Mayo which normally would have taken a lifetime to achieve. But his rise to power also reflected his abilities as a soldier in the field and an accomplished mariner, who performed his military exploits with ruthless determination. In an age of intrigue, double-dealing and compromise, Tibbott more than held his own in his dealings and negotiations with experienced officers of the English Crown. Personal ambition was the primary motivation for his actions, which often led him and his family, as Clifford observed, to 'put their hands far in blood and upon their nearest kinsman'.[34] Yet his actions simply reflected the times, which saw O'Donnell oppose O'Donnell, O'Neill oppose O'Neill, and Gael oppose Gael, in the final struggle for survival of the Gaelic world that had bred them.

CHAPTER SIX

To Serve His Own Turn
1597-1601

DESPITE CLIFFORD'S initial success in Connaught, he made little impact on the situation in Ulster, notwithstanding his assertion that 'the Ulsterman had only to be forced to be overcome'.[1] He managed to place a garrison in the fort on the Blackwater, only to have it promptly blockaded by O'Neill. By June, Clifford was preparing for an offensive against O'Donnell, aided by Tibbott.

Clifford's forces in Connaught were starved of essential supplies and ordnance. So great was the waste of the countryside and so critical the supply situation that corn to feed his army had to be forwarded from Dublin by sea to Galway. This was considered 'a very chargeable and casual method,'[2] the only alternative being the lengthy transport of the army's 'biscuit overland when we can get garrans [horses] for carriage of it'.[3]

At the end of June, O'Donnell sent his MacWilliam into Mayo to round up cattle and drive them into Ulster. Tibbott set off to confront MacWilliam, while Clifford posted himself at Collooney, County Sligo to cut off MacWilliam's passage back to O'Donnell. Tibbott drove MacWilliam and his cattle herds before him in Clifford's direction, with the result that 1,200 head of cattle were captured and 200 of MacWilliam's forces killed. MacWilliam, however, effected his escape back to O'Donnell.

Tibbott's next mission was by sea against his former allies the

Clandonnells, who, it had been reported, were conspiring with O'Donnell. He sailed to Sligo in July in his mother's galleys together with his half-brother, Murrough O'Flaherty, with the intention, or so he claimed, of apprehending the leaders of the conspiracy. By August, however, Clifford had received no communication from him and suspected that he had defected to O'Donnell. With some apprehension, Clifford informed the Lord Deputy: 'I know not of any good reason why he went the journey by sea as having given him his mother and brother amongst them in money and other necessities 200L [200 marks]. I cannot enter into any jealousy of him nor be too much assured of his brother.'[4]

Tibbott was merely playing for time to determine on which side the advantage lay and how best his ambitions could be served within the fluid political situation. English inability to curb O'Neill in Tyrone, the lack of back-up support for Clifford in Connaught, and the growing support for the Ulster chiefs, were ample justification for caution. However, any opportunity to attack MacWilliam was another matter. Consequently, when he later sent Clifford 'the head of Thomas Burke, MacWilliam's brother, and no less mischievous than himself',[5] it was an act more to do with eliminating the opposition than a demonstration of his loyalty to the English crown.

Tibbott's partnership with his older half-brother, Murrough-na-Maor (of-the- stewardships, by reason of the many seignorial rights he claimed and enforced within his territory in Iar-Chonnacht), was to continue intermittently until the end of the war. Pragmatic and opportunistic like his younger sibling, Murrough had aligned himself previously with the English. On that occasion, however, he had sided with Bingham, the sworn enemy of his formidable mother and he had paid the price. Granuaile's wrath was not restricted by maternal considerations when she attacked Murrough's castle, killed some of his followers and plundered his territory in reprisal. But Bingham was no more and the political situation very different.

In September, O'Neill and O'Donnell sent MacWilliam into Mayo with a force of 700 as a decoy to keep Clifford occupied, while they joined forces to oppose an incursion by the Lord Deputy into Ulster.

But Clifford was unable to make any headway against MacWilliam. Spurred by his personal vendetta, Tibbott attacked his kinsman and compelled him to retreat to Ulster. Tibbott's victory brought about the submission of MacWilliam's allies in north Mayo. In appreciation, Clifford made Tibbott captain of a band of 100 soldiers, with pay of twenty-eight shillings per week. The Lord Deputy questioned this unorthodox development of giving a Gaelic chieftain command of a detachment of the Queen's forces. Clifford defended his action because, as he reported, 'without intertainment his [Tibbott's] people wold not have been kept together', and he further concluded, that it was better policy 'to give him meanes than to suffer so many loose men to continue in action'.[6]

The English Council in Dublin expressed its satisfaction also 'upon the drawing of Tibbott ne Longe and the late expelling of the supposed MacWilliam'. They were hopeful that because of it that 'the country would grow to better settling, the rather for that upon the expulsion of MacWilliam and the coming of Tybott, sundry septs of the Burghes, the O'Mallies and other nations that were loose and stood out before'[7] would now submit. But they were somewhat premature in their assessment. They reckoned without the power and persistence of O'Donnell in the struggle for supremacy in Connaught.

Tibbott, however, did not underestimate the power of O'Donnell and the possibility of a Gaelic victory. Consequently, when not opposing MacWilliam as a threat to his own personal position in Mayo, he acted cautiously in the service of the English. So far they had made little headway against the Ulster confederates and the outcome of the conflict was still far from clear. While the possibility of reconciliation between himself and O'Donnell was a slim prospect, hedging his bets, Tibbott maintained contact with the other Ulster confederate, Hugh O'Neill.

❧ ❧ ❧

A brief truce between the Ulster chiefs and the English was established during 1598. Lord Burgh, the Lord Deputy, died suddenly in office and the civil and military authority was placed in the hands of a committee, an arrangement fraught with indecision, suspicion and petty jealousies. Archbishop Loftus and Chief Justice Gardiner were responsible for civil matters, while military control was invested in the elderly but active Thomas, Earl of Ormond. Under cover of the truce, O'Neill and O'Donnell consolidated their positions. Ormond did little to oppose them. This further increased support for O'Neill and O'Donnell, with the result that, as was reported, 'few places were free from commocion, and almost everywhere they went forth in open action of rebellion or conversed in secret practises of conspiracies'.[8]

Further negotiations between the Ulster chiefs and the English authorities foundered on two main issues – the continued blockade by O'Neill of the English fort on the Blackwater and O'Donnell's insistence that his MacWilliam should have the seigniory and lands of the MacWilliamship in Mayo, part of which had been granted to Tibbott. The stalemate was broken in August 1598, when, in an attempt to relieve the Blackwater fort, an army of 4,000, commanded by Sir Henry Bagnell, was heavily defeated by O'Neill, O'Donnell and Maguire at the Yellow Ford. MacWilliam and 1,000 followers fought with O'Donnell in the battle. It was a major victory for the confederacy.

O'Donnell sought to press home the advantage of the victory in Connaught against the pro-English chieftains there. He seized O'Connor Sligo's strategically situated castle in Ballymote and garrisoned it. He then sent MacWilliam back into Mayo, aided by O'Doherty and MacSweeney, MacWilliam's brother-in-law. They swept into Tibbott's lands in Burrishoole and Carra, routed him and plundered the countryside, taking a great prey of cattle. Tibbott and his family were forced to flee their lands and live aboard his mother's ships, moored off the Mayo coast. His English allies could do little to help him. Clifford's force numbered less than 200, while MacWilliam was estimated to have at his disposal 2,000 foot and 200 cavalry. Even if he had enough men, because of the famine-like conditions in Mayo, as Clifford wrote, 'to go by land … will be very hard for no carriage can be got to furnish an army through Connaught, the country is so waste...'.⁹ The only suitable shipping in Connaught at the time was the fleet of three galleys controlled by Tibbott, each able to accommodate up to 300 fully armed soldiers apiece. O'Donnell established his head-quarters at Ballymote and raided unhindered through Connaught and as far south as Thomond, while his MacWilliam maintained pressure on Tibbott in Mayo.

Robert Devereux, 2nd Earl of Essex, was appointed Lord Lieutenant and arrived in Ireland in April 1599 with the largest army ever used in an Irish campaign. While as a soldier and military leader Essex may not have obtained the results expected of him, he nonetheless displayed a keen insight into the intrigue and intricacies which motivated many of the Gaelic chieftains, such as Tibbott. He advised the Queen, 'if your majesty will have a strong party of the Irish Nobility and make use of them, you must hide from them all purpose of establishing English government, till the strength of the Irish be so broken that they shall see no safety but in your Majesty's protection'.¹⁰ But with rumours that the Spanish were to come in the support of the Ulster confederates, Elizabeth was more concerned with adopting more practical methods and in no mood to dwell on abstract theories propounded by her mercurial Lord Deputy. In particular, she expressed her disquiet about the practice, initiated in Connaught by Clifford, of appointing native chieftains as captains. She ordered Essex 'to take care in the Province of Connaught where there are so many Irish bands together and rather to draw some of them to service elsewhere and send English in their stead'.¹¹ But Tibbott continued as captain of his band and there was nothing either Clifford or the Queen could do about it.

O'Connor Sligo, who had lately returned from the English court, renewed acquaintance with Essex and accompanied him on a hosting through Munster. They were later joined by Clifford. But Essex's show of power proved a fruitless exercise. On O'Connor's return to Sligo, he was besieged in his castle at Collooney by O'Donnell. When Essex heard of his friend's predicament, he ordered Clifford to go to Sligo and lift the siege. With the countryside between Galway and Sligo in such a wasted condition. the only alternative route was by sea. And the only ships available were the galleys commanded by Tibbott. It was time for Tibbott to demonstrate his loyalty.

Tibbott brought his fleet from Clew Bay to the port of Galway. There his ships were loaded up with the necessary ordnance, provisions 'and the engines for constructing castles which had arrived from England'.[12] He then sailed the convoy northwards, anchored off Sligo Bay and awaited Clifford's arrival by land.

As Clifford, accompanied by the Earl of Clanrickard and the O'Connor Don, marched towards Sligo, O'Donnell awaited his approach. The Ulster chieftain divided his forces. One division continued with the siege of Collooney, the second was dispatched to the coast to prevent Tibbott from landing and the third guarded the pass through the Curlew Mountains, through which Clifford had to come. On 15 August, Clifford attempted to cross the Curlews but O'Donnell defeated him with heavy losses. Clifford died on the battlefield and O'Connor Sligo quickly surrendered Collooney Castle to O'Donnell. O'Donnell then moved to the Sligo coast where Tibbott and his fleet were waiting offshore.

There are two versions of what transpired between Tibbott and O'Donnell. According to John Baxter, an Englishman, who had accompanied Tibbott on the voyage from Galway:

O'Donnell came to the yland where our shipping did lye, and entreated Tybbott ne Longe, sonn to Granny O'Mayley, to bestowe some wyne on hym and to com out and drynke with him, but Tybbott would not by any meanes goe, yet in the end upon pledges, Capten Coatch, myself and Murragh Nehmer [Murrough-na-Maor] brother to Tybbott went out to O'Donnell and caryed a barrell of wyne. In which tyme of our drincking O'Donnell did shrew unto the sayde Murragh the head of Sir Coniers Clyforde. And dealt secretly with hym to have himself, Tybbott and the reste of their crue to betraye us and take all our shippinge, which they might have done, had not Tybbott bene very faythfull to her Majestie who revealed all unto us. [13]

The *Four Masters*, however, relate an entirely different version of the events:

> When Theobald-na-Long was informed that the English had been defeated and the Governor slain, and that O'Connor had been let out of the castle, the resolution he came to was not to oppose O'Donnell any longer. He afterwards confirmed his friendship with him and O'Donnell permitted the aforesaid fleet to go back again to Galway. [14]

It is uncertain whether some secret arrangement was made at this time between Tibbott and O'Donnell and, to keep their pact a secret from the English, Tibbott was allowed to take the munitions safely back to Galway as proof of his loyalty. What is indisputable is that his allegiance was considered important to both sides.

So concerned were the English about the rumours of Tibbott's defection that the Earl of Essex issued orders to 'assure him of my good affection, of my resolution to the protection of him and his, to heap upon him as many favours and benefits I can in any way'.[15] He begged Tibbott to 'have especial charge of the victual at Sligo, because by it we must relieve our army and perform all the services in those parts'.[16] He also promised that, at the first opportunity, he would rescue his brother-in-law O'Connor Sligo 'and have a revenge for my worthy friend'. At the same time, however, Essex ordered that a 'trusty messenger' be sent to Captain Coche aboard Tibbott's fleet, and he 'must be conjured to look well to the victuals, shipping and troops of soldiers, if upon this disaster, Tibbott ne Longe should forget his duty'.[17]

Doubts persisted about some secret arrangement between Tibbott and the Ulster confederates. At the end of August it was further reported to Essex that 'Tibbott ne Longe was within with O'Donnell and O'Donnell did send out him as pledges O'Dogherty and two other pledges, the best of his country I heard. Tyrone himself says they are agreed, but they will not have any to know it.'[18]

As the struggle for power between both sides continued to fluctuate, Tibbott could afford to stand back and weigh up the advantages to be gained from either side. Where the Gaelic confederacy was concerned, from Tibbott's perspective, the stumbling block was O'Donnell's continued support of his rival, MacWilliam. The English, particularly Essex, in greater need of Tibbott's assistance now that O'Donnell had free rein in Connaught, could afford to make him the more attractive offer. But despite rumours of deals and double deals, by September the focus of Tibbott's efforts was directed again in his personal war against MacWilliam.

By September also it emerged that Tibbott's brother-in-law, O'Connor Sligo, was no more than a prisoner of O'Donnell, despite O'Donnell's promise to restore him as chieftain of Sligo. But O'Connor Sligo's relationship to Tibbott and his friendship with Essex made him too great a risk to be allowed unsupervised rule over his strategic territory. Essex, despite his extravagant promises, was powerless to do anything to help him.

Essex spent twenty-one weeks in Ireland, during which time English power reached its nadir in Connaught, Munster and Leinster under his ineffectual rule. The influence of O'Neill and O'Donnell, on the other hand, spread rapidly throughout the country. On a tour of Munster to rally support, O'Neill propounded a broader aspiration in the war against the English – the struggle of all of Ireland against the Crown. He claimed that the war was motivated by 'the catholic religion and liberties of our country'.[19] He promised support from both the Pope and the Spanish King.

Despite the frantic exhortations from the Queen, Essex seemed unable or unwilling to confront O'Neill. When, rather gullibly, he opted for a secret meeting with the Ulster chieftain, thereby leaving himself open to accusations of intrigue and collusion with the rebels by his enemies at the English court, Essex sealed his fate. Fleeing to England to defend himself, he found little sympathy from his queen, who had him imprisoned for deserting his post.

With the English administration in disarray, O'Neill pressed home the advantage in Munster, and O'Donnell did likewise in Connaught. In Mayo, the war within a war between Tibbott and the MacWilliam continued unabated. With Essex's departure and his English 'allies' for the moment sidelined, Tibbott had to tread carefully. When

O'Donnell offered a truce and promised that MacWilliam would be confined within his own territory in north Mayo, Tibbott agreed, hoping to attain the time and the space to stand aloof until the pattern of the war became clearer.

In December, however, an English plan to 'recover' O'Connor Sligo from his confinement by O'Donnell, reinstall him as chieftain and refortify the ruined castle of Sligo, seemed destined to drag Tibbott into the forefront once more. The English viewed the plan as the only option left to restrict O'Donnell's access into Connaught. And the only person with the ability to achieve it was Tibbott. In a secret recommendation, the English administration further suggested that payment to him for his service should be in the form of 'one tun of sack [i.e. wine] of the impost in Galway, which will please him more than £100'.[20] The plan, mainly because of Tibbott's reluctance to cross swords with O'Donnell in view of their secret truce, did not materialise.

It did not detract the English, however, in their desperation to try and attain his services again, this time when confronted by their greatest fear – sightings of Spanish ships off the western seaboard, bearing arms and munitions to the Ulster chiefs. A plan was recommended to employ Tibbott and his fleet of galleys to search out the Spanish ships and seize their cargo. 'There be three very good galleys with Tibbott ne Longe, son to Grany O'Malley, his brother and O'Malley and will carry 300 men apiece. These, if employed by Her Majesty would do much good in the north. There are no galleys in Ireland but those.'[21] But Tibbott remained determinedly aloof, successfully holding both sides at bay to determine which way the wind blew before committing to either. He had not long to wait.

Charles Blount, Lord Mountjoy, was appointed to succeed the ill-fated Essex as Lord Lieutenant in 1600. He arrived in Ireland in February, accompanied by Sir George Carew as president of Munster. With an army of 3,000, they ruthlessly quelled support for O'Neill in Munster. Mountjoy was a military man rather than an administrator, whose aim was simple and uncomplicated; to stop the Ulster confederacy from spreading to the rest of the country and to prevent the possible loss of Ireland to the Crown. The imminent prospect of Spanish aid added a greater urgency to the undertaking. The stakes were high; the prize was great.

The methods of warfare practised by previous lords deputies and governors had, in Mountjoy's opinion, been the main cause for the failure to bring the conquest of Ireland to a conclusive end. Hitherto the English armies had adopted orthodox methods against an enemy who successfully employed tactics which seldom allowed them to become embroiled in pitched battles. O'Neill and O'Donnell's policy of wasting their enemy's territory had, in effect, rendered the English forces ineffective. Mountjoy was prepared to learn from his predecessors' mistakes and from the methods employed by the Ulster chiefs in their victories over the English. He advised the Privy Council that 'our only way to ruine the rebels must be to make all possible waste of the means for life', but added the warning, 'if we be not supplied out of England, we shall as well starve ourselves as them'.[22] Moreover, he recommended that the war was to be carried out without a winter respite tso that the rebels could not plant crops or replenish stocks. At the same time, he proposed to establish permanent, well-garrisoned forts in the territories seized from the rebels and back his operations by land with a sea invasion of Ulster.

Armed with this formula, Mountjoy moved into Ulster against O'Neill in May, while Sir Henry Docwra landed behind O'Donnell's lines with 4,000 men in Lough Foyle. As the English spread out, a war of destruction ensued. Mountjoy's grim mantra, that famine was the only way to beat the rebels, was carried out to the letter as he set out to destroy crops, burn homesteads, seize cattle herds and give the Irish no respite. O'Neill and O'Donnell resisted the English advance as best they could while anxiously awaiting the promised help from Spain.

While Ulster burned, Connaught remained relatively peaceful. Mountjoy made no attempt to restore English supremacy there in the knowledge that once O'Donnell was defeated in Ulster, Connaught would submit forthwith. If Tibbott's active support could not be depended upon, all Mountjoy could hope for was that he would stand neutral in the campaign against the Ulster chieftains. It was a vain hope where Tibbott was concerned and by spring 1600, he was once again enmeshed in a web of intrigue and double-dealing.

Dermot O'Connor, a scion of the O'Connor Don family in Roscommon, commanded a force of 1,500 mercenary soldiers in Munster. He was married to Margaret, daughter of the once powerful Earl of Desmond, who had been killed in 1583. The Earl's widow, Eleanor, Countess of Desmond, had recently married Tibbott's brother-in-law, Donough O'Connor Sligo. The late Earl's son, heir to the confiscated Desmond estates and now in his twenties, remained a prisoner of state in the Tower of London. His cousin, James Fitz-Thomas, the leader of a growing alliance of Munster chieftains allied to the Ulster confederacy, usurped the vacant earldom and thereby subsequently became disparagingly known as the *Sugán* (straw-rope) Earl.

In December 1599, Dermot O'Connor agreed terms with O'Neill to go to Munster with his mercenaries in support of the *Sugán* Earl of Desmond. On his journey south, Dermot was attacked by the Baron of Castleconnell, Richard Burke and his brother, Thomas, near Grange in Thomond. They were subsequently 'surrounded, prostrated and unsparingly put to the sword'[23] by Dermot. Richard and Thomas Burke were kinsmen of Tibbott.

Meanwhile in Munster, the newly arrived president, the wily Sir George Carew, schemed and intrigued with an ability and an appetite without equal, to remove the *Sugán* earl and destroy the alliance that was growing around him. Given Dermot O'Connor's strength as a mercenary leader, open to the highest bidder for his services and, more significantly, his position as husband to the sister of the 'real' earl, incarcerated in the Tower of London, the complex state of affairs attracted the Machiavellian talents of Carew. He 'resolved to try the uttermost of his wit and power'[24] to turn the situation to his advantage. He found willing accomplices in both Dermot and his wife, Lady Margaret, who, on Carew's promise to free her brother from the Tower and restore him to the earldom (and on receipt of a substantial fee) agreed to conspire against the *Sugán* Earl.

Despite his agreement with O'Neill, O'Connor captured the *Sugán* Earl in January 1600. The *Sugán's* supporters subsequently rescued him and Dermot was forced to flee back to Roscommon. Undeterred by the failure of his scheme, in a further plot to reduce support for the *Sugán* Earl, Carew had the young earl brought from the Tower back to Munster. At the same time he re-hired Dermot O'Connor. He arranged a safe passage for him from the Governor of Connaught, Sir Arthur Savage and from the Earl of Clanrickard, through whose territory O'Connor had to traverse on his journey from Roscommon.

Realising that the return of the real Earl of Desmond would dilute their support in Munster, the Ulster chieftains determined to limit its effect elsewhere. O'Donnell captured O'Connor Sligo, the stepfather of the young earl, and imprisoned him in an island fortress in Lough Esk to prevent any Carew-inspired conspiracy between him and his stepson. In September O'Connor Sligo smuggled out a letter to Mountjoy, urging him to send 'my brother-in-law Tibbott ne Longe… with forces to assist me'.[25]

Supposedly loyal and in the 'Queen's pay', Tibbott and his army were stationed near Gort, County Galway when news was brought to him of the approach of Dermot O'Connor. Tibbott immediately intercepted O'Connor, attacked him and took him prisoner and 'the next morning hanged him with such martial law as I had',[26] cut off his head and sent it to the English authorities in Galway, thereby insinuating that he had perpetrated the deed on behalf of the Crown.

The incident, however, reflects the intrigue and controversy that surrounded Tibbott's actions and which placed a permanent question mark on exactly where his true loyalty lay. Dermot had made an enemy of Tibbott when he had killed his kinsmen, Richard and Thomas Burke. But by his actions against the *Sugán* Earl and by his intrigue with Carew, O'Connor was also an enemy of the Gaelic Confederacy. Did Tibbott act out of personal revenge or as a covert ally of O'Neill? Tibbott claimed it was an act of revenge for his cousins but revenge too for 'the manifold hurts done by him [Dermot] in the several provinces of the realm against all and every [of] Her Majesty's servitors and sub-jects',[27] as he boldly wrote. Clanrickard, however, refused to believe that Tibbott had killed Dermot to protect English interests in Munster but rather to help O'Neill. Clanrickard was adamant that this was Tibbott's real motivation and 'the chefest cause, how so ever it may be disguised'. He urged that the deed be regarded by the Government 'as an indignitie offered to the State' and since it had occurred in Clanrickard's territory, despite the safe passage he had given O'Connor, as a 'perpetual slander and abuse to me and my posterity'.[28]

Clanrickard sent word to Tibbott, who was still camped quite unconcernedly within Clanrickard's territory, warning him that unless he made good the spoils and prisoners he had seized in the incident, he would become 'the greatest enemy you have in the world which (with the permission of God) I will make you and yours feel, if you urge me thereunto'.[29] Carew took up the issue next. He wrote his version of the affair to the Privy Council, denouncing Tibbott and maintaining that he had acted on behalf of O'Neill and O'Donnell. He further accused Tibbott of actively aiding O'Donnell in a recent raid on Thomond, using a company of soldiers paid for by the Crown. 'I know not of one day's service that Tibbott ne Longe hath performed',[30] Carew vowed, and the accusation had a ring of truth.

While the controversy of words raged, Tibbott blithely disowned all knowledge that Dermot O'Connor had been granted a safe passage by the English and boldly proposed that he was due 'great thanks' and 'great reward' from the English for his action. He maintained that he was in Galway because the Earl of Clanrickard had requested him, 'with my power to come to his aid'.[31] While Clanrickard and Carew both demanded Tibbott's imprisonment, Mountjoy decided on less dramatic action, confidentially admitting to the Privy Council that, owing to the power and standing of Tibbott, 'neither could I have apprehended him if I could'.[32] Instead, he ordered that Tibbott be suspended from duty as captain so that the matter could be further investigated. In an attempt to further appease the young Earl of Desmond, Sir Robert Cecil, the Queen's private secretary, promised that if it were proved that the Earl's brother-in-law had indeed been granted formal letters of safe conduct, that 'Tybbot ne Longe shall answer it with his head'[33] for his murder.

Tibbott, however, not only retained his head but, after a short lapse, was also reinstated as captain of his troops, not because he was proved innocent of the killing of Dermot O'Connor but that the English considered that he made a better ally than a foe. To retain even his tacit support was more acceptable than to risk his total withdrawal to the ranks of the Ulster confederates. Whether Tibbott killed Dermot O'Connor out of revenge or to aid the fortunes of O'Neill is impossible to determine so convoluted are the politics pertaining to the affair. If it were the latter, then his alliance with O'Neill was to be short-lived.

Tibbott returned to Mayo and bided his time for the controversy over the O'Connor incident to abate. Meanwhile there was still his vendetta with MacWilliam. He marched into Tirawley and captured his enemy's store of arms. MacWilliam was forced to flee for protection to O'Donnell. But by then, O'Donnell had his own problems to contend with in Tirconaill. Hard-pressed by Docwra and his puppet, Niall Garv O'Donnell, he was in no position to help his protégé in Mayo.

With O'Donnell thus sidelined, Tibbott determined to finally settle the MacWilliamship question himself. He convened a meeting of the Bourke septs who opposed O'Donnell's MacWilliam at the ancient inaugural site at Kilmaine and conferred the title on his close ally and cousin, Richard Bourke, son of the Devil's Hook. With the title at his feet, Tibbott chose to confer it on his subordinate. His action is the most telling indication of how worthless, in effect, the once most coveted title had become and with it the way of life that supported it. What was becoming clear was that ownership of land rather than the possession of an archaic title was the criterion of real power. Tibbott already possessed a major share of the MacWilliamship estates, granted to him by the Privy Council. Moreover, by conferring the title on a subordinate, it showed that he, in effect, considered his own status of more power and significance than the once all-powerful MacWilliamship.

In the broader context, this final struggle for the MacWilliamship in Mayo symbolised the final struggle of the Gaelic world that had bred and sustained it throughout the centuries. Perhaps this fact also resolved Tibbott not only from becoming the last holder of a useless title but also the champion of the archaic world from which it emanated.

Richard Bourke was as much Tibbott's MacWilliam as Theobold Bourke was O'Donnell's; as Sir Robert Cecil noted, 'this new Mac-William and all his partakers will follow the said Captain Tibbott'.[34] He later reported to the Privy Council that 'the Burkes of Mayo dependeth chiefly on Theabold ne Long Burke, who lately usurped the name of MacWilliam for Richard Burke the Devil's Hook's son to make him beat his direction.'[35] The English Government had little option but to acknowledge its inability to curtail Tibbott, even when he committed the treasonable act of reinstating a title long rendered extinct by English law.

It may have been to the long-term advantage of the English to ignore Tibbott's disloyal act. However, for O'Donnell, whose ambitions and those of the Confederacy depended on having unopposed access through Mayo into the rest of Connaught, intervention on behalf of his MacWilliam was imperative. With as large a force as he could muster, he sent his protégé into Mayo once more in a bid to restore his authority. Tibbott, with his MacWilliam, barred the way and, as the annalists recorded, 'a fierce battle was fought between them, in which both were mutually mindful of their ancient grudges and recent enmities'.[36] While Tibbott could be said to have been beaten by O'Donnell's forces on the day, and to have lost a close friend and ally in Richard Bourke, it was an empty victory for his opponent. MacWilliam was subsequently forced to flee back to the north, leaving Tibbott once again undisputed leader in Mayo, not necessarily champion of the English cause there but champion of his own.

By summer 1601, the intrigues and manoeuvres reached a crescendo, as O'Neill and O'Donnell awaited the imminent help from Spain that would bring their long struggle with the Crown to a climax. Tibbott watched from the sidelines as both sides manoeuvred towards the final showdown.

On 23 September, 2,800 troops under the command of Don Juan

Del Aquila landed at Kinsale. By the end of October they were sur-rounded by Mountjoy and a large army. O'Donnell, whose territory had been wasted by the continual raids of Docwra, departed for Kinsale in the knowledge that unless his long and heroic march south ended in a conclusive victory, he could not return to Tirconaill, which would assuredly be overrun by his enemies in his absence. At the end of November O'Neill, after much deliberation, finally headed south.

In mid-December, Tibbott set sail southwards from Mayo with his 300-strong army, too. After years of hedging his bets, he finally showed his preference at Kinsale, fighting with distinction with the forces of Mountjoy. His valour and his 'daring exploits against the Spaniards' were lauded by Elizabeth's successor, James I, who conferred him with a knighthood in 1603.

More than a battle was lost and won at Kinsale. O'Neill and O'Donnell lost the war and whatever hopes they entertained of ruling a country free from English domination. Mountjoy won a war and secured the Tudor conquest of Ireland. After the battle, MacWilliam fled to Spain with O'Donnell. So ended the 300-year-old title, the emblem and the source of much contention and division, dying with the Gaelic world that had conceived and sustained it.

Tibbott's intrigue and double-dealing finally paid dividends. His actions over the years leading up to Kinsale, while they may appear unpatriotic, even traitorous, when viewed in hindsight and out of the context of the period, no more than mirrored the actions of many other 'earls, barons, great territorial chieftains, belted knights and high gen-tlemen offering for money and for land',[37] to ally with whatever side could guarantee them the power and status they craved. This fact is most evident in the composition of the so-called 'English' army of Mountjoy at Kinsale, a battle where it could be truly said, 'the Royalist Irish, the Irish who adhered to the [English] State and its fortunes, defeated the Confederate Irish'.[38]

The stance taken by chieftains such as Tibbott emanated from an overwhelming sense of insecurity, provoked by the destabilisation of their native world, the undermining of its very foundations, its political system, laws and customs and a way of life that had flourished for over a thousand years. The system had encouraged individual rather than corporate ambition and thus when attacked from without had no national ideology, figurehead or focus to inspire chieftains like Tibbott to its defence. Like the myriad of minor chieftains of the period, Tibbott-ne-Long Bourke simply sought to survive the upheaval as best he could. Unlike the rest of them, he was successful.

CHAPTER SEVEN

A Knight of Property
1601-1612

A PROVERB OF THE 16th century which gloomily pre-
dicted that 'the pride of France, the treason of England and
the war in Ireland, shall never have end',[1] was proved par-
tially wrong at least after Kinsale, when the war in Ireland did end and
for a generation peace descended on a broken and devastated country.
Wasted by years of incessant warfare, famine and plague stalked the
countryside. Both protagonists had adopted the scorched-earth tactic,
resulting in the spoliation of crops and livestock. The few towns and
villages that existed were in ruins and the castles and fortresses of the
native aristocracy were laid low. Thousands died from starvation, particularly in Ulster, which in the final months of the war had been
utterly ruined. In Tyrone alone, 3,000 starved to death at a time when
the population of the entire country did not exceed 600,000 people.
Economically the country lay in ruins, its currency debased, its trade
diminished, inflation rampant.

Kinsale was the final step in the Tudor reconquest of Ireland and
with it disappeared any hope that the Gaelic world could reassert itself.
Ireland's Spanish allies departed hastily from her shores, never to
return. With them went O'Donnell, the champion of the Gaelic cause,
who died shortly after his arrival in Spain or, as many claimed, was poi-
soned by English secret agents. On his return to Ulster, broken and
dispirited, O'Neill opened negotiations with Mountjoy in an attempt
to salvage something from the debris. Mountjoy consolidated the

Crown's position and made Ireland secure from further invasion and rebellion by the establishment of armed garrisons in Munster and Connaught. To deter O'Neill from further action, he marched into Tyrone, systematically destroyed the harvest and 'broke down the chair wherein the O'Neill's were wont to be created',[2] at Tullaghoge – a symbolic move, if any were needed, to signify the end of the old Gaelic order.

Elizabeth, in the last year of her long and eventful reign, had lived to see her ambition in Ireland finally realised. The cost to both sides in the nine years, arduous campaign, however, was great. As yet, Gaelic Ireland had only begun to pay the price for its persistent resistance, while England began to slowly recoup her expenditure.

After Kinsale, Tibbott returned home with the remains of his army, having accredited himself well in the battle and earned himself Mountjoy's praise. He settled down to a less turbulent life at Belcarra Castle with his wife, Maeve O'Connor Sligo, and their young family, which now comprised four sons, Miles, David, Theobald and Richard, and three daughters, Mary, Honora and Margaret, and awaited the rewards of victory to emerge. On the strength of his actions at Kinsale, his eldest son Miles was released from custody in Athlone Castle and reunited with his family.

Tibbott's mother, Granuaile, now an old woman of over seventy years, was living out the last few months of her extraordinary life in the stark surroundings of her fortress of Carrickahowley on Clew Bay. Her days of glory, both by sea and land, were gradually receding from the clarity of reality into the haze of folklore and legend, which would preserve her memory for centuries to come.

Tibbott, too, abandoned his seafaring activities in order to consolidate his position on land. The remains of his fleet were now controlled by his O'Malley relations and they continued the tradition of their ancestors into the first few decades of the new century, but without the effectiveness and flamboyance that had been the hallmark of Tibbott and his mother. But old habits were slow to be eradicated completely. Notwithstanding his 'valorous action' on behalf of the English crown at Kinsale, in the transition years that followed, the lure of his defeated native Gaelic world continued to weave its magnetic spell on Tibbott.

The remnants of O'Donnell's army, under the leadership of his brother, Rory, struggled back from Kinsale through Connaught. They attempted to re-establish themselves in Ulster, to await the promised return of their chieftain with further aid from Spain and continue the struggle at home. Rory O'Donnell solicited Tibbott's help to ambush Sir Oliver Lambert, the new Governor of Connaught. Subsequently, Tibbott prevailed on Lambert to advance from Galway along a particular route towards Sligo where, Tibbott informed him, he could better attack O'Donnell and seize the prey that O'Donnell had taken in Mayo and Sligo on his way north. Lambert, however, became suspicious and subsequently discovered that Tibbott was leading him into a trap. He complained to Mountjoy, 'I was no sooner past Castlebar than my spies brought me certain word that O'Rourke, Rory O'Donnell, Donnell O'Connor, with all their rabble, attended 3 days my coming through the pass … I only told Tibbott what I heard and passed it over, being more watchful of the rest of his advises.'[3]

Relations deteriorated between the Governor and Tibbott after this incident. Lambert appears to have been an unpopular administrator and was not greatly liked even by those chieftains who supported the English. Mountjoy shared their dislike. In September, he rebuked Lambert for alienating Tibbott and refused to accept Lambert's assertion that it was hopes of Spanish aid that had made Tibbott side with O'Donnell and O'Rourke. Mountjoy, on the contrary, suggested that the real reason for Tibbott's disloyalty was his personal animosity towards Lambert and disquiet at the Governor's plan 'to dispossesse the principal men of their lands and livings and to get the same into her Majestie's hands'.[4] He further admonished Lambert for his ill-treatment of Tibbott, whom he stated 'hath grievously complained to me of the committal of his cosen Davye Bourke and some hard usage towards himselfe'.[5]

Lambert subsequently made his peace with Tibbott when they met in Galway. From there they set out together to make the arduous journey to Dublin, where Tibbott was warmly received at Dublin Castle by Mountjoy. Mountjoy reinstated him as captain over his band of followers, with an allowance from the Crown and sent him back to Connaught, as he recorded, 'with a resolution which I hope will tend to the speedy quieting of that country'.[6]

The Treaty of Mellifont brought the war to a formal conclusion with a show of intrigue and subterfuge that had been the hallmark of the nine-year conflict. The final act in the Tudor reconquest of Ireland was stage-managed with appropriate craftiness and ingenuity. On 30 March 1603, O'Neill submitted on his knees unwittingly to a dead Queen, Elizabeth I having died six days previously. Fearing that news of her death and the subsequent accession of her Scottish heir, James I (with whom O'Neill had intrigued in the past), would deter O'Neill from submitting, Mountjoy suppressed news of the Queen's death until the submission documents had been signed and sealed.

However, the terms that O'Neill secured from Mountjoy were indicative of his power and status on the one hand and the desire of Mountjoy to adopt lenient and conciliatory measures in dealing with the defeated leader on the other. Forfeiting his right to be The O'Neill, he agreed to renounce his allegiance to Spain and accept garrisons and sheriffs throughout his territory. He was allowed retain ownership of his vast lands, as well as jurisdiction over his principal underlord, O'Cahan. In effect, as far as property was concerned, O'Neill acquired personal possession of lands that, by Gaelic law, belonged to his clan. A similar settlement was made with Rory O'Donnell, who was created Earl of Tyrconnell.

The death of the old queen was in every way the end of an era. It had been an age of great and colourful figures on both sides of the divide: Elizabeth, Mary Queen of Scots, Sidney, Perrot, Essex, Philip of Spain, O'Neill, O'Donnell, Bingham, the Earl of Desmond and Ormond, Richard-in-Iron and Granuaile. All had contributed to an age which, despite its inherent cruelty and bloodshed, had a certain romantic splendour and excitement. Now the wars and military conflicts had ended and a wasted country began the long struggle back to some semblance of normality. It was a deceptive and unstable peace that settled over Ireland but it did allow time for the country to become fertile and orderly, as well as providing a suitable climate for the extension of English law into every aspect of life hitherto governed by Gaelic law.

If soldiers and military strategists instigated the conquest of Ireland, it was completed by legal experts, adventurers, profit-seekers and entrepreneurs who sought possession of Gaelic lands, property and assets by legal or quasi legal means or by whatever means opportunity placed in their path. While English military dominance had been established over the whole country at the time of Elizabeth's death, the ownership of the land of Ireland remained largely in Gaelic hands. Under Elizabeth's successor, James I, the battle for the land of Ireland began in earnest. It was a battle waged by lawyers, surveyors and speculators, armed with maps, pen and parchment and obscure deeds. By the middle of the century it would have dramatically altered the ownership of the land of Ireland forever.

The accession of the Scottish King to the throne of England at first ppeared to herald a tolerant era in Ireland. O'Neill was restored to his earldom and the Act of Oblivion was passed in 1604 by which those who had rebelled against the Crown were pardoned. There was a general expectation that a new era of religious tolerance was about to dawn. It was, however, an unfounded expectation.

A proclamation issued by the new Lord Deputy Chichester declared the end of the 'servitude and dependence of the common subjects upon their great lords and chiefs',[7] and, in effect, the formal ending of the Gaelic laws, to be replaced by the laws of England. Sir John Davies, the newly-appointed Attorney General for Ireland, in his frequent circuits throughout the country, established for the first time the principle of English common law and the replacement of the Gaelic law of gavelkind by English landlordism.

A royal commission for defective land titles was established, whereby the legality of the ownership of land under English law was examined and the present occupiers had to prove legal claim and title to their possessions. This was one of the most disturbing aspects of the new regime, particularly for the native and gaelicised Anglo-Norman chieftains who, for the most part, held title to their lands according to the Gaelic practices of tanistry and gavelkind. In Connaught, the Composition of 1585 had attempted to legalise the land titles of the chieftains there, but this was now found to be defective, because the Composition had never been formally ratified.

Tenure of land by Gaelic law, more often bequeathed by oral tradition and custom than by written submission, was further complicated by inherent customs of gavelkind and by the recognition of the rights of tenure of illegitimate sons. Now counter-claims to land titles were presented by different members of the same clan on the slightest chance of success; by a stronger local chief or lord at the expense of a more vulnerable one; by English adventurers seeking new investments; and by the Crown, which had many pretexts at its disposal, such as forfeiture and confiscation for past rebellious acts, whether pardoned or not. Trickery, forging of leases and claims, and threats, both physical and legal, became accepted methods in the unholy scramble for Irish land and property at the beginning of the 17th century. The old clan system slowly crumbled and succumbed to the all-encompassing greed for land by both native and newcomer alike.

After Kinsale, the level of land purchases increased even more as lack of money forced the defenceless chieftains of the minor septs to offer their land for sale, lease or mortgage to more fortunate neighbours or relations. But such transactions were not concluded easily. To establish claim to Gaelic-owned land was a complicated procedure. By right of Gaelic law several members of the same family could have an equal claim to the same property, as Tibbott's dealings with the MacEvilly clan demonstrated. Further complications arose if any one of the co-owners had sold, mortgaged or leased his share to a third party. Parts or shares in actual properties, such as castles, mills, fisheries, and weirs were also inherited, with the result that a potential purchaser might well have to undertake many separate transactions for the one building or piece of land. Hence, there could be many separate deeds relating to a single property. Further difficulties were encountered when the claim of the vendor was disputed by the admittance of an older claim, often originating centuries earlier.

A new and complex society began to emerge following the disintegration of the old Gaelic society. From the old Gaelic and gaelicised Anglo-Norman ruling families, such as Tibbott's, emerged a new ruling class, sharing a common background and religion but now rapidly adopting and adapting to English laws and customs. The early Elizabethan settlers, often sharing the same religious affiliation as their Gaelic and gaelicised Anglo-Norman neighbours, were considered less as outsiders, owing to the influx of a new wave of English and Scottish Protestant planters. These planters, adventurers and entrepreneurs showed little consideration for the rights of the previous occupiers, Gaelic and gaelicised Anglo-Norman alike. The remnants of the old Gaelic and gaelicised Anglo-Norman nobility, in turn, sought to consolidate their hold on the lands and properties that, in many cases, had been invested in them by Gaelic law, giving them a life-interest only. The lesser chieftains, as well as the native peasantry, bore the brunt of the greed of all.

On 4 January 1604, King James I knighted Tibbott in recognition of his 'loyal and valorous service'. He was styled Sir Tibbott (ne Longe) Bourke. The letters patent, officially confirming the honour, were preserved in Westport House. They are written in Latin on six pages of parchment, the colour and writing still as vivid as the day they were drafted. They are adorned with the De Burgo Arms, Tibbott's personal arms, the arms adopted by his eldest son and heir, Miles, and by a portrait of King James I.

Tibbott's mother, Granuaile, died about this time at the great age [for the time] of seventy-three years. She is most likely buried on Clare

Island at the mouth of Clew Bay, both her home and her 'kingdom' for the greater part of her long and eventful career. Whether or not she lived to see her son become 'Sir' Tibbott is not certain but, if tradition is to be believed, she herself had been proffered a title from James's predecessor, Elizabeth, but had refused the honour.

On receipt of his knighthood, Tibbott forwarded a petition on behalf of himself, his stepbrother Murrough-na-Maor O'Flaherty, and his nephew by the half-blood, Donal O'Flaherty, 'praying His Majesty to accept of their respective surrenders of their estates and to re-grant the same by letters patent'.[8] Later in the year, the King in a letter patent 'given under Our seal signet at Winchester, the 25th day of September', ordered the Commissioners to 'enquire what mannors, seignories, landes and herediataments the said Sir Theobald righfullie holdeth, of any estate of inheritance by discent or other lawfull meanes'.[9] As was customary, the commissioners appointed by the King had firstly to determine 'the quantity and limits of the land whereof he is reputed owner. Next, how much himselfe doth hold in demesne and how much is posset by his Tenants and Followers and thirdly what Customes, Duties and services, he doth yearly receive out of those lands.'[10]

In Tibbott's case, such an investigation was more necessary than for most. His claim to lands belonging to the MacWilliamship, to lands held by him in trust for his sept, as well as to his personal estate, was made by right of both Gaelic and English law. As early as 1594, by virtue of the agreement he had entered into with Conyers Clifford, he was granted lands in the barony of Carra belonging to his kinsmen, Shane Bourke Mac Hubert, Ulick and Shane Bourke MacMoyler. With two legal systems still in operation and with claims being submitted and investigated by right of both, Tibbott sought individual ownership to as much property as he could lay claim to. If he did not, it would fall prey to the wave of new English planters who had descended on Connaught after Kinsale. The more powerful the claimant and the better versed in the legal process, the more likely he was to succeed, usually at the expense of less powerful and less knowledgeable neighbours and relations.

The new English administration also sought to abolish the system whereby chieftains, such as Tibbott, who, harking back to the old Bremen code, negotiated on behalf of their tributary clans and clients, receiving payments and services from them in return. This development was largely welcomed by the minor clans and septs who were often prevailed upon to partake in the arrangement against their will.

In December 1603, a decree was issued by the Earl of Clanrickard, chief commissioner of Connaught, in such a case involving Tibbott and the O'Malley clan. The O'Malleys complained that 'Sr. Tibbott Boork Knight [did] daylie practise and devise to procure authoritie ... over them'. They asked that he be instructed to desist in his actions against them and forbidden 'to burthen charge or ympose them with anything'.[11] In this instance, Tibbott was in breach not only of English law, but of Gaelic law as well, whereby traditionally the O'Malley clan paid no tributes or services to the Bourkes but only a 'rising out' in time of war. The Earl of Clanrickard, no friend of Tibbott, decided in favour of the O'Malleys, and Tibbott's right of exaction over them was denied.

Tibbott risked further alienating his O'Malley relations by claiming land in the Barony of Murrisk. He executed his claim as the only heir of his mother, Granuaile, to whom the said lands were bequeathed as the only child of her mother, Margaret, who, in turn, had inherited them as sister and sole heir of the former owner, Dowdara Mac Donnor Oge Mac Connor O'Malley, Tibbott's maternal great-grandfather. Tibbott denied the counter-claim of the O'Malleys, which held that Hugh O'Malley was the son of Dowdara. Instead, he maintained that Hugh was in fact 'a bastard begotten and born out of wedlock upon the body of one reputed a common whoore and never married unto the said Dowdarra'.[12] In response, the O'Malleys stated that the said Hugh O'Malley, not having any male heirs, had divided the lands between his cousin Teig O'Malley and Tibbott; that during the last rebellion Teig, 'fearing that the people thereabouts would join the said rebellion and being a person civilly bred in the English pale he forsook the said country',[13] whereupon Tibbott and some of the MacGibbons 'taking advantage of his absence entered into the premises and have since occupied the same'.[14] The outcome of these complex proceedings resulted in Tibbott being granted ownership of the greater part of the disputed lands.

This case was typical of the period, involving a claim and counter-claim under both Gaelic and English principles, involving the laws of gavelkind, primogeniture, tanistry, fosterage and illegitimacy, as well as inheritance through the female line. To unravel the right of either claimant was a virtual impossibility. Many decisions in such cases were ultimately dependent on the status and power of the parties involved. On this occasion 'Sir' Tibbott Bourke, being the more influential claimant, won the day. Using every legal and quasi legal mechanism at his disposal in the early years of the new century, Tibbott acquired, by purchase and mortgage, the lands and properties, including 'the great mill of Cooley' and many fisheries and castles of the foremost clans and septs in Mayo – O'Malleys, Bourkes, O'Conroys, MacGibbons, MacPhilbins, Barretts and MacEvillys. Some of the septs, ignorant of English law and fearful that their lands would fall into the hands of English planters, were persuaded to appoint Tibbott and his son, Miles, 'as their attorneys and patentees'.

Tibbott's dealings with the MacEvilly clan of Mayo, for example, are unique in Irish historiography in that they are an example of land trans-actions between two Gaelic parties, based on principals of Brehon law for which documentary evidence is still extant. Tibbott's involvement with the MacEvilly clan began with his fosterage with the chieftain, Myles MacEvilly, in 1582. Subsequently MacEvilly conferred the clan estate on his foster son. This appears to have been no more than a tac-tical ploy on MacEvilly's part to obtain the protection of Tibbott's father, the then MacWilliam, against an English undertaker named William Bowen. An officer in the English army, Bowen sought to attain Castlecarra, part of the MacEvilly estate, by right of an ancient deed of feoffment sold to him by Peter Barnewell, Baron of Trimbleston in the Pale. The Baron of Trimbleston traced his right to Castlecarra back to 1300, to a deed vested in Nesta, the grand-daughter of the original Norman grantee of the estate, Adam de Staunton.

In 1597, on the death of the chieftain Myles MacEvilly, Tibbott com-menced the purchase 'for a certain sum of money' of the MacEvilly estate. Owing to the complexities of Gaelic inheritance system, it took him over a decade to complete the transaction. The clan's principal seat,

Kinturk Castle, Tibbott's foster home, had been part inherited by Ever Mac Myles, Edmond Mac Thomas and Sarah ny Richard Mac Breoyne MacEvilly. In 1597, Tibbott purchased Ever's third of the property, 'together with twenty two quarters of land to the same belonging'.[15] In 1604, Edmond stated in a deed: 'I doo gyve graunt bargaine sell and confirme unto the said Sr Tibbott Bourke, knight, the third parte of the Castell of Kinturk by the midell with a third part of the Bawen and all the lands tenements and herediataments of the said third belonging.'[16] Sarah MacEvilly, by a deed dated October 1605, sold Tibbott her 'third part of the Castell of Kinturyck viz the sellar [seller] and the third part of the Bawen and third parte of all and singular lands tenements and herediataments belonging or in any wyse appertaining to the heritadge of Slight [Sliocht, i.e. sept] Breoyne MacEvylle, to me by course of inheritance belonginge'.[17] By 1611, Tibbott's transactions with the MacEvillys had given him ownership of Kinturk Castle, with twenty-two quarters of land, the manor castle and house of Manulla, with four quarters, a share in the castle, town and lands of Kilboynell (later to become Castlebourke) together with 'the messuages, buildings, orchards, gardynes, moores, meddowes, waters, watter courses, fishinges, emollements and other hereditaments'[18] pertaining to each property.

In the first three decades of the 17th century, the transfer of lands and properties from Mayo clans like the MacEvillys, O'Malleys and Barretts to Tibbott continued unabated. The 'legal' documents by which this major change in ownership of land was effected are preserved among Tibbott's papers in the Westport House manuscript collection. These brittle, faded, parchment relics are a poignant testimony to the all-pervasive fear and uncertainty that beset these indigenous clans as they faced an uncertain future following the overthrow of their native world. Unfamiliar with the new laws, language and customs of the victor, they willingly accepted Tibbott and his family as 'one of their own', to act as a buffer between them and the alien legal system to which they were now subjected and to protect them from the acquisitive onslaught being mounted by outsiders. By so doing, they became mere tenants of the ancestral lands of their forbears.

Like other native landowners of the period, Tibbott availed of the principals of Brehon custom where they worked to his advantage. His status in the locality *vis-à-vis* other clans and the 'protection' he afforded them, as well as the practices he employed in the administration of his newly acquired estate, were more in keeping with a MacWilliam than with a knight of the realm. He paid his tenants mainly in kind and practised a form of *metayage*, renting part of his lands in return for the third or fourth sheaf (i.e. one-third or one- quarter of the produce) and also giving and receiving cattle in payment. In the years of transition between the Brehon and English law after Kinsale, cattle held their place as a unit of exchange and continued to be an important commodity of exchange in dowry, jointure and mortgage settlements.

Tibbott took possession of his former foster home, Kinturk Castle, and, for a time, adapted to the less turbulent lifestyle of a country landowner. The anglicisation of Gaelic chieftains, like Tibbott, took many years to accomplish. The transition was firstly most noticeable in their style of dress. Gradually they abandoned the use of the braccae or tight frieze leggings and the long loose-sleeved *léine*, to be replaced by the hose and doublet after the English fashion. The characteristic Gaelic woollen cloak, however, survived for many decades. A recommendation that the availability of English apparel should be restricted in Ireland owing to the cost of same and 'that none should wear silks or richer stuffs nor gold or silver lace or satin lace nor combri nor Holland but either noble man or minstrels or ladies of honour of great state or whores'[19] would seem unnecessary in a country where money was extremely scarce and where barter and payment in the old Gaelic manner still prevailed.

A shortage of money, however, did not appear to curtail the assemblies and feasts for which the houses of the chieftains were noted. Kinturk Castle resounded to the sounds of harper and piper when Tibbott hosted such social gatherings, known as 'banishes' and 'cosheries'. Bards and rhymers, together with the all-important 'caroughs' (professional gamblers), joined Tibbott and his party to make merry. Contemporary reports indicated that such feasts were often of three- and four-days duration.

One such feast would have occurred in Derrymacloghtny, County Galway on the marriage of Tibbott's eldest son and heir, Miles, to

Honora Bourke, daughter of Sir John Bourke and granddaughter of the Earl of Clanrickard. It was perhaps fitting that the descendants of the two original branches of the Connaught De Burgos should be united at the start of a new era. Miles and Honora took up residence in Belcarra Castle.

✤ ✤ ✤

While the redistribution of land was a major feature of the early years of the 17th century, other developments were also taking place. Mountjoy died in April 1606 and O'Neill (Tyrone) effectively lost the only remaining buffer between him and his enemies in London and Dublin. Although restored to their estates by the King, neither Tyrone nor Tyrconnell (Rory O'Donnell) had become reconciled to their positions, which lacked the authority, privilege and status they had formerly enjoyed. Harried and derided, their powers were steadily eroded by the encroachment of the English administration, as well as Scottish and English planters into their territories.

Mountjoy was succeeded by Sir Arthur Chichester, the strong-willed governor of Carrickfergus, who aimed to establish a presidency in Ulster further to undermine the authority of the vanquished Ulster chiefs. These developments, coupled with the suspicion and distrust with which their every move was monitored, finally resulted in 1607 in the Flight of the Earls – perhaps the most enigmatic episode in Irish history. The earls of Tyrone and Tyrconnell forsook their patrimony to seek solace and protection in the royal courts of Europe, leaving their extensive territories and their dependent clans to the mercy of Scottish and English settlers.

Prior to the Flight of the Earls, the final tragic chapter in the demise of Gaelic Ireland was played out fittingly within a climate of yet more subterfuge and intrigue. Both Tyrone and Tyrconnell were accused of plotting with the Irish in exile in Spain – those who had fled the country after Kinsale – in an attempt to revitalise Gaelic resistance. After the Flight, details of the 'plot' were divulged by Christopher St Lawrence, Baron of Howth, on his return from military service in Flanders. He made certain disclosures and accusations to the English government against, not only Tyrone and Tyrconnell, but also against Tibbott.

The Lord Deputy was initially sceptical about Howth's revelations and observed, 'I like not his look and jesture when he talks with me of this business.'[20] Given the climate of anti-Catholic suspicion and alienation that prevailed in the English government, heightened by the Gunpowder Plot of 1605 and, since the flight of the Ulster chieftains added some substance to Howth's disclosures, an investigation into the affair was ordered. The investigation revealed that during August 1607, prior to O'Neill and O'Donnell's departure, intelligence had been received at Dublin Castle which implicated the Earl of Tyrconnell, the Earl of Tyrone, Sir Thomas Burke (brother of the Earl of Clanrickard) and 'Sir Thibbott Burke' of 'involving Spanish aid for the overthrow of the English'.[21] Tibbott was named as one of the conspirators by an old adversary, David Mac Ulick Bourke, who voiced his suspicions to the President of Connaught, the Earl of Clanrickard, who in turn promptly informed Chichester.

In September, Chichester ordered Tibbott to appear before the Vice-President of Connaught, Sir Robert Remington, to answer the charges. Tibbott pleaded inability to leave Kinturk, owing to ill health, whereupon a 'serjeant-at-arms' was ordered 'to stay there for him till he be able to travel'[22] and to bring him in for questioning. By October, Tibbott had recovered sufficiently to present himself at Athlone Castle where he was immediately confined to prison. Meanwhile, his step-brother, Murrough-na-Maor O'Flaherty, was also brought in from Iar-Chonnacht. They were taken from Athlone to Dublin Castle. After a detailed examination by Chichester and the Council, no evidence emerged to prove conclusively that Tibbott and Murrough were part of the conspiracy. After one month's confinement in the Castle, they were allowed to return to Connaught.

In 1608, however, Chichester obtained further evidence implicating Tibbott of collusion with exiled Gaelic chiefs in Spain. Reverting back to the 16th-century ploy of hostage-taking, this time Chichester seized Tibbott's son, Miles, and sent him to England, in the company of Sir Anthony St Leger, as a pledge for Tibbott's future loyalty. While the evidence may have been inconclusive, Chichester was taking no chances. The Lord Deputy warned Tibbott to look to his position in Mayo, 'seeing he has strong competitors there for all the lands he possesses, which he is sure to hold no longer than he is supported and defended by His Majesty'.[23]

It is quite likely that Tibbott knew about the conspiracy and, had been approached by the conspirators. But as a major landowner in Connaught he also had his share of enemies. In acquiring his huge estate in Mayo, he had stood on the toes of many of his relations and neighbours who sought out any opportunity to destroy him. By accusing him of treason, the English undertakers and land speculators hoped to acquire his lands for themselves. As an English official in the Irish service commented at the time, the whole affair was no more 'than a practice of his adversaries to bring him into disgrace and danger'.[24]

In October, Tibbott was one of a number of Gaelic captains who were discharged from their duties as leaders of private armies in the pay of the Crown. The government viewed the existence of these native armies with deep mistrust. Subvented by the government, they were primarily used by lords like Tibbott to further their own interests locally. In view of the continued doubts voiced over his loyalty, and his suspected contacts with the exiled Irish in Spain, a private army under Tibbott's command was deemed too great a risk.

With his power thus reduced, coupled with the close scrutiny on his every movement by his adversary, the Earl of Clanrickard, Tibbott decided to face down his detractors. He boldly returned to Dublin and demanded that he be either called to trial or absolved and that his bonds for good behaviour be dissolved. Reluctantly Chichester was forced to concede that he could not 'with a good conscience keep a man of his sort in prison without some pregnant cause appearing against him'.[25] He released Tibbott from the bonds of good behaviour but urged him to reconcile himself with the Earl of Clanrickard. Tibbott had blustered his way out of danger but his name continued to be linked with foreign conspiracies for many years to come.

In July 1610, the Catholic Archbishop of Tuam, Florence O'Mulconry, who had travelled to Spain with Red Hugh O'Donnell after Kinsale and is described by the English State Papers as being 'an agent for all Irish matters that the Pope's crew would have brought to pass there',[26] landed secretly in Cork. He brought with him 'a great packet of letters from Spain and Rome to the nobility and chief gentlemen of Ireland about Tyrone's present coming into this Kingdom with armies ready prepared'.[27] One of these letters was addressed to 'Sir Tibalde Burck, alias Longe, in Connaghte'.[28]

The letter was brought to Chichester's attention by the Protestant Bishop of Limerick. However, while Tibbott may have been contacted and his support solicited, there was no evidence that he actively participated in the plot. Yet the English authorities were suspicious and Sir Oliver St. John, in a letter to the Privy Council, warned that Tibbott 'was still a person to watch' in Connaught and that 'the O'Flahertys and Mayles [O'Mallies], the worst of all the Irish in the Kingdom, and a number of Clandonnells, a near bad sept of Gallowglasse, and all there are either by alliance or dependence linked to Sir Tibbott'.[29]

Despite the continued foreboding of the English administration in Dublin, Tibbott and his eldest son, Miles, were granted a pardon for past offences from the King in July 1610, in a final attempt towards establishing definitive claim to the extensive property and lands they had accumulated in counties Mayo and Galway.

The notice of the pardon is preserved at Westport House and reads:

> Memorandum that Sir Theobald Bourk of Kanturk in the Co. of Maio Knight appeared personally before us at Conge the fourteen day of August, 1610 and then and there found surrities for the observance and performance of his Mastie moste gracious pardon to him and others granted and dated at Dublin this nynthe day of July in the yeares of the reigned of our sovraigne Lord King James of England France and Ireland the eight and of Scotland the forty third.[30]

The pardon, together with the finding of the Commissioners, would finally determine the nature and extent of the lands that English law would formally confer on Tibbott.

CHAPTER EIGHT

The Gaelic Viscount
1612 - 1629

OR THE FIRST TIME it could be claimed that the English
king's writ ran throughout the entire country, albeit with varying
degrees of effectiveness. The Attorney General, Sir John Davies,
lyrically observed 'the clock of the civil government is now well set and
all the wheels thereof do move in order; the strings of the Irish harp,
which the magistrates doth finger, are all in time and make a good
harmony in the commonwealth.'[1] Davies urged that the Crown should
respond to 'this civility' and ensure that both native and foreigner be
treated equally under English law, concluding that, in time, if treated
fairly, the native population would learn to obey and acknowledge the
king as their sovereign. But Davies's advice was not acted upon and while
the country remained relatively peaceful, discontent seethed under the
surface and threatened, as one far-sighted observer remarked, 'the next
combustion from our degenerate English Irish'.[2]

In 1613, an event occurred which, far from reconciling this large
and vocal group, placed a wedge between them and the Crown which
would eventually fester until their grievances exploded into armed
resistance. While the laws and customs of Gaelic Ireland had been
replaced to a large extent by the laws of England, the Crown had been
unsuccessful in its attempt to make the Gaelic world conform in the
matter of religion. The most powerful group, the gaelicised Anglo-
Normans or old English, together with the survivors of the old Gaelic
nobility, had refused to conform to the new religion. The anxiety they

had experienced relating to the legality of tenure of their estates under English law was further heightened by the realisation that adherence to their religious beliefs was viewed by the English government to be synonymous with disloyalty and that, consequently, the government might seek to deprive them of their property on a religious pretext. This group was to become known as the 'Recusants' and was to play an eventful role in the affairs of the early decades of the 17th century.

In the initial years of James's reign, religious conformity in Ireland was not pursued with any greater vigour than under Elizabeth. The existing recusancy laws were less severe than those prevailing in England. The anti-Catholic legislation introduced by James I after his accession, and the Gunpowder Plot which followed, had alienated the English Catholic nobility and gentry from the king and the government. It was now considered appropriate to enforce conformity throughout Ireland as well.

To this effect, as well as to enact other legislation to cater for the changed political circumstances, it was decided to convene a parliament in Dublin. (The previous parliament in Ireland had sat in 1585.) Chichester and the Irish Council prepared legislation to impose greater restrictions on the practice of the Catholic religion. However, it was obvious from the start that the bills would not be passed so long as there was a Recusant majority in parliament. In the Upper House, a Protestant majority was assured, but the Recusants had a substantial majority in the Commons. Consequently, Chichester decided to contrive the required Protestant majority by creating new boroughs in areas that would ensure the return of a Protestant member, regardless of whether the designated area was of sufficient size to warrant the status of a borough. The Recusants protested but to no avail. Elections for the fabricated seats were held and the convening of parliament set for 18 May 1613.

Tibbott was elected to represent County Mayo, together with Sir Thomas Bourke of Ballyloughmask, in the new parliament. Sir John

Bingham and Thomas Peyton were elected to represent the newly created borough of Castlebar. As the most extensive landowner and premier leader in Mayo, both by virtue of his origins and of his recently acquired English honours, Tibbott was an obvious choice. He was, however, at one accord with the aims of his Catholic co-religionists and opposed the borough creations. Tibbott and Sir Thomas Bourke were the first native Irish to be elected to represent the county in parliament. (In 1585, it had been represented by John Browne of the Neale and by Thomas Williams.) On receipt of his summons to attend the parliament in Dublin, Tibbott was faced with an arduous journey, on horseback. The country roads were scarcely more than ill-defined tracks and the increasing numbers of raparees and highwaymen added to the dangers encountered by the traveller. The scarcity of inns made it necessary to seek food and lodgings in the houses of the local lords through whose lands he travelled.

Dublin was a small but expanding city with a population of about 50,000 people. It was an English city in its customs and in the lifestyle of its citizens. Its medieval walls encircled a warren of narrow, dark streets, lying to the west and north of the castle on the south bank of the Liffey. With the exception of St. Mary's Abbey, St. Michan's Church and the 'Innes' or law courts, the city had expanded little on the north side of the river. The Liffey was spanned by one bridge, stretching from the 'Innes' to Oxmantown Gate at Usher's Island. Trinity College was in the process of construction and was considered at the time to be 'near Dublin'. The river lapped the city walls because the quays were not constructed until many decades later. The most populous area lay within the walls and to the west of the Castle. Some development was taking place outside the city walls to the west and south of Francis Street, Patrick Street and James Street. Tower gates guarded entrances to the city. Ringsend was gradually superseding Howth as the main port for both cargo and passengers, and barges and small boats sailed up the river on the tide.

On completion of the long journey from Mayo, Tibbott entered the city via the tower gate at St. Michan's, crossed the 'Old Bridge' and entered the city proper via Oxmantown. He rode slowly along the narrow streets and alleys, some less than five feet wide, many still unpaved. The bustling and congested streets were further 'pestered with hucksters sitting under hulks and stalls',[3] selling their produce, while carriages, carts and men on horseback jostled for position in the traffic jams of the day. Beggars, prostitutes and petty thieves were plentiful, while coffee houses and bookshops were just making their appearance around Castle Street and Skinner's Row. The city was well endowed with taverns and ale-houses and Tibbott might well have quenched his thirst at such establishments as the Nag's Head, The Sugar Loaf or the White Hart. There was an acute scarcity of lodging houses, aggravated by the arrival in town of the members of parliament. Tibbott would have found accommodation in a private house, as was customary, in the vicinity of the Castle where the parliament was due to sit. At night, the city was dark and menacing, with no street lighting, irregular policing, frequent street brawls, muggings and murders. The great bell of Christ Church rang daily at nine in the evening, to announce the time of retirement, and in the morning at four to rouse the citizens to the new day.

While on parliamentary duty, Tibbott received thirteen shillings and four pence per day expenses. The parliament sat from eight or nine in the morning until midday on most days of the week, while the afternoons were generally devoted to committee work. Tibbott took his seat among the Recusants on 18 May.

From the outset, the main contention concerned the question of the legality of the newly created boroughs, which had effectively reduced the Catholics to 100 members out of a total of 232 in the Commons. Describing themselves as 'the knights and burgesses of the ancient shires and corporations' the Recusants demanded 'an examination to be made of the lawfulness or unlawfulness of the supposed members'[4] of the newly-created boroughs before they would agree to proceed with the business of the House. A heated debate followed before both parties agreed that a speaker should be elected. The Lord Deputy proposed Sir John Davies. The Recusants proposed Sir John Everard. Pandemonium broke out in the hall as each side rushed to the Speaker's chair and physically attempted to seat its respective candidate. Everard was eventually forcibly removed. He and his supporters left the House in protest, shouting as they departed 'you that are in the house are no house and your speaker no speaker'.[5] The parliament was adjourned for some days. When it reconvened, the Recusants in both houses still refused to attend and so the parliament was officially prorogued until October 1614.

Tibbott made his way homewards to Mayo after his brief participation in an institution and in an atmosphere that was alien to his background and to his character. His presence at parliament spelled both an end and a beginning. Hitherto, like his ancestors before him, as a Gaelic chieftain working within the Brehon code, it was he who dispensed and had made the rules governing his territory, now he was a mere participant in a process over which he had little control.

During the recess, the Recusants, over Chichester's head, forwarded their grievances to the King, complaining about the creation of the illegal boroughs and also the treatment meted out to them by Chichester's government. The King delivered his response in August 1614, declaring that the Recusants had no legitimate cause for grievance. In relation to the boroughs, eight were to be deprived of representatives, two were declared void, while three were adjudged to have no right of representation whatsoever. This resulted in the overall membership of the Commons of 108 Protestants and 102 Catholics, but, with the Protestant majority so reduced, Chichester considered it unwise to move the bills against the Recusants.

The 1613 parliament was significant because it marked a further expansion of English constitutional procedures in Ireland and brought into the open the conflict that had been smouldering between the Recusants and the government. Its legislative output, however, was minimal. When the parliament was reconvened in October, two acts were eventually passed: the Act of Attainder of the Ulster chiefs, and an Act for the suppression of piracy (which must have caused many eyes to turn in Tibbott's direction). The Recusants had successfully blocked the proposed legislation against them and were to enjoy the same degree of religious toleration as they had before the parliament convened. Yet their future prospects looked grim. The eight boroughs temporarily suspended would, in the future, return Protestant members and restore a sufficient majority to ensure the passing of the postponed legislation.

The parliament was dissolved in October 1615 and Tibbott returned home to resume his more usual role as landowner and local magnate. Parliamentary procedures, no matter how eventful, had little relevance to everyday life in Mayo, where experience of English law was confined to the sessions and to the legal battles over land, waged in the Courts of Chancery, of which Tibbott had ample experience. Otherwise a rural lifestyle, extracting a livelihood from the land and overseeing the administration of his large estate, became his principal and essential occupation.

While the pastoral economy of the 16th century continued in the west of Ireland, more settled agricultural practices were also being introduced. Land under tillage was increasing; village settlements, markets and fairs were also becoming established. The country's currency was still recovering from the debasement policy of the late Elizabethan years and, because of the scarcity of actual coin, cattle maintained their position as the basic unit of exchange. Booleying, or the practice of transhumance, still survived in the mountainous regions, while horses, sheep and swine continued to be reared extensively. Fosterage was to continue to cement relationships and dependence between clans and families. Tibbott's own grandson, Theobald Bourke, was fostered with William Kelly, to whom Kelly in 1652 bequeathed his interest in Donamona Castle. Rents continued to be paid to Tibbott in kind by his tenants, and many a bushel of wheat and side of salted pork was received at Kinturk in lieu of services and rents.

Tibbott's family were now grown men and women. Miles and his wife, Honora Burke, resided at the castle of Belcarra, a short distance from Kinturk. The marriage had produced a son, Theobald. In 1615 Tibbott's eldest daughter, Mary, married Calvach (Charles) O'Connor

Don, heir to the high-kingship of Ireland. In 1607, Charles had been engaged to one of the Countess of Desmond's daughters but the marriage did not take place because of English opposition to the match. At the time of his marriage to Mary, extensive lands and the castle of Knockalaghta in County Roscommon were settled on Charles, who eventually succeeded to the main O'Connor castle and demesne at Ballintobber.

However, the settlement made on Charles upon his marriage to Mary was concluded amid great controversy, because of a claim lodged by Dermot, the son of Charles's father by a previous marriage. Dermot contested in the Court of Chancery that the agreement made between Tibbott and Sir Hugh on the marriage of Charles and Mary was 'very disadvantageous to himself' and accused Charles's mother that 'she did give out and caused it to be divulged for a common report that he [Dermot] was not born in lawful wedlock and that consequently the said Charles was son and heir to Sir Hugh'.[6] Dermot, however, was unsuccessful in his claim to the O'Connor Don estate, which was eventually settled on Charles and Mary and their descendants.

As was customary, Tibbott gave a large dowry in livestock, household goods and money on his daughter. This union between the direct descendants of the king of Connaught and Richard de Burgo, his conqueror, reflects how the wheel had turned full circle in the intervening centuries, from the invasion of the O'Connor territory by the De Burgos in the 13th century, through the decades of dissension and disorder, to the gaelicisation of the descendants of the De Burgos and their coexistence with the native population and now the anglicisation of both O'Connors and Bourkes.

Tibbott's third son, Theobald Riabach (the strong), married the daughter of Walter Bourke of Turlough and resided at the castle of Cloghans in Tirawley. Tibbott's two younger sons, David and Richard, were as yet unmarried, as were his other daughters, Honora and Margaret, who continued to reside at the family castle of Kinturk.

In Ulster the policy of plantation was being pursued with vigour. Obscure deeds, in many cases forged, were being presented by unscrupulous lawyers. Vague crown claims to vast estates were being established, many stretching back to the Norman invasion. One quarter of Ulster was set aside, specifically for plantation by the Crown, while new titles confirmed the King's ownership to the rest. Royal claims now extended to vast areas of the province. Dispossession of previous occupiers both native and Old English was rampant. As co-religionists, this further hardened their resolve against the government and moved them into closer alliance with each other.

In Connaught the plantation policy was less widespread. For the purpose of stabilising land tenure and, at the same time, to bring closure to the Gaelic practice of clientship, the King ordered that the measures of the old Composition should be revived and receive formal sanction. Consequently, new surrenders of lands were made to the Crown by the Connaught landowners, fees were paid and patents granted to formally establish title to their land. But the King's policy was opposed on two accounts. Firstly, the provisions of the Composition under which the new titles were to be confirmed 'and the indiscriminate regularisation of its findings would certainly have perpetuated injustices'[7] because the claims of the various chieftains and lords who had initially signed it in 1585 were often inaccurate. To establish the current occupiers in firm title of their lands, the King intended to give free pardon to those who had previously rebelled against the Crown. But by so doing, he would in effect deprive both the Crown and, more especially, English land speculators of access to vast estates that otherwise would be forfeited because of the rebellion of their original owners. Such was the opposition to the scheme in England that 'the final stage in the process of validating the new titles, by enrolling the patents and surrenders in the Court of Chancery, was never completed'.[8] Chieftains like Tibbott were forced to compete with the newcomers and resist challenge to the title of the lands they occupied.

In January 1616, such on inquisition was ordered into the validity of Tibbott's title to the substantial estate he had accumulated.

Accompanied by his son Miles, Tibbott made submission to the inquisition of the lands he claimed by right of inheritance from his father's personal estate, the MacWilliamship inheritance, inheritance by right of his mother and the lands that had more lately come into his possession by grant, purchase and mortgage. He produced deeds and documents to back his claim, brought witnesses to support his statement, where no written documents existed, and generally relied on his wits to put forward the strongest case to secure his possessions. An ensuing grant from the King, dated 20 March 1617, is in itself a testimony of his astutness and tenacity in defending the lands he had accumulated. What he had acquired, either by right or by slight of hand, he intended to keep and defend and preventing them from falling into the hands of others.

The grant gave him title to extensive estates across the baronies of Carra, Burrishoole, Murrisk, Erris, Tirawley, Gallen and Kilmaine, with outright title to twelve castles and part title to four others, including 'the fifth of the castle and bawn of Cahirnamarte',[9] the former residence of his mother's half-brother, Donal-na-Piopa O'Malley, together with many of the islands in Clew Bay. The grant further stipulated that 'all the lands in the barony of Carra … are created the manor of Ballinecarrow with 400 acres in demesne … the lands in the barony of Borrisowle are created the manor of Ballinknock … those in the barony of Murriske are created the barony of Danigin … those in the barony of Gallen are created the manor of Belanmore … those in the barony of Erish, are created the manor of Cloghans … all with the like demesne and power of creating tenures, licence to hold courts leet and baron; to have free warren and park; to enjoy all waifs and strays in all the said manors', together with the right to collect tolls, to have markets and fairs on specific days 'all to be holden as of the castle of Athlone, by knights' service and saving all rents reserved to the Crown by any other letters patent and now of record'.[10] The grant, in effect, made Tibbott the single largest landowner in County Mayo.

Tibbott had prospered and had used the depressed economic state of the country to his advantage, offering his protection and financial assistance to less well-off neighbours in return for mortgages and leases, competing effectively with wealthy Galway merchants and English speculators in the process. Once the concept of English tenure had been established and primogeniture accepted by Tibbott and his peers, the basic principal of Gaelic law – the relationship between the chieftain and his followers – became legally redundant. Henceforth the criterion for assessing a chieftain's power and status was not the number of his client lords and followers but the number of acres he possessed. In the early 17th century, 'the Irish lords recognised the same advantage in owning large estates as did the wealthy merchants and new English planters',[11] and Sir Tibbott Bourke did so quicker than most.

While the small freeholders began to subdivide their holdings in order to provide farms for their sons, Tibbott also acquired additional land to provide new estates for his younger sons. Already established at Belcarra Castle, Miles would eventually, by right of primogeniture, succeed his father both to his title and to his estate. Tibbott purchased lands and a castle in Carra barony for his second son, David, while Theobald received the manor and lands of Cloghans in Tirawley. Richard, his fourth and youngest son, received lands in the baronies of Murrisk and Carra. All four sons, in their own right, extended their properties by further purchases of land and mortgages from local free-holders. On her marriage to Murrough O'Flaherty of Aughnanure, Tibbott's daughter, Honora, received a substantial dowry from her father, as did Margaret on her marriage to Theobald Bourke of Turlough, County Mayo.

However, while the King had re-conveyed the lands to Tibbott and to other landowners by new letters patent, yet another complication emerged when the patents failed to be enrolled by the clerks, despite a sum of £3,000 having been paid by the grantees for this purpose. As the finances of the English exchequer grew more critical, the King desperately sought additional revenue. The unconfirmed title of the Connaught lords presented him with an opportunity to escape from his financial dilemma. Under threat of plantation, the Connaught 'proprietors offered to purchase a new confirmation of their patents by doubling their annual composition ... and to pay a fine of 10,000

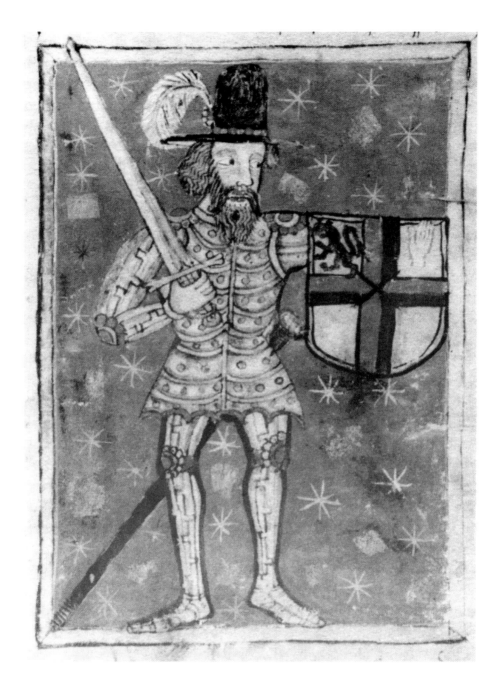

Richard de Burgo, Lord of Connaught
Courtesy of Trinity College, Dublin

Above: Gaelic Chieftain and Kerne
(Image of Ireland 1581)

Granuaile
Courtesy of Westport House, Co.
Mayo

Left:
Sir Richard Bingham,
Governor of Connaught

Letter from Tibbott-ne-
Long o Lord Burghley,
1595
(SP1 63/179)

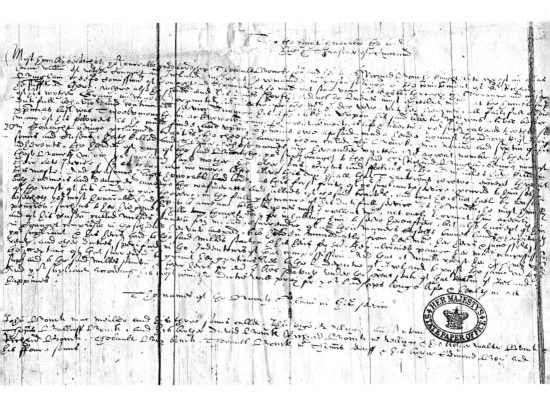

Elizabeth dei gratia Anglie Francie et Hibernie Regina fidei defen-
sor etc. noverit etc. gratia nostra speciali ac ex certa scientia et mero motu nostro ac de ad-
ordina nostro gratoque habilitatis ac deputati nostri generalis regni nostri Hibernie etc. de advis-
et consulimus dilecto subdito nostro Richardo Bonke alias Richard Fuller Bonke ac
gentia ac natura de alippia ane et secundarior tenentium et acquisitum anno
nostri Hibernie finattur etc. manerija terra tenentia et hereditament omnia cum eo
tenetur predicta rector manerior terr Itentor et hereditamentor terr retror plen
in vassalor ac apoliats et eorundem ac patria nostra violatorea ac pturbetor
huius quoties et prout necesse fuerit pro servitio nostro predicta atque defensio
regimen vitamque civilem inter bonos subditos nostros infra limites per
officio Generali nostri infra eosdem limites amuster ait etc. mque ut possit
libera ecclesiastica et castra patronabilea anna expensita quandocumque
vel gubernatorem nostrum tamen comissionem nostram priumire nostre Countie iussa fi
predicta officium aut utilitatem subditor nostror infra limites predicta aut alias
officiu authoritatem manerija casta terr Itentia hereditamenta terr rete
prefato Richardo Bonke alias Richard Fuller Bonke durante dicta anna ratio
nostra atque obserbet serviat coluet peddit et pimplett omnia et angela tende
gra gra nostra patentibz timez que ex pte dict Viri servicium eandem futur
valeat tamen aut de rectitudine priuissor ac eor altruisma aut de alia
fiat in partibz viiimie fiat aut aliquo attrinto terr ordinat amte pbia

Letters Patent Elizabeth 1, 1581 to Richard-in-Iron Bourke
(Westport House MSS)

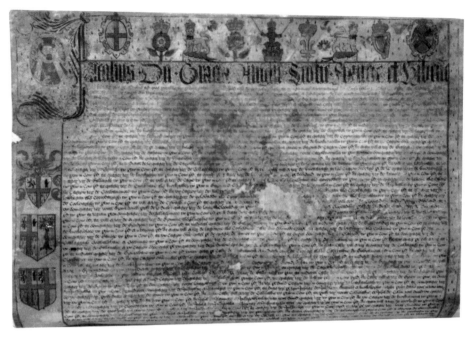

Letters Patent of Knighthood, James 1. 1603 (*Westport House MSS*)

The meeting of Granuaile and Queen Elizabeth 1 in 1593

The right Honorable Sr Theobald Burke kt Viscount Burke of Mayo deceased the 18 of June 1629. he had to wife Maude Dr of Charles O Connor Sligoe, by whome he had issue the right Ho: Miles Viscount Burke, Dauid, Theobald, Richard, Mary, Onora, and Margaret, was buried in the Church of Balintober in the County of Mayo.

Fees not payed ye Certificatin by Athlone

The certificat taken by Athlone, ye fees received by Ulster,

Left:
Tibbott's Death Notice (*Funerals Entry Book- Genealogical Office, Dublin*)

Ballintobber Abbey, Co Mayo (*Courtesy Dept of Environment*)

Kinturk Castle, Co Mayo (*Courtesy Dept of Environment*)

Right:
Tibbott-ne-Long's tomb in Ballintobber Abbey (*Courtesy Dept of Environment*)

pounds'.[12] They had little option. The King readily accepted the 'proposal', and duly suspended the threat of plantation.

Until his death, Tibbott continued to increase his estate, using the Courts of Chancery to establish claims on whatever pretext presented itself. While this was sometimes at the expense of his politically weaker or financially less well-off neighbours and relations, it was simply a question of survival. Competition for such lands was fierce from outside speculators and undertakers. Tibbott, in turn, was frequently summoned to defend his title, usually by outsiders, who used similar pretexts, as well as casting doubts on his loyalty, to try to dispossess him.

Controversy continued to dog Tibbott's steps, despite his wealth and newly found status as a knight of the realm. In 1620, a merchant ship, en route to Scotland from Spain with a cargo of wine and provisions, sailed into Clew Bay and anchored off Burrishoole. It was captained by an Englishman named Robert Luccopp. Tibbott and his son, Miles, were visiting nearby Castleaffy, Tibbott's former foster-home, together with their wives and a number of friends. According to their later testimony, Miles 'and his wife were invighted aboard the sayd ship to make merry'.[13] Tibbott declined the invitation. Later he apparently changed his mind and came out himself by boat, with the intention of buying some of the merchandise, as he later testified. However, Luccopp's decision to break his voyage in Clew Bay was motivated by reasons other than trade. His real intent was to exact revenge for the murder of his brother, which had occurred in the same place sixteen years previously. And Tibbott was high on his list of suspects.

While Robert Luccopp was anchored in Burrishoole, Tibbott invited him and his company to dine at Castleaffy. It was later claimed that Tibbott's invitation was no more than a ruse to lure Luccopp away from his ship. Tibbott's son, Miles, his cousin, David Bourke and some of his followers boarded Luccopp's ship and, on Luccopp's return from dining at Castleaffy, murdered him and his crew, seized the ship and its cargo and set sail out of the bay. The ship, whether accidentally or deliberately, was wrecked farther along the coast and the cargo pillaged. Whether or not this was done with Tibbott's approval was suspected but unproven. Tibbott's evidence was that although he did recollect that 'a Scotch ship was there about that time',[14] he claimed to know nothing regarding the murder of the captain and crew.

After the incident, to avoid implication in the affair, Miles went to England on the pretext 'to compound for a lease which his father holdeth from the Earle of Ormond'.[15] The Government ordered an investigation into the incident. On his return to Ireland, Miles was arrested on suspicion of being 'accessory and privy to the killing of Robert Luccopp and the taking of his ship'.[16] Tibbott and his half-brother, Murrough-na-Maor, were also arrested and lodged in Dublin Castle for examination before the Council. Since no sustainable evidence could be found against them, they were subsequently released. Miles was sent for further examination before the Privy Council in England. While the case against him was unproven, he was nevertheless imprisoned at the Gatehouse at Westminster where he remained for over a year. During 1622 he submitted a petition to the Privy Council to either be released or brought to trial. With no substantive evidence forthcoming, he was eventually released.

While many such murky incidents continued to mark Tibbott's public life, his personal life seemed serene by comparison. The faithful and companionable relationship he enjoyed with his wife Maeve O'Connor Sligo, was remarkable in an age in which multiplicity of wives, concubinage and divorce were prevalent among the Gaelic and gaelicised aristocracy. Their domestic harmony was in contrast to the difficulties that arose between his son and heir and his wife, Honora Burke. According to the surviving evidence, it was claimed that Honora 'so misbehaveth herself during the time of his living in England' that Miles 'forsooke the said Onora'.[17] She forfeited her substantial marriage portion in the process, left Belcarra and returned to her father's house in County Galway. While Honora appears to have been the defaulting party, her father nevertheless initiated legal proceedings against both Miles and Tibbott in an attempt to recover his daughter's marriage portion of £500, together with land, as well as the bond of £1,000, which both parties had entered into prior to the marriage. The case was presented in Court in May 1625 and from the contents of the surviving documentation, it appears that Miles and Tibbott emerged the eventual winners. After divorcing his first wife, Miles remarried some years later.

While the complete depositions are no longer available on this historic divorce case, there is sufficient information to show that marriage settlements between aristocratic families of the period were very much business propositions, involving complex and rigid legal contracts. If either party broke the terms of the contract, the legal process was unhesitatingly used to compensate or penalise the offending party. During the 17th century such marriages were usually arranged by the parents for their children and 'in such a system, where love cannot enter into marriage, except occasionally by chance, and where the most that can be hoped for is that common interests and associations may in time engender mutual respect and possibly affection, marital infidelity might well be expected to be very usual'.[18] That a woman should be cited in such an action and accused of 'misbehaving' herself in her husband's absence was less usual at the time, because the expected result of such misdemeanour – forfeiture of her marriage portion and banishment from her husband's property – was ample deterrent. Unlike the old Gaelic system, which afforded equal opportunity to both the female and the male partners to bring legal action against their spouse for infidelity, few, if any cases, came to Court in the 17th century where the husband was cited for similar misbehaviour.

Charles I succeeded his father, James I, to the throne of England in March 1625. He inherited depleted state coffers, a war with Spain, and Ireland rumoured, as ever, to be in collusion with the Spanish enemy.

In May Tibbott was accused by the authorities in Dublin Castle of being involved in a new conspiracy with secret agents of Spain and Rome: that he was intriguing to receive the 'exiled sons' of Tyrone,

Tyrconnell and O'Sullivan in Mayo. They were expected to arrive on a Spanish ship in Broadhaven Bay to embark on a new rebellion to recover their lands and livings, then in the possession of English planters and undertakers.

Tibbott and Miles were instantly arrested and taken to Dublin Castle where they were interrogated by the Lord Deputy and the Council. The evidence against them consisted of unsigned letters, which had conveniently been found by an agent of the Crown blowing in the wind near Ballintobber Abbey, close to Tibbott's castle of Kinturk. The letters contained details of Tibbott's supposed treasonable plans. However, Lord Deputy Falkland, expressed doubt as to their authenticity and shrewdly observed that 'some arguments persuade mee to doubt all may bee practice of Enemyes whoe are malitious towards the Gentlemen for private respects'.[19] On the other hand, because of Tibbott's previous record and to forestall any such rebellion, he recommended that father and son should be restrained in Dublin until the matter could be further investigated. Not wishing to risk alienating two such influential lords, particularly if the rumours of a rebellion proved to be true, Falkland was at pains to point out to them 'that their restraint did rather proceed from circumspection and duty than of ill opinion'.[20] While it was subsequently established that foreign agents had been entertained by Tibbott at Kinturk Castle, there was no evidence to prove conclusively that he was implicated in the proposed rebellion. After a short period of confinement, Tibbott and Miles were allowed return to Mayo.

In April 1626, Tibbott's half-brother and long-time ally, Murrough-na-Maor O'Flaherty, died. This second son of Granuaile, by her first marriage, had become the most powerful and wealthy lord in Iar-Chonnacht. He died at his castle of Bunowen and, in accordance with his wishes, was buried in the Abbey of St. Francis in Galway city. Although older in years than his enterprising half-brother, Murrough had been content to serve under Tibbott's command, both by land and sea, during the final years of the 16th century. They were kindred spirits, tied not only by blood but also by their actions and outlook. Both eventually accepted the inevitable disintegration of the Gaelic world of their birth and its replacement by an alien but potentially rewarding system and both prospered accordingly.

Murrough left six sons and two daughters. His eldest son, named Murrough-na-Mart (of the beeves), succeeded him. He was knighted in 1637 by the Lord Deputy, Sir Thomas Wentworth, and confirmed in his title to his estates. Murrough-na-Maor's will, dated 13 April 1626, has survived (see *appendices*). He appointed Tibbott and his son, Miles, trustees of the dowries forthcoming from his estates to his daughters and provided money, 'when he is ready and determined to goe beyond the seas to studie', for the education of his youngest son, Patrick.

In February 1626, in a gesture described expansively by the King as a reward for 'his faithful service' and 'eminent affection' to the Crown, Tibbott was raised to the peerage. The King commended Tibbott for 'his warlike valour ... his daring exploits against the Spaniards when they landed not so very long ago ....' By Privy Seal, he directed the Lord Deputy to inform 'Sir Theobald Burke of the County of Mayo, Knight, that he was to have the said honour and title and dignitie of Viscount Burke of Mayo to him ... and the heirs males of his body'.[21] Tibbott was ordered to present himself at Dublin Castle where the investiture was performed by the Lord Deputy.

The title viscount, the fourth in order of precedence following duke, marquess and earl, came to be used in England as a designation of nobility from around 1440. The style of address was Right Honourable and the title-holder was addressed by the Monarch as 'Our right trusty and well beloved Cousin'. The title was conferred on Tibbott by letters patent dated 21 June 1627 (see *appendices*). They referred to 'Theobaldus Burke, a gilded knight, sprung from a sometime illustrious stock in England who has won fame, not only by reason of his broad acres and the nobility of his origin, but especially by reason of his sincere fidelity towards us and our predecessors, and by reason of his warlike valour.'[22] There was no acknowledgement of his Gaelic ancestry, through his mother Granuaile, by now considered an impediment in the new world of the conqueror. But titles were not granted by Charles I merely in lieu of past glories and loyal deeds. They were also a lucrative means to replenish the royal coffers. In 1627, an

Irish viscountcy was charged at a rate of £1,500 to the recipient so honoured. Tibbott's son and heir, Miles, was conferred with the title of Baronet of Nova Scotia and was permitted to use the designation 'sir' as a form of address during his father's lifetime.

The personal arms chosen by Tibbott at the time of his knighthood in 1603 are preserved on the Letters Patent of his creation at Westport House. The arms are similar to the arms he later chose as viscount, which are preserved in the Book of Funeral Entries recording his death. Tibbott's personal arms are a variation on the arms of the Connaught De Burgos. They contain a shield but do not show a motto or supporters, as in the arms of later Viscounts Mayo. In 1629, the shield is topped by the viscount coronet, with a lion rampant sable in the first quarter and a hand dexter sable in the second quarter. The dexter half of the shield is divided by a cross. The lion is the emblem of courage in heraldry. In Gaelic, the word *leomhan* (lion) was also the emblem of a warrior chieftain who epitomised the three qualities of the lion – bravery, ferocity and liberality, the traits for which the Gaelic poets of the previous century had lauded Tibbott. The cross frequently appears on the shields of families of Norman descent, such as the Bourkes, and is thought to have indicated the participation of an ancestor in the crusades of the Middle Ages. On the sinister half of his shield, Tibbott had impaled the symbol of his wife's family, the O'Connor oak tree. After the 1627 conferring, the lower two quarters of the dexter half of the shield show the ermine symbol, long associated with the robes of the nobility, and particularly with the formal robes of a viscount.

In July 1627, Tibbott and Myles were appointed Commissioners for County Mayo, to raise money for the upkeep of the king's army in Ireland. The money was designated to be in lieu of special favours promised by the King to the Recusants. Tibbott and his son collected the not inconsiderable sum of £1,000 in County Mayo. In May 1628, (not before an additional payment of three annual subsidies of £40,000), the King eventually approved the long-awaited special favours, the 'Graces', as they became more popularly known.

The Graces covered a wide range of concessions, which included protection of land title, a ban of sixty years on any Crown claim to estates in Ireland, the army to be maintained in garrisons instead of being quartered on the country, reduction in court fees, curtailing the powers of local and court officials and the lifting of restrictions on certain exports from Ireland. For the Recusants, the most important concession was the freedom to sue out their liveries without having to swear an oath of allegiance to the Crown. For a brief period it appeared that the Recusants had won the battle to establish their rights, but their victory was to be short-lived. Suspicions that the Government had no intention of putting the provisions into effect were heightened when the parliament, to be convened in Dublin, to ratify the agreement between the Recusants and the King, failed to be convened. Perhaps it was this failure of the English monarch to honour his commitment that drove Tibbott and his son to seek redemption from the exiled elements of the Gaelic and Catholic opposition one final time.

In 1628, documents implicating Tibbott and Miles in further plots involving the exiled Gaelic lords in Spain and in the Lowlands were brought to the attention of the Lord Deputy. It was reported that Miles, together with Thomas Fitzgerald of Desmond, leader of the remnants of the once powerful House of Desmond in Munster and subsequently imprisoned in Dublin Castle, were among a company of twenty horsemen who travelled throughout Galway and Clare soliciting support for 'invasion or innovation'.[23] The deputy Governor of Galway further reported that Miles, 'eldest son of Lord Mayo came into Ennis [where the County assizes were held] to beg for help' and warned 'the act is base and bold and may be a bad gloss to a worse text'.[24] As with the previous intrigues, however, it came to nothing. Despite their overt allegiance to the Crown and their newly won titles and honours the old but doomed cause of the restoration of Gaelic supremacy continued its mesmeric hold on Tibbott and his family to the end.

Theobald Bourke, Tibbott-ne-Long, Lord Viscount Mayo, died at Kinturk Castle on 18 June 1629, aged sixty-two. Tradition says that he met his end by murder at the hands of his brother-in-law, Dermot O'Connor, who stabbed him to death on his way to visit the monks at

Ballintobber Abbey. Tradition has also maintained that the deed was committed at a place aptly named *Cnocán Thiobóid* (Tibbott's hillock). The incident has been further preserved in a local curse still used in the area when bad luck and a sudden end is wished on someone – 'turas Thioboid na Lung go Baile and Tobair leat' (Tibbott-ne-Long's journey to Ballintobber to you).[25]

There is no factual evidence to support this version of Tibbott's demise. No reports of the murder of a viscount appear on the record books of the time. It is more likely that the incident originated from the slaying of a Bourke by an O'Connor near the Abbey centuries earlier. Tibbott's memory, however, has been enshrined in Irish folklore and tradition, in poem and in song, a tribute to his status as a leader of his community and to the impact he made on the times in which he lived.

He was buried in Ballintobber Abbey, in a building erected at the south side of the chancel. This building is presently the sacristy. 'As an example of 17th century carving, the tomb resembles an altar with rudely carved figures of the 12 Apostles'[26] and it is considered a fine example of 'that transitional Hiberno Romanesque cum Gothic style in which the Mayo craftsmen seem always to have excelled themselves'.[27] The tomb once bore the somewhat inaccurate inscription, 'Here lies the body of Sir Tibbott ne Long Burke, first Lord Viscount in which tomb all his posterity was buried, whereof four were Lords and Earls.' Some of his direct descendants were buried elsewhere. The tomb was subsequently defaced during the Cromwellian period but, together with its fine stone canopy, is relatively well-preserved to the present day.

Notice of Tibbott's death was recorded in the official *Funeral Entries Book* at Athlone Castle by his son and heir, Miles. The funeral entry read:

> The right Honorable sr Theobald Burke Kt Viscount Burke of Mayo, deceased the 18 June 1629. He had to wife Maude, dr of Charles O'Connor Sligoe, by whome he had issue, the right Ho: Miles, Viscount Burke, David, Theobald, Richard, Mary, Onore, and Margaret, was buried in the Church of Ballintober in the County of Mayo.[28]

An addendum to the notice, inscribed by the clerk of the day, disap-provingly notes: 'Fees not payeed'.

✤ ✤ ✤

The life of Tibbott-ne-Long Bourke, Gaelic chieftain turned English knight, vividly reflects the traumatic era in which he lived and in which he played such an active and interesting role. He came to prominence when his native Gaelic world was mounting its final stand against the physical and psychological power of a stronger and more modern nation, who viewed the alien and outmoded civilisation of its smaller neighbour as a threat to its own security. Ireland's potential in land, produce and raw materials, attracted English attention, as much as its potential as a base for England's enemies. This was the age of explo-ration and acquisition and during the late 16th and early 17th centuries, Ireland looked a safer bet to English entrepreneurs and adventurers than the far-off Americas.

The instability of the Gaelic ruling system, with its independent chieftains and lordships, its internal feuds and dissension, gave a certain sense of inevitability to the takeover by a politically more astute and powerful neighbour. That it should be England rather than France or Spain, for example, that became Ireland's eventual overlord, is perhaps due more to geographical proximity than to any intervention of fate.

Born into the Gaelic ruling class, Tibbott-ne-Long sought to retain his inherited position by whatever means presented themselves within the ever-shifting political parameters, as England threw down the gauntlet. When his native Gaelic world failed to mount an adequate defence to the English challenge, Tibbott's motivation, like many of his contemporaries, became essentially one of survival. Nationalism or patriotism had little input on the policies and actions of the O'Neills, the O'Donnells or the Bourkes of Gaelic Ireland. Survival and personal advancement were the principal motivations for all. A strong and skilful warrior and a shrewd tactician, Tibbott at first resisted the encroachment of the English administration on his territory and on his privileged position as a Gaelic chieftain. However, as the Gaelic side continued to be beset by the inter-tribal feuds and grudges that ever tended to be its inherent weakness, it became apparent which side was more likely to emerge victorious. When that side acknowledged Tibbott's potential as a warrior, a mariner and a leader, spurned through petty jealousies and disputes by his native peers, Tibbott made terms to secure his and his family's future and commenced an uneasy alliance with the Crown.

The Gaelic world did not collapse without a prolonged and bitter struggle, but personal issues tended to confuse, overshadow and weaken its overall resistance. Tibbott's alliance with the English experienced many relapses when his position and status as a leader in Connaught appeared at risk. The fact that he survived politically in the atmosphere of intrigue and subterfuge that marked the campaigns of both sides, and that he secured and advanced his position in the political and social morass, marks him as agile, able and shrewd as the forces who sought to overthrow him. And when the sounds of battle faded, against the acquisitive hoards of English planters and undertakers who descended on the properties and estates abandoned by many of his more powerful Gaelic contemporaries, Tibbott stood his ground. Within an alien legal code, he demonstrated his undoubted abilities by successfully defending and extending his patrimony against all comers.

In the past, Irish history chose to create heroes out of the Gaelic chieftains and lords who fled the country after Kinsale. The few, like Tibbott Bourke, who remained forced the challenge of the ensuing change and upheaval and who prospered within the new system, were either demonised or air-brushed into historical oblivion.

CHAPTER NINE

The Descendants
1629-1767

T IBBOTT'S LAST WILL and testament has not been preserved. However, some idea of the conditions of his will can
be gleaned from the Stafford Inquisition of County Mayo
which took place a few years after his death.

The survey was undertaken in July 1635 by the Lord Deputy
Wentworth in order to confirm the King's title to the land of
Connaught. It contains the most detailed extant account of the ownership of land in County Mayo before plantation. It shows the pattern
of ownership that had obtained there since the time of the Anglo-
Norman invasion. It also includes the more recent land speculation of
the first thirty-five years of the 17th century by native chieftains such as
Tibbott, by wealthy Galway merchants, who had purchased much of
the mortgaged property of the smaller Gaelic proprietors, and the land
acquired by newly-arrived English adventurers and speculators.

The results of the survey show that Tibbott amply rewarded his
wife, Maeve O'Connor Sligo, for the turbulence and insecurity of the
early years of their married life and for her constant and loyal affection.
The Inquisition stated that 'Maud, dame dowager of Mayo' had been
left in possession by her husband of 'the castle, bawn and house of
Kinturck … as part of her jointure during life, the reversion after her
death to the Lord Viscount'.[1] Together with Kinturk and the adjoining
lands, Tibbott bequeathed her a life interest in lands he had acquired
for his sons, Theobald, David and Richard, in the baronies of Murrisk

and Carra, to revert to them on the death of their mother. On her own behalf, in 1625, Maeve purchased further lands and mortgages from Edmond Staunton, Mylie MacEvilly and Hubert McPhilbin in Carra barony and, together with the thousands of acres inherited from her husband, she was left a very wealthy widow.

In the relatively short history of the title, there were to be eight lords viscount Mayo. On Tibbott's death, his eldest son, Miles, became the 2nd Lord Viscount Mayo, according to the English law of primogeniture and by the provisions whereby the viscountcy had been initially conferred. Miles had conformed to the Protestant religion on his second marriage to Isabelle Freake, widow of Sir John Benboe and daughter of William Hodges of Ilchester. He had three sons by his first wife, Honora Burke, whom he had divorced – Theobald, his successor, John and Edmond – and a daughter, who married John Moore of Bries in County Mayo. His eldest son, Theobald, who outwardly at least had also conformed, was educated at the University of Oxford, under the famed Archbishop Laud.

Religious conversion in Ireland at this period was motivated by political expediency. To advance within the new English system, outward conformation was practised, particularly among the nobility and landed classes. The Oath of Supremacy had to be sworn by anyone holding official or judicial positions in the new administration. But, as one commentator noted, 'such oaths were taken quite carelessly and were regarded, as a rule, almost in the light of political formalities'.[2] 'There was nothing unusual, especially among the well-to-do classes, in two members of the same family professing different creeds… a man might attend a Protestant church for some reason of policy, while sending his wife and children to Mass on the same day.'[3] And Tibbott's family was no different. His younger sons, Theobald, David and Richard, as well as his daughters and his widow, continued to adhere to the old religion.

Tibbott left the lion's share of his large estate to his eldest son, Miles. His inheritance stretched across the baronies of Carra, Murrisk, Burrishoole, Tirawley, Erris, Gallen and Kilmaine. His younger brothers each received lesser estates, with the proviso that if, on their deaths, they had no male heirs, their lands would revert back to the viscount of the day. Miles was also in receipt of substantial rents from other properties in almost every barony in the county. In 1633, he bought the mortgage of the 'parcell of the quarter of Cahernamart and the first sgte. of the Castle, Bawne and Barbican and common of Cahernmart'[4] from his kinsman Dermot O'Malley for the sum of 'fouer and six pounds ster. and curr. lawful money of and in England of good fine and pure silver....' The survival of more ancient customs were yet evident in the 'tributes' forthcoming to Miles out of the barony of Murrisk, 'a cheifrie of £3, a beef, 40 quarts of butter, a basin of meal and a basin of malt yearly',[5] tributes which harkened back to the 'cuttings and spendings' of the old Gaelic system.

David, the second son, was left in possession of the castle and lands of Manulla and further increased his inheritance by purchasing additional land in Carra. He married Hugh O'Donnell's sister, Mary, who had previously been married to Tadhg O'Rourke of Breifne until his death in 1605. David married secondly the daughter of Richard Howard of Dublin. He died without issue and his lands reverted to the viscount.

Theobald Riabach, Tibbott's third son, married the daughter of Walter Bourke of Turlough, County Mayo and inherited the manor and castle of Cloghans and the surrounding lands in Tirawley.

Richard, the fourth son, inherited the castle and lands of Lisgowell, Carra Castle and other lands in the barony of Murrisk, and, in a conveyance dated 1 May 1629, the 'castle of Cathair-na-Mart' from his father. All four sons added to their original inheritance by the purchase of additional lands and property in their own right.

In 1632, Thomas Wentworth became Lord Deputy of Ireland in a climate of great discontent from among the Irish Catholic nobility. They had paid the King the large sums of money demanded for the implementation of the Graces, but on the ending of the war with Spain, yet again Charles had reneged on his promise. It would take both a skilled and ruthless Lord Deputy to weather the effects of such a breach of faith, and Wentworth did not lack the skill or the degree of ruthlessness required. With a policy that was to eventually alienate him from every group in the country in equal measure, he set himself the task of making the administration in Ireland powerful and independent, loyal only to the King.

Previously, in November 1630, Miles, together with the earls of Westmeath and Fingall, the Viscount Gormanstown and the barons of Howth and Slane, had forwarded a petition to the Lords Justice that in lieu of the substantial contributions they had made to the King, if the Graces were not to be sanctioned, the following grievances might be considered:

1. That titles of more than sixty years old be no longer inquired into and that the holding of a Parliament be ascertained.
2. That the charges made by the Church for clandestine marriages be stopped.
3. That fees of the clerk of the market and the charge of suing forth recognisance for building churches be abated.
4. That the commission appointed to see how much of the subsidies had been paid be re-appointed.
5. That free export be allowed.
6. That no advantage be taken for not enrolling the surrender of Connaught according to his Majesty's instructions in former years.[6]

The list was an indication of the developments taking place throughout the country, especially in relation to religion and land. With the King's repudiation of the Graces, an outburst of religious intolerance against Catholics had taken place during 1629 and 1630. Proclamations had been issued by Wentworth's predecessor, Falkland, forbidding the exercise of ecclesiastical jurisdiction emanating from Rome and ordering the dissolution of religious houses. While neither Catholic clergy nor laity suffered much more than inconvenience at this time, the future significance of this hardening of government resolve against Roman Catholics did not augur well for the future. The intolerant trend, coupled with the renewed threat of a plantation in Connaught, made the future appear bleak, especially when many of the land titles inherited or purchased by the old Gaelic lords like Tibbott and his sons had not, as yet, been confirmed by the King.

With the arrival of Wentworth, whose main objective was to increase revenue from Ireland for his hard-pressed King, the resolve of the native Catholic landowners to resist attempts to penalise them, either by land confiscation or by inhibiting their religious freedom, hardened. Political intrigue and conspiracy intensified as each group in the diverse political arena sought to secure and enhance its position within the system, while Wentworth exploited each group's animosity towards the other for his own and the King's benefit.

✤ ✤ ✤

While national affairs of state loomed large at this time, local political developments were equally important to lords like Miles Bourke. In 1632, he proffered a petition to the King requesting that the village that had grown around his castle at Belcarra be appointed 'in the interest of the public good' as the principal place to hold all future assizes and court sessions for the county, instead of being held at random places. He also requested 'that the gaol being kept at Conge, in the most remote part of the county, the inhabitants did not only suffer in their estates, by the journeying of the disorderly prisoners with their guard through the country, to the place where the judges met; but justice also many times was prevented by the ordinary escape of notorious male-factors.'[7] In reply the King directed the Lord Deputy to examine Miles's petition in July 1632 and, if it were deemed in order, to grant the same by patent for a period of thirty-one years. Later in 1637 Miles was granted permission to establish a by-weekly market at Belcarra and also to hold an annual fair there on the feast of St. Matthew. The anglicisation of the social, as well as the political, structures in Mayo continued apace.

The continued threat of plantation, however, hung like a sword over the heads of the Connaught landowners. The uncertainty affected every aspect of their lives and their ability to plan for the future. An example of how insidious was the threat is evidenced in a deed of settlement, dated 5 June 1630, on the marriage of Miles's son and heir, Theobald, to Elizabeth Lewis, preserved in the Westport House manuscript collection. In the settlement, it was recorded that provision for Elizabeth's jointure (the property to be settled on her in the event of her husband's death) 'cannot as yet bee legally assured with the said Dame Elizabeth out of the lande of the saide Lord Viscount Mayo for that a plantation being intended to bee made in the County of Mayo, where the said lands doe lye it is not knowne what lande of the sayd Lord Viscount will bee allotted and laid for his Majesties fourth pt'.

In November 1634 Miles represented County Mayo in the parliament convened by Wentworth in Dublin. The unsuccessful attempt by the English government in 1613 to render the native and old English members powerless was reversed by Wentworth who 'by refusing to allow parliament to deal with any business other than that presented to it by the government ... made constructive opposition impossible. And by arranging for the election of a group of government officials, who held the balance of power in the House of Commons, he was able to play Catholic against Protestant to secure approval of a government policy which included the repudiation of the more important of the Graces.'[8]

Thus the Irish parliament, the only means of redress left the native and Old English lords, became, in Wentworth's hands, another weapon to be used against them. As opposition to government policy was thus rendered impossible, Wentworth was in a position to govern the country with total disregard for local interests or the interests of the diverse groups which now constituted Irish society. A quarter of the land of Connaught was earmarked for plantation, with no distinction made between the Old English and native Irish lords. Planters in Ulster were penalised for failing to fulfil the conditions of their grants, while proceedings were initiated against the newly-established Presbyterian church which the Scottish planters had introduced into Ulster.

Wentworth spared no group in his actions on behalf of the Crown and thus alienated himself from all.

✤ ✤ ✤

In Mayo, Tibbott's widow, Maeve, was living out her remaining years at Kinturk. In 1635, a year before her death, she commissioned a chalice to be made in memory of her husband and herself and presented it to the Abbey of Murrisk. The inscription on the base of the chalice reads:

> *Ora pro animab (us) Dni Theobaldi Vicecomitis Mayo et uxorus*
> *ejus Meov ny Cnochoure qui me fieri fecerunt pro Monasteio de*
> *Mureske*
> *Ano. Dni 1635*

> (Pray for the souls of Theobald Lord Viscount Mayo and his wife
> Maeve O'Connor, who caused me to be made for the Monastery
> of Murrisk in the year of our Lord 1635)

It is interesting that the donation should be made to Murrisk Abbey, rather than to the adjacent Ballintobber Abbey. Tibbott's relationship with the O'Malleys, through his mother, Granuaile, was perhaps the motivation. The chalice was in use in Murrisk Abbey until the dispersal of the friars in the mid-1700s. The then Prior, Rev. Philip Staunton, went to reside with his niece, Mrs Sarah MacCormack, at Creevagh, Ballintobber. After the Prior's death in 1797, she loaned the chalice to Rev. Patrick Burke P.P. in Ballintobber Abbey, where it was in use until 1862. It was subsequently given by the Rev. J. Browne to Valentine Blake of Tower Hill House for use in his oratory. In 1880, Major J. Blake presented it to the Right Rev. J. MacCormack, Bishop of Achonry, the grandson of Sarah MacCormack, who restored it to Ballintobber-Burriscarra parish, where it has since been preserved in Carnacon church. Maeve, who died in 1636, is buried with Tibbott in Ballintobber Abbey.

✤ ✤ ✤

Wentworth was recalled to England in 1640. Muted while he was in power, the Recusants gave full vent to their grievances and anger on his removal.

The division developing between Charles I and his parliament in England began to have a decisive influence on events in Ireland. At first the King's dilemma in England appeared to the advantage of the dis-contented groups in Ireland. The Irish parliament co-operated with the parliament in England in preparing charges of treason against Wentworth, which eventually led to his execution in 1641.

The Catholic Old English and Gaelic lords attempted to capitalise on the King's difficulties, in order to wring from him the promised concessions. They wanted the Irish parliament to play a more inde-pendent role in the government of the country and to be in a stronger position to safeguard their property and their personal and religious freedom. The King, however, refused to agree to what he regarded as a threat to his authority in Ireland. The Catholics had little alternative but to accept yet again his promise of goodwill because the alternative – a victory by a militantly Protestant English parliament – would present them with an even greater threat.

As the crisis between crown and parliament deepened in England, the Catholic Gaelic lords in Ulster, whose lands had been exploited by extensive plantation, gave vent to their grievances in an armed rising under the leadership of Sir Phelim O'Neill. The rising spread rapidly to other parts of the country. The insurgents insisted that they had risen in support of the King in his fight against his parliament and in defence of their own rights and property. They were soon joined by the Old English lords, 'who made common cause with their fellow Catholics because they too were suspicious of the English parliament's intentions because the government in Ireland had made it clear that it did not trust them and could not defend them and because they were satisfied that the northern Irish remained loyal to the King'.[9]

In Connaught, Roger Jones, Viscount Ranelagh, was appointed president of the province. He established his headquarters at Athlone with a small troop of horse and two companies of foot soldiers. The government of Galway was vested in the Earl of Clanrickard. Miles was appointed joint-Governor of Mayo, with a commission to safeguard 'the preservation of all his Majesty's loyal subjects in those parts'.[10] To this effect, Miles raised six companies of foot soldiers in Mayo and succeeded initially in maintaining peace in the county. However, developments elsewhere in the country and in England were soon to affect his life and that of his son, with disastrous consequences.

The rebellion in Ulster soon spread to Mayo. The insurgents, many of them dispossessed of their lands, made frequent attacks on the new Protestant settlers. The unsettled state of the country in general, and the prospect that the rebellion might eventually restore them to their property, motivated many of the dispossessed to acts of violence against those who now occupied their lands. Many of their attacks were directed against members of the new settler community who were least in a position to defend themselves, such as Protestant clergymen and their families.

As joint-Governor, Miles tried to maintain law and order within the county, but soon found his position untenable. As an appointee of the English government, and as a Protestant, in name at least, he had to show some pretence of enforcing the law. But his actions had also to be undertaken with an eye to developments in Mayo and in the rest of the country. Many of the insurgents were his neighbours and friends. Complaints of harassment and attack from the Protestant community in Mayo flooded into Kinturk. One Protestant clergyman later claimed that the rebels entered his house 'presented their sharp skeans to his throat, robbed him … of all his household goods, books, cattle, horses, provisions and other of his goods and chattels worth about £500 and forcibly expelled him from his church, livings and lands worth £100 per annum'.[11]

Miles pursued some rebels who had taken cattle from another settler as far as Ballyhaunis where the rebels fortified themselves in a mill. An eyewitness later testified that Miles did not seem anxious to apprehend the culprits and 'after some intercourse between the Lord of Mayo and these rebels by messages going betwixt them, the Lord of

Mayo gave them protection. And then after much shouting and joy, besides both parties being intermingled, they lodged that night at the Abbey of Ballyhaunis, amongst a company of friars, the Lord of Mayo being there present amongst them.'[12]

This ambivalence towards the rebels is more understandable when the prevailing conditions are taken into account. Miles was still regarded more Gaelic chieftain than Anglo-Irish lord because of his ancestry and he was expected to be sympathetic to the rebellion. It was difficult and dangerous to be seen to openly oppose neighbours, relations and friends, particularly on behalf of a government which itself was embroiled in an armed struggle between its king and its parliament. Moreover, the 'rebel' army in the north had gained much support throughout the country from the Old English and Gaelic lords under the guise of supporting the King against his parliament. Miles had to use his newly acquired power as joint-Governor of the county with caution.

The rebels soon demanded more: that he should unequivocally demonstrate his allegiance to them by openly joining the rebellion and supporting them in their attacks on the English settlers in Mayo. Perhaps in an attempt to play both sides, Miles drafted some of the insurgents into the army under his command, given to him to maintain law and order and to use 'as he thought fit for his Majesty's service'.[13] According to the later testimony, it was at this time also that Miles and his family, with the exception of his second wife and his daughter, reverted back to their former religion and openly attended Mass.

As the attacks on the Protestant settlers continued, many fled their newly acquired lands to seek protection from local Protestant landlords, like Henry Bingham at Castlebarry. Bingham was subsequently besieged by a sept of the Bourkes led by Edmund Bourke from the Owles. Bingham sent for help to Miles, who came 'with an army, drove away the said Edmund Bourke, and entered and possessed the castle'.[14] To ensure the welfare and protection of the settlers, it was decided that Miles would convey them under his protection to the Galway border and hand them over to the care of the Earl of Clanrickard. The group numbered about sixty men, women and children, including the Rev.

John Maxwell, Bishop of Killala, Rev. Varges, Dean of Killala, Rev. Crowe and seven other Protestant ministers, their wives and children.

On 13 February, Miles conducted the group from Castlebarry to his castle at Belcarra, where they remained overnight. The following day they journeyed on to the house of John Browne of the Neale. The next morning, according to his own testimony, Browne 'was importuned by the said Bishop and the said Lord of Mayo to go along with them to Shrule'.[15] From the Neale the party journeyed on to Kinlough where they were given lodging by Walter Burke. The following morning the party arrived at Shrule on the border between Mayo and Galway.

In the inquiry conducted ten years later by a Cromwellian commission, differing versions of the events that occurred at Shrule were given in evidence. It appears that Miles had engaged Edmund Bourke (who had perpetrated the initial attack on the settlers when they had sought shelter in Castlebarry) and his forces to help convey them to Galway. It was implied at the inquiry that Miles was in total accord with Edmund Bourke and had complete knowledge of the fate planned for the Protestants under his protection. However, according to Miles' son Theobald, his father, in fear of his life, had no option but to allow the rebels to accompany him. At Shrule, Miles informed the Protestants that, since his jurisdiction ended at the Mayo border, he could not accompany them into Galway but that once they crossed over the bridge that divided the two counties they would be protected by the Earl of Clanrickard. The settlers entreated Miles and John Browne to accompany them. In fear of their own safety, they refused and rode away from Shrule leaving the settlers under the 'protection' of Edmund Bourke.

As the settlers crossed over the bridge, they were set upon by both Edmund Bourke's forces and a company of Galway rebels who awaited them on the other side. According to one eyewitness, 'some were shot to death, some stabbed with skeans, some run through with pikes, some cast into the water and drowned and the women that were stripped naked throwing themselves upon their husbands to save them were run through with pikes'.[16] When Miles's son, Theobald, who, unlike his father, had remained on the Mayo side of Shrule bridge, saw the Protestants being attacked, he thereupon, according to his own testimony, ran 'over the bridge with his sword drawn, offered to assist the English and rescue them from their enemy until a shot or two was made at him; whereupon one John Garvey and others, took him and conveyed him away for the safety of his life'.[17] Theobald's testimony was borne out by another witness, who further stated that John Garvey, the Sheriff of Mayo and brother-in-law of Edmund Bourke, took hold of Theobald and 'by the assistance of some of the company carried him by force over the bridge and then brought him a horse and bade him to be gone after his father for he could do no good there but could be killed or endangered if he opposed them'.[18] A few of the settlers managed to escape, owing to the intervention of the abbot of the nearby Ross Abbey, who prevailed upon the rebels to stop the massacre. Others were sheltered by local people.

It is beyond question that Miles was implicated in the events at Shrule. He was privy to, or at least must have guessed, the fate that lay in store for the Protestants as soon as they were out of his jurisdiction. The cries and shouts of the victims and their attackers would have reached his ears as he rode away that Sunday morning from Shrule to Cong. When a messenger arrived at Cong and informed Miles of the extent of the massacre, he reported that 'Lord Mayo went instantly into a chamber and there wept bitterly, pulling off his hair and refusing to hear any word of persuasion and comfort, or to be patient, having no manner of means left him at that time to be revenged for that inhuman and bloody massacre'.[19]

No immediate investigation into the incident at Shrule could be initiated, because of the unsettled state of the country. Miles and Theobald subsequently joined the Catholic Army, an alliance of the Old English and native lords, who fought in the King's name against the forces of his parliament. In August, Miles was appointed to represent Mayo in the Provincial Confederate Council and was made Governor of the county, 'having for his guard and attendants 100 foot and 50 horse allowed him in pay'.[20] Later in the year he was appointed to the Supreme Council of the Confederate Army at Kilkenny.

A central organisation to direct the course of the Catholic cause was to be put into effect at Kilkenny in October 1642, but events had changed dramatically by the time the meeting was due to take place. In England, the King's differences with his parliament had finally erupted into war. In Ireland, the descendants of the exiled Gaelic nobility, many of them professional officers in the armies of Europe, began to return home to place their military skills at the disposal of the Catholic Army. The situation as it then evolved in Ireland became confused and complicated.

Five different armies, espousing divergent causes, competed with one another. The King maintained an army in Ireland under the command of the Earl of Ormond. The English parliament maintained a smaller army in Ireland. As yet, it had made little impact, because the primary aim of the parliament was to defeat the King in England. The Scots maintained an army of foot to protect the Scottish planters in Ulster. The original Catholic Army had divided into two separate factions, namely the Old English, who were prepared to agree to moderate terms to achieve their rights, and the native Irish, led by the returned exiles, commanded by Owen Roe O'Neill and the Italian Papal Nuncio Rinucini. To them the outcome of the struggle between king and parliament in England was secondary to the restoration of full freedom for Catholics in Ireland and the return of all confiscated property and lands to the native Irish. The campaign in Ireland dragged on, with much time and effort 'wasted in haggling and bargaining with Charles, while the really formidable enemy, the English parliament, had built up its strength'.[21]

Miles and his son, Theobald, were named as persons to whom the right of the imposition of martial law in Connaught had been granted in the King's name. However, the pull of their Gaelic ancestry, as well as the allegiance of their neighbours and friends, proved too great. In January 1644, Miles resigned from the Supreme Council and, with his sons and brothers, threw in his lot with the native cause. They were especially friendly with Owen Roe O'Neill and his son, Henry. During the winter of 1648/49, when part of O'Neill's army was wintering in the mountains of North Leitrim, 'Owen and Henry were with their wives with Sir Theobald Burke, in Westport in County Mayo. The ladies made occasional visits to Galway city to give the impression that they were living at a secret address in that area.'[22]

When the parliamentary forces under Cromwell finally deposed of the King and asserted their power in England, they turned their attention to Ireland. Their aim was not only to overpower both loyalist and native armies but also 'to provide immediate employment for the army and to capitalise guarantees and securities given to the financiers',[23] who had funded their campaign in England. In other words, the land of Ireland would help pay Cromwell's bills for his rebellion against the king. The properties of both Irish loyalist and native landowners were reckoned to be admirable reward for his soldiers and would help repay the financial backers of the parliamentary cause in England.

Miles, 2nd Lord Viscount Mayo, died in 1649. He was succeeded by his son, Theobald. Miles' English-born widow, Isabella Freake, lived on for a few years at Kinturk. Unlike his father, Miles did not appear to have left his widow in even reasonable comfort. In 1654, she was allowed by the government 'on account of her old and decrepit age and her low and necessitous condition … 35 pounds to bear the charges of her voyage to England'[24] where she eventually died in 1663.

In 1630, Theobald had married Elizabeth Lewis of Yorkshire, a descendant of the Earl of Shrewsbury, by whom he had two sons, Theobald and Miles, and two daughters. His daughter, Margaret, married Sir Henry Lynch of Galway, while Maud married John Browne, son of John Browne of the Neale and ancestors of the present Marquess of Sligo of Westport House. On the death of his first wife, Theobald married secondly, Eleanor, daughter of Sir Luke Fitzgerald of Tecroghan, County Meath, by whom he had one son, Luke, who later became an army captain. The editor of Roger O'Flaherty's *Iar Chonnacht* ascertained that his epitaph was visible in a ruined abbey two miles from the ancient church of Ballinakill, County Galway and that it read:

> Here under is interred, Captain Luke Bourke, son of the Right Hon. Theobald Lord Viscount Mayo and Elynor Fitzgerald of Tier … han, who died 10 March 1684.[25]

Oliver Cromwell arrived in Ireland on 16 August 1649 with an army of 18,000 foot and 6,000 horse soldiers and a great supply of guns and materials of war. He proceeded to subdue all opposition to the English parliament in Ireland by methods of indiscriminate brutality against those who actively opposed him, as witnessed at Wexford and Drogheda, and of a more lenient attitude to those who did not. After the subjugation, the lower classes of the native population were left relatively undisturbed. It was to be the Old English and old Gaelic landed class, who had backed the wrong horse in England, who were to experience the full effects of Cromwell's revenge. Their properties were to provide the means to repay his creditors.

Ireland's wealth was her land and that commodity was earmarked to repay the services and loans, which Cromwell had accumulated in his campaign against the King. To this effect a civil examination of Ireland was undertaken. 'It divided landholders in Ireland into two groups – those who had been guilty of involvement in the rebellion and those who had not. The first were to lose all their estates and all their property rights; the second were to be allowed to own a proportion of the amount of land which they had held.'[26] But not in the same place. Ireland was divided into two parts: Connaught, including Clare, to which landowners who were successful in proving their innocence of involvement in the late rebellion were to be transplanted; and the remaining twenty counties, which were earmarked as government property and, in the main, were to be used to pay back Cromwell's creditors and soldiers.

Those transplanted from their estates to Connaught in turn dispossessed native landowners there. Murrough O'Flaherty, Theobald's first cousin, had also fought on the side of the Catholic Confederation and was subsequently dispossessed of his extensive lands in the Barony of Ballinahinch in Connemara, his castle of Bunowen razed to the ground. Part of his estate was granted to Art MacGeoghegan from Castletown, County Westmeath, whose own estate had been granted to Cromwellians. Unlike his cousin, Murrough later failed to be restored to any part of his lands and died landless and destitute in 1666. His case was representative of many of the former old Gaelic families in Connaught.

At the same time as the plantation, a high court of justice was established to try those accused of involvement in the murders of English Protestant settlers in 1641. The court for the province of Connaught commenced its proceedings on 17 December 1649 in Galway. Theobald was arrested and tried for his alleged involvement in the killing of the Protestant settlers at Shrule. Those who sat in judgement on his case were mainly newly arrived Cromwellians, including Sir Charles Coote, Peter Stubbers, Humphrey Hurd, Francis Gore, John Deboraugh, Thomas Davis, Robert Ormsby, Robert Clerk, Charles Holcroft, John Eyre and Alexander Steples. For the new-comers, the trial was looked on both as a retribution and, in view of the defendant's large estate, an opportunity.

The trial commenced on 30 December and lasted until 12 January. Submissions were taken from survivors and eyewitnesses at Shrule. Theobald gave evidence of his attempt to rescue the victims, a fact substantiated by the testimony of other witnesses. Moreover, Theobald could hardly be held responsible for his father's inability or unwillingness to protect those entrusted to his care. But while the case against Theobald was weak, the Cromwellian commissioners viewed the extent of Theobald's vast acres as sufficient reason to find him guilty. By a majority vote of seven of the commissioners – Gore, Davis, Clerk and Holcroft voting against – he was convicted and sentenced to be executed by firing squad. The execution took place at Galway three days later. It was stated that the firing party missed their target three times until 'a corporal, blind of an eye, hit him'.[27] The estates of the Viscount Mayo were forfeited to the Cromwellians and the greater part parcelled out among transplanted persons and military adventurers of the Commonwealth. Theobald's widow, Eleanor, was allowed 'to enjoy so much of her jointure, as was then waste and undisposed of'.[28]

Theobald's son and heir, also named Theobald, then a minor and in fosterage with William Kelly at Donamona Castle, was, in effect, dispossessed. In 1653, he was obliged to submit a petition to the English government for maintenance. The government agreed to pay for his board and lodging and for his education, provided he resided in Dublin. Having a dispossessed minor in residence near his father's former estates was, perhaps, too much a reminder to the new owners of the injustice that clouded their acquisition. Theobald was subsequently placed in the care of John Stephens, master of the English Free School in Dublin, and given an allowance of £20 per annum. This was increased to £30 in 1656. On completion of his studies in Dublin, with his inheritance confiscated, he had little alternative but to seek refuge with his mother's family in England, where he remained until the restoration of King Charles II in 1660.

On the restoration of King Charles II, Catholic Ireland looked forward to a new era of toleration. In view of their loyalty and their efforts on behalf of his father, the Catholic lords confidently expected that the new King would restore them to their confiscated lands. While appearing sympathetic to their plight, the King was, however, more mindful of the fact that he had been recalled from exile by the Commonwealth army who expected Cromwell's land settlements in Ireland to be upheld. Charles II was in a dilemma and, in keeping with the practice of his Stuart ancestors, made promises to both sides. He promised the Cromwellians that they would retain their newly acquired property and the Catholics that they would recover their confiscated estates, a promise which made the Duke of Ormond remark, 'there must be now discoveries made of a new Ireland, for the old will not serve to satisfy these engagements'.[29]

Theobald, heir to his father's estates, was brought back from England to the care of his stepmother, Eleanor, the Dowager Countess of Mayo, in expectation of the restoration of his estates. He resided with his younger brother, Miles, and his half-brother, Luke, at Kinturk Castle, part of Lady Mayo's jointure. Despite their status and once extensive estates, their condition was extreme and the family was forced to apply for government assistance. In 1660, two pensions were granted 'to the Lady Mayo' for the upkeep of herself and the three children, one for '30s a week for 14 weeks'[30] which was extended for a further six months.

Eventually an Act of Settlement was passed by the English parliament in 1662, which provided for a limited number of named royalists to receive back their former estates, while the new occupiers of these estates were to be compensated with 'other' lands. When no such lands could be found, a second Act was passed entitling the royalists to the return of just part of their confiscated estates. Courts were established to hear the claims of the dispossessed owners but were hurriedly terminated before all cases could be presented. Thus many claimants failed to be reinstated to any part of their property. For the few hundred who did succeed in recovering some of their property, the legal process was made deliberately slow, cumbersome and expensive.

On 14 May 1661, Theobald took his seat in the Irish House of Lords. On 18 July, he presented a petition for the restoration of his estate. But it was to be a lengthy and complex process. Prior to the rebellion of 1641, in an effort to protect their estate, his father and grandfather had conveyed some of the lands in trust to friends and relations, while, in the aftermath of the rebellion, other lands had fallen into the possession of those described as 'adventurers, soldiers, Forty-Nine Officers, transplanters and Connaught purchasers'. The new owners, some of whom had been dispossessed of their lands elsewhere by Cromwell, did not part easily with their newly acquired property. It took four years before Theobald was finally restored and then to only part of his inheritance. The colour, both in processing his case and, because rents from the disputed lands were not forthcoming, in sustaining himself and his family throughout the lengthy process was excessive. Consequently he contracted large debts, which would have to be repaid from his assets. In 1662, the House of Lords had a clause inserted on his behalf in the Act of Explanation. The clause provided that lords, like Theobald, who though 'innocent of rebellion had yet lost their estates',[31] should be restored. In April 1666, Theobald was finally restored to '50,000 acres of land and 5 manors in the county of Mayo'.[32]

However, the restoration was worth more on paper than it was in practice. The conditions stipulated that Theobald must make reparation 'according to value' to the current occupiers of the lands, who had been transplanted from their own properties elsewhere in Ireland. Theobald was consequently forced to borrow additional money and to mortgage much of his estate. After the turmoil and uncertainty of the previous two decades, his lands were also in a run-down state. Further money had to be borrowed to repair and re-stock the property. Most of the finance for these undertakings came from his more affluent brother-in-law, John Browne, son of John Browne of the Neale.

While the fortune of Tibbott's immediate descendants had floundered, the fortune of John Browne had flourished. In 1669, he had married Theobald's sister, Maud Bourke. A successful and able lawyer, with a large practice in Dublin, John Browne had inherited an estate in County Mayo. Owing to Theobald's inability to repay the loans, much of his estate came eventually came into the possession of his brother-in-law, 'partly by purchase from … [Theobald] and partly by purchase from severall transplanted persons whose title [to the lands] had been allowed and confirmed by the hon. the now Commissioners appointed for hearing and determining the claymes of transplanted persons and partly by severall purchases for one and the same lands both from [Theobald] and from severall transplanted persons, by manner whereof the said John Browne hath beene at greate charge'.[33]

Land transactions at this time of political unrest and uncertainty were a muddled and murky business, with claims and counter-claims emanating from the original owners, planters, dispossessed and the transplanted alike. To sort out the rights and claims of any party in this legal minefield was a virtual impossibility. As a lawyer by profession, John Browne was more *au fait* with the legal complexities than his brother-in-law. Although in a later deposition preserved in the Westport House Papers entitled *The Answer of Col. John Browne* in which he defended his land dealings, it is apparent that the complexities and uncertainties of land tenure in the west of Ireland was beyond even his legal expertise. That his hard-fought-for lands would eventually come into the possession of the great-grandson of John Browne, the sheriff of Mayo, against whom he had fought and who had been killed by his Bourke relations in 1583 would hardly have been appreciated by Theobald's great-grandfather Tibbott-ne-Long.

To salvage something from the ruin of his inheritance, Theobald also mortgaged, leased and sold land to other proprietors in the area. He borrowed money from every available source, including 'Thadie O'Malley, gentleman' for 'the full sume of forty pounds, good and lawful money and currant in England',[34] ironically a kinsman and descendant of a family from whom his great-grandfather had originally acquired part of the Mayo estate.

Theobald married Ellen, daughter of Sir Arthur Loftus of Rathfarnham, and secondly the Lady Ownes. His death took place on 5 June 1676. Perhaps not surprisingly, in view of the enormity of his financial situation, it was reported to have been 'occasioned by too large a quantity of laudanum, to compose him to rest, after taking physick in a fit of sickness'.[35] He was buried in St. Patrick's Cathedral, Dublin. He left no issue and was succeeded by his brother, Miles.

Miles, 5th Viscount Mayo, inherited a debt-ridden estate. In 1677, for a sum of '5 shillings', he formally signed the general release of part of his estate in the baronies of Carra, Murrisk and Burrishoole to his brother-in-law, John Browne, except a small part, including 'the four quarters of Castleburk for use of the said Myles Lord Viscount Burk of Mayo and the lady Jane his wife for and during the tearme of their naturall lives.'[36] Castlebourke, formally Kilboynell Castle, was to become the residence of future viscounts Mayo. In 1576, for the sum of £400, he sold further lands in Burrishoole. By 1679, his indebtedness to John Browne amounted to the sum of £5,000. Such was the impecunious state of the 5th Viscount and his family that John Browne also agreed to pay for 'the maintenance or supporte of the said Myles, Lord Viscount Mayo and the lady Jane his wife and their children'.[37] Miles died at Castlebourke in March 1681, leaving a two-month-old infant, his only son Theobald, as his heir. Miles was buried in Ballintobber Abbey.

Theobald was cared for as a child by his step-grandmother, the redoubtable Eleanor, second wife of the third Viscount. With her son,

Luke, the Countess became embroiled in a protracted lawsuit with John Browne over the payment money relating to rents and mortgages in contracts previously concluded with him by her husband and by her stepson. In her depositions to the courts, it is obvious that her extreme financial state was also, in large part, due to the non-payment of rent by the tenants on the Mayo estate, despite many 'lawsuits against the tenants of some of the said lands for to recover the said rent charges'.[38]

The many changes in the ownership of the disputed estate over the previous two decades had provided the tenants, in effect, with a rent-free period of tenure. The Court's verdict was that the Dowager Countess of Mayo was to be allowed a life interest in the heavily mortgaged lands in dispute which, on her death, were to be passed to the holders of the mortgages, among them John Browne, on payment of one thousand pounds.

At the close of the 17th century, the misfortune that encircled the Mayo estate reverted on John Browne. He found himself in similar financial straits as his in-laws when the war in England between two rival kings, James II and William III, and in Europe, between Louis XVI in France and The Holy Roman Emperor, Leopold I, was fought out in Ireland.

A staunch Jacobite, John Browne became a colonel in the army of King James II and fought with Patrick Sarsfield at Limerick, with two regiments provided at his own cost. From his ironworks at Knappagh, Foxford and Westport, he supplied the Jacobite army with firelocks, bayonets, cannonballs, swords, grenades, pickaxes, spades and other equipment. The correspondence in the Westport House papersfrom many of the principal participants, including King James II, Sarsfield, Tyrconnell and Berwick, testify to the substantial amount of ordnance and equipment supplied by John Browne to the Jacobite cause and for which, for the most part, he received no payment. In 1690 for the defence of Sligo alone, he supplied 965 cannonballs (of sizes 3-5 pounds), 220 shovels, 56 spades, and 85 pickaxes. In July of the same year, he was ordered by Patrick Sarsfield to send all his 'gunsmiths and blade makers at Westport, well guarded, and with all their tools and utensils to ye town of Galway' [39] to supply the army there. The defeat of the Jacobite cause in Ireland heralded John Browne's financial ruin.

While Sarsfield and many of his fellow-Jacobins sought solace and a new future abroad, to become immortalised as the Wild Geese, John Browne returned to Mayo to salvage what he could . His estate comprised 113,440 acres in County Mayo, 41,122 acres in County Galway, of which total only 39,117 acres were deemed to be profitable, yielding an annual rent of £3,456. He was heavily indebted to both Catholic and Protestant creditors, including, ironically, the young Viscount Mayo, for money owed to his father for land Browne had purchased from the Mayo estate, as well as his indebtedness for the marriage settlement of his daughter. A mortgage debt of some £760 owed by him to Theobald's father, Miles, had, with interest and arrears, increased to £1,500 by the end of the war.

John Browne's lands were subsequently confiscated. He was imprisoned for debt. An Act of Parliament was specifically enacted to attempt to unravel his financial situation. Many of his debts were acquired by Englishmen Gideon Johnston and William Chambers, who instituted legal proceedings for full restitution of the same. The Act legalised the claims of his Protestant creditors only. 'But his affairs were so involved and his creditors so numerous, that a second Act soon followed appointing the Barons of the Exchequer as trustees to superintend the sale of his estates and the distribution of his assets.'[40] By 1704, all his lands in County Galway and in the baronies of Gallen, Kilmaine, Tirawley and Erris, as well as the greater part of lands in the baronies of Carra, Burrishoole and Murrisk in County Mayo, were sold off. His remaining estate centred on a few hundred acres around Westport and Aghagower.

An attempt to improve the fortunes of both families was, perhaps, the reason for the marriage, by special dispensation, in 1702 of John Browne's daughter, Mary, to her first cousin Theobald, the 6th Viscount Mayo. The marriage agreement stipulated that 'one thousand pounds more as marriage portion of the said Theobald Lord Mayo,'[41] in addition to the sum already owed, was to be paid to Theobald on settlement of John Browne's estate. But Browne's financial situation continued to deteriorate, leaving his son-in-law, as one commentator noted, with 'not a penny in his pocket'. Since payment from John Browne's estate was to be made to his Protestant creditors only, Theobald, as was reported, 'resolved to go to church' to salvage something from the ruin. On 19 June 1709, he conformed to the Established Church of Ireland in St. Audoen's Church in Dublin and subsequently took his seat in the House of Lords. His marriage to his cousin Mary Browne produced the two succeeding viscounts. They also had five daughters, *viz,* Jane, who married Morgan O'Flaherty of Lemonfield, County Galway; Maud, who died young; Elizabeth, who married William Mitchel of Surrey, and was upper housekeeper of Somerset House; Mary, who also died young; and Bridget, who in October 1731 married her cousin John Gunning of Castlecoote, County Roscommon. Their daughters, Maria and Elizabeth, known as the 'gorgeous Gunnings', became the toast of 18th-century English society. One married the Earl of Coventry and, on his death, the Duke of Hamilton; the second married the Duke of Argyle.

Theobald (commonly known by his nickname 'Lord Cheek') and his family resided at Castlebourke. Kinturk Castle, the residence of previous viscounts, which had come into the possession of John Browne, had by this time fallen into decay. Despite his marriage to Mary Browne, Theobald, in a petition to Queen Anne from whom he sought a pension, accused John Browne, whom he described as 'a papish lawyer', of having defrauded his father, 'a gentleman of very weak capacity' of his estates. In his rebuttal, John Browne claimed that the petition of his son-in-law 'was filled with misrepresentations almost from beginning to end'; that much of the land he had purchased in good faith from the Mayo estate had, in effect, been already in the ownership of others and that he was forced to purchase the interest of the new owners as well as his in-laws, resulting in considerable additional expense and involving 'many lawsuits and troubles'. The Bourke-Browne land transactions of the late 1600s, one of the few for which records survive, is a microcosm of the legal confusion throughout Ireland which emanated from the collapse of the old Gaelic system of land ownership, rebellion and confiscation.

Theobald was the last viscount to reside full-time in Mayo and who continued to adhere to many of the Gaelic customs of his forebears. He was noted for the hospitality of his house and at the many social gatherings held at Castlebourke, the company was often entertained by travelling bards, among whom was the famed harpist and poet Turlough O'Carolan. He was a frequent visitor and composed and dedicated his well-known air 'Tighearna Maigheo' to his hospitable patron. (James Hardiman in his *Minstrelsy*, however, ascribes the song to David Murphy, a dependant of the Viscount, and claims that it was set to music by a harpist called Thady Keenan.) The 6th Viscount died in 1741.

Theobald was succeeded by his eldest son, Theobald, as the 7th Viscount Mayo. By this time little remained of the Mayo estate. Because Tibbott-ne-Long had originally purchased the lands and mortgages of his less well-off neighbours, now the once huge estate had been sold, field by field, to pay the creditors and to settle the debts incurred by his descendants. The original estate became confined to a few hundred acres around Castlebourke and lands in the west of the barony of Murrisk. Theobald married Ellis, eldest daughter of James Agar of Gowran, County Kilkenny in 1726 and had two sons, Theobald and Agar, who both died in their childhood. Theobald held the title for barely one year, dying in London in 1742, aged thirty-six years. He was interred with his ancestors in Ballintobber Abbey where his wife erected a monument, which bore a lengthy laudatory inscription, to his memory:

> A faithful Friend, a dutiful Son,
> An affectionate Brother,
> And a tender Husband:
> He passed through Life
> With unblemished honour, beloved and esteemed
> By all that Knew him.
> His manners were easy:
> His temper gentle and humane:
> The Knowledge of his high Birth

Had no other Effect upon him,
Than to make it his Study, in all the Offices of Life
To life up to the Character, to which he was born;
Being sensible that the truest Nobility
Is that of the mind;
And to possess it to the highest degree
Is to walk steady in the paths of Virtue;
Which he did to the day of his death. [42]

In 1745, his widow married Francis Birmingham, eldest son of Edward, 20th Baron Athenry, and Bridget, eldest daughter of John Browne of Westport, her late husband's cousin. On his death she was created Countess of Brandon and was recorded as being 'the first peeress in her own right in Ireland.'[43] She died at her residence in Merrion Square, Dublin in 1789, aged eighty-one.

John Bourke succeeded his only brother as 8th Viscount Mayo. He married Catherine, only daughter and heiress of Major Whitgift Aylmer, owner of extensive estates both in England and Jamaica.

Catherine's family was descended from the John Whitgift, Archbishop of Canterbury 1583-1604. The son of his cousin and heir, John Whitgift, married Elizabeth, daughter of Samuel Aylmer, from whom the family name emanated. The connection of the Whitgift and Aylmer families with the West Indies, and with the island of Jamaica in particular, was established by the mid-17th century at the time of the overthrow of the Spanish on the island by Cromwell's Parliamentary forces. A Captain Whitgift Aylmer was recorded in 1666 as owner of over 2,000 acres of land in the parishes of St John, St. George and St Thomas-in-the-East, while in 1704, his brother, Samuel Aylmer of St John, was in possession of 200 acres in the Parish of St Dorothy. At the time of his death at the age of sixty-seven in 1707, Whitgift Aylmer had risen to the rank of colonel and had further increased his Jamaican property. He was buried in the St Catherine's Cathedral, Spanishtown. His son, also called Whitgift Aylmer, at his death in 1720, in turn bequeathed his estates 'my sugar works and plantations at Guanaboa, my negro slaves, horses, mares and mules ... the ginger in the ground...' [44] to his only daughter, Catherine Aylmer.

As a younger son, John Bourke had little reason to expect to succeed to the viscount Mayo title. Through his brother's untimely death and the early demise of his nephews, however, he became the 8th viscount in descent from Tibbott-ne-Long. Like many younger sons from the landed and the wealthy merchant classes of the west of Ireland, he had gone to seek his fortune in Jamaica. At the time of his marriage to Catherine Aylmer, he was known as the 'Honourable John Bourke, esq of Jamaica'. By his marriage to the Aylmer heiress he became quite wealthy. There is, however, no evidence that he spent any of this wealth to enlarge or improve his Mayo estate, which was confined to Castlebourke and a few hundred acres of land.

He had one son, Sir Aylmer Bourke, who died aged five years and was buried in St Mathew's Church, Irishtown, Dublin, and a daughter, Bridget. The last officially recognised viscount in the direct line, John spent most of his lifetime in England, with summer visits to his Irish estate. His agent, James Bourke, lived with his family in Castlebourke and managed the estate in his absence. John died at his residence in Pall Mall, London on 12 January 1767 'after a long and painful illness' as reported by the *Freeman's Journal*, and was buried in St James's West. In his will he bequeathed to his wife all his 'personal estate in the Island of Jamaica and in the Kingdom of Ireland',[45] as well as an estate in Oxfordshire. He appointed his wife, Catherine, his sole executrix. She subsequently married Edmond Jordan of Legan, owner of the Old Head estate in the barony of Murrisk.

The 8th viscount's only daughter and heir, Bridget, married Edmund Lambert of Boyton House, near Heytesbury, Wiltshire in 1758. He was a direct descendant of Richard Lambert, Sheriff of London in 1572. Under their marriage settlement, dated 28 April 1758, the 8th Viscount Mayo stipulated that 'one moiety' of his estate was to be settled on his son-in-law for his life, the other on his wife, Lady Mayo. Both moieties were later inherited by the only son and heir of the marriage, Aylmer Bourke Lambert, who was born at Bath in 1761. A famous botanist, he resided in Grosvenor Street in London and, for a short time, at Castlebourke. In 1795, in controversial circumstances (see *Chapter 10*), he conveyed the remainder of the Mayo estate to the great-great grandson of Colonel John Browne, John Dennis Browne, 3rd Earl of Altamont, later 1st Marquess of Sligo, for the sum of £29,702, payable in staged payments over a period of years. It is significant to note that part of the estate being sold included land in the barony of Murrisk which was inhabited by 'the freeholders of Asgalan,'[46] and cousins of the last viscount.

Kinturk Castle, after a brief occupation by John Browne, gradually fell into decay. It is now an impressive ruin on the shores of Lough Carra, standing stark and bare, a silent testimony to Tibbott-ne-Long and his descendants, a once powerful family, incorporating the strange mix of Gaelic, Norman and English ancestry, so characteristic of the blood-mix of Ireland's aristocracy.

After the death of the 8th Viscount Mayo, the title was deemed to be dormant for want of male heirs. But the illustrious designation continued to allure and entice. In keeping with the life of its first grantee, Tibbott-ne-Long, the title Viscount Mayo was set to become embroiled in controversy and legal argument.

CHAPTER TEN

The Viscount Mayo Title
1767-1814

O N   T H E   D E A T H of the 8th Viscount Mayo in 1767, the title was deemed dormant by the authorities. The following year, however, a claim to the title, honour and estate was lodged by David Bourke as the only surviving cousin and male heir of the 8th viscount. This claim set in train a controversy that remains unresolved to this day.

David Bourke was the only son and heir of Theobald Bourke (nick-named Blind Toby, being blind in one eye) of Asgalan, in the Parish of Kilgeever, in the Barony of Murrisk, some two miles west of the present-day town of Louisburgh. His mother was Anne Crean, daughter of William Crean of Brickens and Ballinvilla, County Mayo. His family had held their lands in Asgalan 'at pleasure' and free from rent from successive viscounts Mayo. Tibbott-ne-Long had initially acquired the lands from the O'Malleys before 1630 when, in a survey at that time, he is designated as having a 'chefrie or rent charge' of '1 quarter at Askalane'.[1] Aged twenty-three in 1768, David Bourke was unmarried. To help further his claim and to circumvent the penal obstacles then pertaining to Catholics, he converted to the established Church of Ireland and is reported to have 'read his incantation in Westport'.[2]

David claimed the title Viscount Mayo as the direct descendant of Richard Bourke, the fourth son of Tibbott-ne-Long. Those who sought to discredit his claim contended that Tibbott did not have a fourth son. Contemporary evidence would prove otherwise. In the *Book of Funeral Entries,* the official register that recorded Tibbott's death, Richard is listed as the dead viscount's fourth and youngest son. During his lifetime, as already mentioned, Tibbott granted his son Richard an estate in the baronies of Carra, Murrisk and Burrishoole. Among the Westport House manuscripts one, dated 14 February 1636, records that Miles, the 2nd Viscount Mayo, leased additional lands to his brother, Richard. Moreover, various inquisitions, including the *Stafford Inquisition of the County Mayo,* lists Richard, together with his brothers, as proprietors of lands previously owned by Tibbott-ne-Long. More significantly in the *Book of Survey and Distribution (1641)* for County Mayo, Richard, together with his brother Miles, 2nd Viscount Mayo, are listed as having joint interest in one quarter of 'Askalon', comprising 214 acres of profitable and 300 acres of unprofitable lands',[3] lands that by 1768 were in the possession of the family of the claimant, David Bourke.

In 1769 the 'genealogy of the Right Honourable David Bourke, Ninth Viscount Mayo,' certified by William Hawkins, Ulster King of Arms, Chief Herald of Ireland (see *Appendices*) stated that he was 'lawfully descended in a direct line from the Honourable Richard Bourke, fourth son of Theobald Bourke created viscount Mayo 21 June 1627'.[4]

> Know ye therefore that the said King of Arms by the power and authority to me granted by his present Majesty King George the third under the great seal of this Kingdom of Ireland to hereby certify that David Bourke now the ninth Viscount Mayo of the said Kingdom is lawfully descended in a direct line from the Honourable Richard Bourke fourth son of Theobald Bourke, created Viscount Mayo … In testimony whereof I have hereunto put my hand and affixed the seal of my office the 15th Day of February 1769.

The last three viscounts Mayo, Theobald, Lord 'Cheek' (6th viscount), his eldest son, Theobald (7th viscount) and his younger son, John (8th Viscount), from the extant evidence, acknowledged David's family as their only and legal heirs. During his lifetime Lord 'Cheek', in particular, was a frequent visitor to Asgalan and publicly acknowledged David's father and his family 'to be next in succession to the title of Mayo ... [as] the last two lords Mayo had no probability of leaving issue male, they being long married and their respective wives being advanced in years'.[5] Lord Mayo often entertained his Bourke relations and, on one occasion in 1740, when dining with David's father and mother, Lord 'Cheek' noticed that David's mother, Anne, being 'then big with child and very much out of spirits...spoke to the said Anne and desired her to be cheerful and to take great care of herself for that if the child she then bore was a son he could be Lord Mayo, if his own two sons, Sir Theobald and John Bourke...died without issue' and, as the witness to the conversation later testified, 'an event which at that time was likely to happen and which has since happened'.[6]

In his will, dated 7 November 1737, after providing for his two daughters, Lord 'Cheek' also made the unusual provision that should his sons have no male heir, and if, after ninety-nine years, there was 'a remainder of fee simple of my real estate', he instructed that the remains of his estate 'shall go and accrue and be and remain with such person as shall have and be entitled to the Honour and Title of Mayo provided he be a Bourke and the heirs male of his body...that my said estate...shall always be attendant upon and accompany the Honour and Title of my Family...'.[7]

In addition the evidence, both genealogical and by sworn depositions, submitted by David Bourke to the Lord Lieutenant of Ireland, Lord Townsend, to corroborate his claim to the title seems unimpeachable. The honourable Elizabeth Bourke, second daughter of the 6th Viscount, then aged sixty-one (see *Appendices*) testified that 'she hath always heard it reputed in her Family and does believe it to be true that Theobald, the first Lord Mayo had four sons...'.[8] According to her written testimony, 'her father and her brothers and their relations all considered David Bourke to be the legal claimant to the title of Viscount Mayo' and she believed that 'the said David, now called Lord Mayo, is the person justly entitled to the title...'.

Since the three previous lords viscount had died within twenty-six years of each other, there were many people within the locality still alive who had known all three and who testified in written submissions to support the claim of David Bourke. Relations of the late viscounts, such as John Bermingham, who had 'married a niece of Lady Mayo on or about the year 1725',[9] and Peter Lynch, son of Sir Henry Lynch, a close friend of Lord 'Cheek', as well as numerous tenants of the Mayo estate, all testified on his behalf. The testimony and genealogical proof was, however, to prove ineffectual against more powerful and devious forces that sought to thwart his claim.

By the late 18th century, the Bourkes of Asgalan, despite their pedigree, were a family of little means. Like many aristocratic families descended from younger sons, over succeeding decades, their fortune had substantially diminished and their status had become, in effect, little more than that of tenant farmers. In the age of the notorious 'squireens', David's grandfather and father were known for their wild and reckless behaviour. They were 'ramblers', had lived for a time in France and, when at home, were frequently involved in local riots and faction fights. On numerous occasions they had incurred the anger of the 6th Viscount, 'who lamented that nothing made him so unhappy as that people so nearly related to him should behave in such a disorderly manner'. He had confided to a friend, William FitzMaurice, who testified that it was his fervent wish that his disorderly relations had remained abroad 'and it would be a happy circumstance for one of them to be called home in the title and estate of Lord Mayo'[10] when the time came.

Despite his personal and material unsuitability David Bourke was the legitimate heir apparent. His claim was subsequently 'referred by the then Lord Lieutenant to the Attorney and Solicitor General who reported favourably on the case'.[11] To pursue such a claim in the courts involved substantial expense and David Bourke had little means. The Countess of Brandon, who had been married to Theobald, the 7th viscount, and Owen O'Malley, the father of Sir Samuel O'Malley, 'from a consciousness and belief ... of the undoubted rights of the said David who was however in very narrow circumstances...' offered to assist him financially to pursue his claim. The Countess, then resident in Merrion

Square in Dublin, and Sir Owen provided David with 'clothes and fitted [him] out in a suitable style and caused proceedings to be commenced towards establishing the said David in his right to the Title'.[12] What should have been a relatively open-and-shut case turned out to be a manipulated miscarriage of justice.

Edmund Lambert, husband of the daughter of John, the 8th viscount, set out to obstruct David's case to safeguard what remained of the Mayo estate for himself, his wife and his son. He subsequently lodged claims to the remaining lands, and employed more strong-armed tactics against David Bourke's supporters on the estate. According to the sworn testimony of Walter Gibbons of Carrahorn, County Mayo, his father-in-law, Edward Hynes, who had been a tenant of the Mayo estate, was threatened by Lambert, who would 'distress him for rent and make him an English tenant if he did not sign the said paper', declaring the David Bourke 'was not heir to the title and estates'.[13] Hynes refused because 'he had always heard and did in his conscience believe that said claimant David was lineally descended from Richard-an-Iarainn and was true and lawful heir to the honour and estates of Mayo.' It was also alleged in the testimony that much damage was caused to the property and livestock of the tenants who refused to sign, while those who consented were indulged by Lambert, some of them receiving beneficial leases.

David Bourke remained in Dublin while his claim was being pursued with the support of the Countess of Brandon and Owen O'Malley. The principal counter-claim of his opponents centred on their assertion that Tibbott-ne-Long did not have a fourth son. This, however, was deemed unlikely by the Chief Herald's office, who reckoned that the 6th viscount would have been aware of his ancestry and would have been 'well-acquainted with his kinsmen and friends that must have known the first viscount Mayo and have given that young nobleman a clear recital of the family to fill up that short space of 52 years from 1629 [the year of Tibbott's death] to 1681 [the year of the 6th viscount's birth]. And so,' the authorities concluded, 'it must be admitted that Theobald the First Viscount Mayo left a son Richard from whom the Petitioner derives his title'.[14] The Prime Serjeant-at-law also lodged an objection on the grounds that descendants of Tibbott's third son, Theobald, could still be alive. The genealogical authorities considered this to be highly unlikely and stated that it was not possible that 'Sir Theobald, the 6th Viscount Mayo, could have gone to remote parts to seek some distant branch of the family that had a title to the honour, if he had an uncle and a cousin'.[15]

More than genealogical questions, however, prohibited David Bourke's claim. The possibility of someone, a half-step above a tenant farmer, a Roman Catholic by birth and by inclination, despite his recent recantation, lacking the social graces and material wealth to support the venerable title, was also frowned upon by members of the aristocracy both in Dublin and in Mayo. This was the 'golden age' of the Irish Protestant Ascendancy. Their Parliament in Dublin legislated and catered exclusively for them. At the time David Bourke presented his petition, the Lord Lieutenant, Viscount Townsend, was faced by a veritable barrage of requests for titles and promotions in exchange for votes from Irish parliamentarians. 'Viscounts who had sons and nephews in the lower house wanted earldoms. Barons wanted to be viscounts, commoners to be barons.'[16] The possibility of a vacant title becoming available to appease the demand was fortuitous. Moreover, the complexities and subterfuge that surrounded the estate of the viscounts Mayo, particularly from the time of the Restoration, and the confusion that still adhered to many of the land titles on the estate, made those with vested interests in the same intent on obstructing David Bourke's claim.

The case continued to drag on for some years and the pressure began to tell on David Bourke. He was described as 'a weak and ignorant man', and the possibility of being raised to the peerage had not made him mend his wayward temper and behaviour. When 'he offended the said Countess [of Brandon] she discontinued to support his rights'. He was dealt a double blow when his second supporter, Owen O'Malley, began to experience financial difficulties of his own and was eventually 'confined in the Marshalsea of the Four Courts in Dublin where he died.'[17] These events left David without the financial means to pay the heavy legal costs necessary to prosecute his claim.

The power of the establishment finally won out when in 1781 the title Viscount Mayo was declared extinct in the male line. It was subsequently conferred by patent dated 13 January 1781 on the Right Honourable John Bourke of Kill and Moneycrower (a former Commissioner of the Revenue and Excise), Baron of Naas and MP for County Kildare. The Bourke family of Naas was descended from John Bourke of Moneycrower, who had been a captain of horse in the army of the Duke of Ormond in 1641. He subsequently settled on lands at Kill, where he died in 1690. By the early 1700s, the family had an estate at Palmerstown, County Dublin. The family claimed descent, ironically from the descendants of Tibbott-ne-Long's 16th-century old adversary, O'Donnell's MacWilliam.

John Bourke was subsequently created Earl of Mayo on 24 June 1785. He had two sons, one of whom, Joseph Deane Bourke, was by coincidence, the incumbent Protestant Archbishop of Tuam at the time David Bourke made his submission. In 1792, Joseph Deane Bourke succeeded his brother as the 3rd Earl of Mayo.

David Bourke died in 1790 in 'lodgings' at Smithfield, Dublin, a broken and destitute man, protesting his claim to be the rightful Viscount Mayo to the end. According to the testimony of Anthony O'Connor, a physician, who administered to him on his death bed, 'unto the hour of his death'[18] David Bourke claimed to be the Viscount Mayo, which claim Dr. O'Connor, who testified under oath, believed to be true. David was buried in St Michan's Church in Dublin. It is a measure to the degree of uncertainty which continued to surround the title (which by then had been conferred on John Bourke of County Kildare) that the *Freeman's Journal,* 27 April 1790 recorded: 'Died: The Right Honourable, David Bourke, Lord Viscount Mayo'.[19] Later, on 2 December of the same year, it also recorded the death of the Earl of Mayo who, it stated, had attained his earldom by right of his title, 'Viscount Mayo'.

David Bourke died unmarried and without issue. His uncle, Richard Bourke of Ballyhaunis, claimed the title Viscount Mayo as the next male heir and as the only surviving brother of Theobald Bourke (Blind Toby) of Asgalan. Richard was married to Bridget, daughter of Randall Mac Donnell of Eallaghmore, County Mayo. Like his nephew,

Richard was in poor circumstances but, unlike David, he was elderly and did not have the financial backing of wealthy patrons to pursue his claim. The Countess of Brandon had died in 1789 and the O'Malleys had their own financial difficulties to contend with. In any event the likelihood that such a 'poor and old man',[20] as he was described, being successful in depriving someone as influential and wealthy as the Earl of Mayo of the title was remote, given the prevailing political, social and religious climate. Richard Bourke died in 1796 and was buried in the Augustinian abbey in Ballyhaunis. He was survived by his third but last surviving son and heir, Michael Bourke, of Lavalaroe, a town land near Ballyhaunis.

During his father's lifetime, Michael Bourke secured legal advice regarding the on-going disposal of the Mayo estate by the son of the last viscount's daughter, Aylmer Bourke Lambert, a famous botanist. In 1782 he had married Catherine Webster, a widow, living at the auspicious address of 'Hampton Court, Middlesex'.[21] In 1794, Michael Bourke instructed his solicitor to lodge a claim to lands in counties Mayo and Kilkenny on behalf of his father, Richard, as next legal heir, which were in the process of being disposed of by Aylmer Bourke Lambert. Other claims to the Mayo estate also materialised at the same time from 'John Gunning and others'[22] but, as with David Bourke's claim, these were unsuccessful. Aylmer Bourke Lambert subsequently sold the greater part of the estate to the Earl of Altamont, descendant of John Browne. Among the Westport House Papers is an agreement, dated 22 September 1795, between Aylmer Bourke Lambert and John Denis, 3rd Earl of Altamont for the sale of the Mayo estate[23] in staged payments for £29,702. The transaction was not finally concluded, however, until after 1810 when Howe Peter Browne, 2nd Marquess of Sligo, instructed his mother to 'pay off whatever mortgage has been made to pay Lambert'[24] but, he cautioned, not before the deeds to the lands, which Lambert claimed to have misplaced, had been located. Aylmer Bourke Lambert retained Castle Bourke and 470 statute acres on a lease for '3 lives'.[25] This was subsequently sold by his heirs by auction in 1862 and was acquired by the 3rd Marquess of Sligo.

Political events culminating in the 1798 Rebellion and the

subsequent Act of Union 1800 both delayed and perverted Michael Bourke's efforts to establish claim to the title. By the time he submitted a petition, signing himself 'Michael Bourke, Viscount Bourke of Mayo' in 1808 to the Lord Lieutenant, Charles, Duke of Richmond, the possibility of achieving his goal had receded even further. By 1808 Michael Bourke's circumstances were, like most of his fellow Catholic countrymen, deplorable. 'Their dwellings are primitive ... the walls and floors of clay, the roofs of sod and thatch ... a hearth without grate or chimney ... their food potatoes or oaten cakes, sour milk and sometimes salted fish ... few among them can read or write',[26] according to one contemporary account. In light of the disaffection of the majority Catholic population from the legislature and organs of government, which often manifested itself in acts of violence, an anti-Catholic bias prevailed in every aspect of government. The arrival in April 1807 of the Duke of Richmond as Lord Lieutenant and his subsequent public contention that it was not 'practicable or possible ... to put the Catholics upon an equal footing with Protestants'[27] further entrenched the bias.

Notwithstanding these obstacles, Michael Bourke set about establishing his right 'to the estates and honours of the Viscount Bourke of Mayo'.[28] Born in 1755 in Manulla, where his father had initially lived, Michael was sixty-three years old at the time he promulgated his claim. Together with the depositions that had been submitted on behalf of his first cousin, David, Michael presented eleven further sworn affidavits to substantiate his claim. Among those was one from Sarah Durcan née Bourke, an illegitimate daughter of Blind Toby, another from Margaret Lyster, daughter of Margaret Gunning of Castlecoote, cousin of the 8th Viscount, and the Reverend James Martin, who had been employed by the agent of the Mayo estate, James Burke, 'to instruct his children in the French language'. The affidavits all testified that Michael was 'the fourth cousin in the male line of collateral descent, to the late John, Lord Viscount Bourke of Mayo who died without issue male'.[29]

Despite the substantive evidence Michael Bourke's claim was unsuccessful. Like his cousin and uncle before him, he lacked the criteria that might have helped him succeed – influence, status and wealth. For despite his noble ancestry, he had been reduced to the status of a tenant farmer and the exigency of his financial circumstances hindered his advancement. He died, unmarried, sometime after 1814. Michael's younger brother Edmond, who predeceased him, would appear to have had a son, also named Edmond, next in line as claimant to the title. No claim, however, was submitted in Edmond's name.

The 'rambling' predilections of his father and his uncles, alluded to by the 6th Viscount, found other possible claimants to the title living in the vicinity of Aughagower, near Westport at the beginning of the nineteenth century. All that is known of Miles and Stephen Bourke is that they were the younger brothers of Theobald (Blind Toby) and Richard, the second claimant, and that both are buried in Aughagower. Both were married; Richard to an Anne Gibbons and Stephen to a woman whose surname was Garvey. While details of Richard's family, if any, have not been recorded, it appears that Stephen had at least one son.

Due to the paucity of records for the period, however, and given the deteriorating political and social conditions in Ireland, culminating in 1845 in the Great Famine and the resultant mass death and emigration that followed, especially in the west of Ireland, the trail to find further claimants to the Viscount Mayo title from the family of Tibbott-ne-Long petered out.

The title, as it now stands, still adheres to the earldom of Mayo and to the present and 11th Earl of Mayo, Charles Diarmuid John Bourke.

Perhaps through the auspices of this biography of the original holder of the venerable title, a twenty-first-century descendant of Tibbott-ne-Long might yet emerge to reclaim the title of Viscount Mayo.

Appendices

APPENDIX ONE

*The order of James I, 1603, establishing a Commission of Inquiry
to investigate lands claimed by Tibbott-ne-Long*

JAMES REX

RIGHT TRUSTIE, etc. Where Sir Theobald Bourke, Knt.
Exhibited a petition unto us, as well in behalfe of himselfe, as
of Morrogh O'Flaertie and Donell Ikoggie O'Flahertie, of
Jeherconnaght, his twoe brothers by the halfe blood; besechinge that
wee would bee pleased to accept of their severall surrenders of all their
mannories, seignories, landes and herediataments, and the same severally to grant to them and their heirs. Wee desiringe our subjectes
should hold their owne according to English tenure, and that their possessions should bee settled in a certaine and perpetuall course of
discent, for their encouragement to live in a civill course, to the benefit
of their lawfull progenie, etc., do hereby require you to cause our com-
missioin to bee passed, etc., to enquire what mannors, seignories,
landes and herediataments, the said Sir Theobald rightfullie holdeth of
any estate of inheritance, by discent or other lawfull means; and
further, what mannors, seignories, etc., the said Morrogh and Donell
have in the county of Galway by the tytles; and, after such inquisition
made and restored, our pleasure is, that our said subjects bee admitted
to make their severall surrenders; and immediatelie after, that you cause
our grant to bee made into them, severally and respectively, of all their
said mannors, seignories, landes and herediataments, soe found to bee
of their several inheritances; to holde to them and their heirs, severallie,
by knight's service in capite, reservinge all beaves, risings out, rentes,

services and dueties, formally chardged, by composition or other matter of record in the council booke of that release or province, or in any of our courtes of record in Dublin; insertinge in said patent all covenantes, reservations, etc. meete for the furtherance of our service in those partes, and usuall in like grauntes, with a province that our said grauntes bee not prejudiciall to the rightes of any other our subjects, nor available to alter, frustrate or infringe our generall compositions made hereto fore, in the tyme of our late deere sister, betweene her and the inhabitancies of the said countries, wherein the said landes are scituate, etc.

Given under our signet at Winchester the 25th day of Spt. In the first Yeere
To the Earle of Devenshire, our lieutenant of Ireland.

SOURCE: Public Record Office, London, Ms No. 501 No. 130

APPENDIX TWO

Abstract of the will, dated 13 April 1626, of Morrogh na Moyre
O'Flaherty of Bunowen

I N T H E N A M E O F G O D , Amen, I Morough Na Moyre
O'Flahertie of Bunowen in the baronie of Ballinahinch within the
County of Galway, Esquire … do make my last will and Testament
in manner and form followinge: First, I bequeathe my soule to God
Almightie, and my bodie to the grave to be buried amongst my
ancestors in St. Frances' Abbey neere Galway. I bequeath, and my said
will is, that all my castles, manors and lands heretofore estated to my
eldest sonne and heire Murrough-na-Mart O'Flahertie, shall be
absolutelie in the said Murrogh, his heirs and assigns for ever; and all
the castles and lands heretofore estated to my second sonne Edmond
O'Flahertie, shall be absolutelie to him and his heirs and assigns for
ever. Item, that my third sonne Bryen O'Flahertie and his heirs shall
have the Cleggan, excepting only the Aiery and hawks upon
Barnanoran reserved to the said Morrogh-na-Mart. Item, that my
married wife Onora Flahertie alias Bourke shall have three quarters and
a half of (the lands of) Ballindoone whereupon the Castle and town of
Bunowen stands, and the half quarter of Bally mc Enilly
(Ballyconnelly) thereinto adjoining, without rente, and after her
decease (the said lands) to be and remaine to the said Morrogh na
Mart. Item, that mee fourthe sonne Teige O'Flahertie shall have to him
and his heires the quarter of Kilkieran and Iwniscrevar out of the lands
allotted to Morrogh, and that Teige shall have no power to alienate or
mortgadge the said lands without the license of the said Morrogh na
Mart. Item that my second sonne Edmond shall pass an estate into my
sixth sonne Hugh and his heires of the quarter of Ballinikille with a

proviso that the said Hugh shall not alienate or mortgage or sell without the license of Edmond or his heires. My will is that my said children, Edmond, Brian, Teige and Hugh and their heires shall yearly pay to Morrogh na Mart and his heires 3 shillings out of every quarter for ever, and that they and their heires shall answer all suits and services due to the manors of Bunowen and Ballinahinse, and from henceforth shall be obedient to the said Morrogh. Item, that my said sonne and heir Morrogh and the rest of my sonnes Edmond and Bryan, and my said wife Onora, shall in one entire payment paie to my fifth sonne Patricke who is become a scholler £20 when he is ready and determined to goe beyond seas to studie, together with £10, everie yeare during his continuance beyond the seas. Item, that my daughters Soragh O'Flahertie and Owna ne Flahertie shall have such portions for their preferment in marriadge out of all the lands allotted to my said three eldest sonnes, proportionately as to the discretion of Sir Tybbot Bourke Knt. or his sonne and heire Myles Bourke and Sir John Bourke Knt. Calling to their assistance two or more of my nearest friends in Galway as shall be thought fit … Item, I give to my said wife Onora all my plate, cowes, garrans and sheep with my household stuffe, besides her third of all my lands. In witness I have hereinto putt me hand and seale on the 13th day of April in the year of Our Lord God 1626.

Morrogh Na Moyre O'Flahertie

SOURCE: *Galway Archaeological and Historical Society*, Vol. II, App.A, p. 54

APPENDIX THREE

Notice from Charles I to the Lord Deputy, February 1626, proposing to confer the title Viscount Mayo on Tibbott-ne-Long

To the Lo: Dep:
for Sir Theobald Burk

RIGHT TRUSTY. We cannot but consider the improvement of that our kingdome since the beginning of the reigne of our most deare father deceased, when many of the principall gentlemen and inhabitants are growne not only by plentifulness of their estates able to suppourt titles of honour but also by their loyal affectione to our service well deserving our princely favour in that kind. And therefore having lately received very good testimony of our well beloved subject Sir Theobald Burke of the county of Mayo Knight, that he is a gentleman not only of a large estate in those qurts., but of an auncient English race and one who did performe many faithfull services to our Crown in the last rebellion, both before and after the Spaniards arrival there. Wee have thought good to advance him to the honour and title of a Viscount of that our Realme, requiring you accordingly by the advice of sume of our learned Councell there, to cause our letrs patents under the greate seale of that our Kingdome in due forms of law to be made unto the said Sir Theobald Burke whereby wee doo authorise you to make ordaine constitute and create him Viscount Burke of Mayo in our said Realme of Ireland. To have and to hold the said honur, stile, title and dignitie of Viscount Burke of Mayo to him the said Sir Theobald Burke and the heires males of his body heretofore begotten and to be begotten. With all rights, priviledges prominences, prerogatives, commodities and imunities of a viscount of that our Realme in as ample and large and beneficall manor as any other viscount doth or ought to hold and enjoy the same. And theis our letres shall be as well unto you our Deputy and Chauncellor there now being, as to any other Deputy thiese Governor or governors, chancellors to keep of the great Seale of that our Kingdome with howe after for the time shalbe and to all other officers and Ministers there to whom it shall or may opptaine, and to every of them; sufficient warrant and discharge in that behalf.

Given under our signet at our palace of Westminister, the eight day of ffebruary in the second year of our reigne.

SOURCE: Public Records Office, London.

APPENDIX FOUR

Extract from Letters Patent of Charles I conferring the title
Viscount Mayo on Tibbott-ne-Long

A S W E A R E A W A R E that our beloved Kingdom of Ireland has won very great renown both in the time of our father of very happy memory and in our own; and more than in proceeding ages has advanced both in civilisation and in wealth; while we acknowledge (this) singular blessing of God, so we are very pleased that such an opportunity has been given us whereby a tribute of a distinguished Chief may be made to his own subjects; especially as among other things which are of much importance to the State for our own and our subjects welfare from that (State). Very few men have sprung to fame who could suffer (more) in proportion to the extent of their possessions, and could merit greater marks of distinction in accordance with the nobility of their birth and the fame of their heroic virtue.

Wherefore, as Theobaldus Burke a gilded Knight, sprung from a sometime illustrious stock in England has won fame not only by reason of his broad acres (Late fundiis) and the nobility of his origin, but especially by reason of his sincere fidelity towards us and our predecessors, and by reason of his warlike valour; the one of which was revealed in his immovable constancy of mind, even when the Kingdom was ablaze with internal conflagration; the other by his daring exploits against the Spaniards when they landed not so very long ago; we think it right and that on a double title we should bring back the reward of a worthy subject and one who has ever deserved right well of his chief.

Now as there can be found nothing more noble and distinguished than Titles of Honour by which Chiefs can and are wont both to reward their subjects who have deserved well for previous exploits, and to urge them on to higher things – because too they remain for future ages an indelible mark of Kingly favour and of a subject's valour, we of our Kingly favour and munificence have decided to enrol the said Theobaldus among the number of the Peers of our Kingdom of Ireland and to promote him to the rank of a hereditary Viscount. Let ye know therefore, that we, by virtue of (these) aforesaid (i.e. dispatches) attending the said Theobaldus with our continued favour, wishing to compensate and glorify with a title of honour his favours and good works in this our said Kingdom of Ireland, of our special favour ....

Translated from Latin
SOURCE: *Lodge's Peerage*, Vol. IV, p. 236

APPENDIX FIVE

Restoration of Theobald, 4th Viscount Mayo, 1660

WHEREAS Richard, Earl of Westmeath, the Viscount Mayo, the Viscount Galway, the Baron of Athenry, the Baron of Brittas, and Viscount Kilmallock, have constantly attended his Majesty's service in this parliament, that regard may be had to their better encouragement, and the support of the dignity of the House of Peers; that therefore it may be provided, that the said Richard Earl of Westmeath and Viscount Mayo etc. may be first restored unto and enjoy their respective former estates, belonging to them or any of them, in reversion or remainder, before any estate be restored to any person or persons, who are not, by his Majesty's gracious declaration, to be restored to their former estates, before a reprisal be first laid out and delivered, according to the said declaration, to the adventurers, soldiers, or others, possessing the same respectively, they the said Earl etc, first satisfying and paying such reparations, according to a just value thereof, as have been made upon their several respective estates, any act to the contrary thereof notwithstanding.

SOURCE: *Lords Journals*, 1.315

APPENDIX SIX

*The Last Will and Testament of John, 8th Viscount of Mayo,
died 1767*

Extracted from the Registry of his Majesty's Court of Perogative in Ireland

I N T H E N A M E O F G O D Amen, I John Lord Viscount Mayo of
the Kingdom of Ireland residing in Pall Mall Westminster make
this my last will and testament. I give my dear wife Lady Catherine
Mayo all my personal estate in the island of Jamaica and in the
Kingdom of Ireland and likewise my coach and horses here and
moreover the plate which belonged to her or any of her family. I give
to my said wife all her watches, jewels, rings and ornaments of her
person used by her wearing apparel and linen. I give to my wife the use
of all my other plate and my household goods and furniture during her
life and after her decease I give the same to Aylmer Bourke Lambert the
son of my daughter and wife of Edmund Lambert Esq. And in the case
he shall die before he shall attain the age of twenty one years I give the
same to my said daughter for her sole and separate use and to be by her
disposed of as she shall think fit notwithstanding her Coverture. I give
to my said wife and her heirs my estate in Oxfordshire purchased of
John Reed. I give to Mr. Theobald Bourke of the County of Mayo my
Agent in Ireland the sum of forty pounds. I give the residue of my
estate to my said dear wife Lady Mayo her heirs Exers. Admors. And
Assigns for ever and I nominate constitute and appoint my said wife
the said Catherine Lady Mayo sole Executrix of this my will and do
hereby revoke all former and other wills by me at any time heretofore
made provided always and it is my express will and desire that my said
wife shall have hold and enjoy all such part and so much of my personal estate which I have herein before given to her during her life only

without being in any manner compelled to give any security or securities to any person or persons who shall or may happen to be entitled to the same or any part thereof under or by virtue of this my will in respect of such personal estate after the death of my said wife Lady Mayo other than and except my said wife shall at any time during her life be pleased voluntarily to give her own bond or other security that behalf which I leave at her discretion to do or omit as she shall think proper and not otherwise. In witness thereof I the said John Lord Viscount Mayo have hereunto set my hand and seal this twenty ninth day of October in the second year of the reign of our Sovereign Lord King George the third and in the year of our Lord one thousand seven hundred and sixty two

[Mayo seal] signed sealed published and declared by the said John Lord Viscount Mayo as and for his last will and testament in the presence of us who have subscribed our names as witnesses thereunto in his presence:
John Smith Chas Foudrimier Phil. White.

The Last Will and Testament of the Right Honourable John Lord Viscount May in the Kingdom of Ireland but late of London in the Kingdom of Great Britain dec^d (having and so forth) was proved in Common Form of Law and Probate granted by the Most Revd Father Richard and so forth to the Right Honble. Catherine Lady Viscountess Mayo the sole Ex^x named in will she being first sworn by Commission Saving & so forth dated the 13 Day of April 1767.

Copy which I attest.

John Hawkins
Reg^r

APPENDIX SEVEN

The testimony of the Hon. Elizabeth Bourke, sister of John,
8th Viscount Mayo, 10 January 1769, in support of the claim
of David Bourke.

S HE HATH HEARD and believes that the title of lord Vis^t
Mayo hath descended from the creation of the said title in a
course of succession to Theo^d the 6th Lord Mayo who was
Dep^{ts}. Father and afterwards descended in succession to Theo^d and
John the two last Lords Mayo who were Dep^{ts} brothers. And saith that
the said John the last Lord Mayo died without issue male on or about
the 12 January 1767 and that said John was the last of the issue male of
Miles, the eldest son of said Sir Theob^d the first Lord Mayo and saith
she hath always heard it reputed in her family and does believe it to be
true that Theobald the first Lord Mayo had four sons only to wit; Miles
his eldest from whom Dep^t is lineally descended, David his 2^d Son who
died without issue male, Theobald his 3^r son who had three sons all of
whom died without issue male and Richard his 4th son and hath also
heard it in general reput^d in her Family and believ^d it to be true that s^d
Richard died leaving only one son called Theo^d who died having 4 sons
to wit; Miles, Richard, Theobald and David and that the said Miles
and Theobald and 1st and 3^d Sons of said Theobald, the son of Richard,
died without leaving any issue and that Rich^d his 2^d son died leaving
five son's all of whom as Dep^t hath heard and believes died with issue
male.

Hath heard and believes that David the 4^t Son of said
Theobald left issue 6 sons to wit Theobald Bourke commonly called
Blind Tibbott or Toby, his eldest son, Patrick John Richard Miles and
Stephen & hath frequently heard her said brother and others declare to
the purpose aforesaid in conversation relative to Dep^{ts} Family and saith
that the said Blind Tibbott was very frequently at Dep^{ts} Father's House

in the county of Mayo during the life of the Dep[ts] father and her said brothers and he and his issue male were considered by Dep[ts] her Father and Brothers reputed by her Family in general and their acquaintances and relations as the persons next in succession to the title and Honours of Lord Mayo on the event of the Dep[ts] Brothers Theobald and John dying without issue male which was in general thought not to be very unlikely to happen.

That said Theobald or Blind Toby left one son only called David at the time of his death which happened in or about the year 1745 and that the said David was a minor at the time of the death of his father and that said minor upon the death of his father was in like manner as his father had been during his life esteemed to be the person next entitled in succession to the Honour and Title of Lord Mayo upon the death of 8[d] Lord John Dep[ts] Bro[s] who was the last Lord Mayo without issue male and Dep[t] does believe that said David now called Lord Mayo is the person justly entitled to the title of Lord Visc[t] Mayo as the heir male and lineal descendant of Sir Theobald Bourke the first Lord Mayo and saith he hath been in general known and stiled as such ever since the death of Dep[ts] Bros. Lord Mayo in the year 1767 without male issue.

SOURCE: Lindsay mss. Public Record Office. Dublin

APPENDIX EIGHT

Memorial of Michael Bourke claiming to be Lord Viscount Bourke of Mayo

To his Grace Charles Duke of Richmond, the Lord Lieut. General and General Governor.

The memorial of Michael Bourke claiming to be Lord Viscount Bourke of Mayo

HUMBLY SHEWETH

T HAT YOUR MEMORIALISTS ancestor Sir Theobald Bourke Knt. was created Lord Viscount Bourke of Mayo by King Charles the First by letters patent becoming date 21 of June in the third year of his reign, which letters patent granted the honours to him the said Theobold and his heirs male of his body lawfully begotten.

That the said Theobold died the 18th of June 1629 leaving issue by his wife Maud dau. of Charles O'Connor of Sligo Esq. and four sons 1 Miles, 2 David who died without issue, 3 Theobold whose male issue is extinct and 4 Richard memorialists ancestor.

The said Miles 2nd Viscount and the heirs male of his body always enjoyed the title and honours granted by the said patent and took their seats and sat in parliament as Lord Viscount Bourke of Mayo until the year 1767 when John the 8th Viscount died leaving an only daughter Bridget who became the wife of Edward Lambert Esq. On the death of the said John the heirs male of the body of the said Miles 2nd Viscount and oldest son of Theobold the 1st Viscount failed and became extinct and the dignity descended to and upon David Bourke the 9th Viscount, son of Theobald, son of David, son of Theobald, son of

[189]

Richard, 4th son of the 1st Viscount, who put in claim for the honour and it was referred by the then Lord Lieutenant to the then attorney and solicitor general. That the said David, a man of weak intellect by some misconduct disgusted the Countess of Brandon, widow of Theobold the 7th Viscount, by whom his case was supported and she in consequence declined giving him any further assistance and he being in needy circumstances was unable to carry out the proceedings necessary to establish his right to the honour. That the said David died without issue in the year 1790 when the honour descended to and upon your memorialist's father Richard as his uncle and heir viz. brother of Theobold, father of the said David. The said Richard died 1 April 1796 and Memorialist is his son and heir.

Your memorialist humbly sheweth to your Grace that he is now next heir male of the body of Theobald the 1st Viscount Bourke of Mayo and therefore humbly makes his suit before your Grace and prays such order may be made in the promises for the relief of your memorialist as shall be thought just.

And your Memorialist will pray,

Michael Bourke
Viscount Bourke of Mayo

SOURCE: Lindsay mss, Public Records Office

Genealogy

1.   Lower MacWilliam
2.   Viscount Mayo Pedigree
3.   David Bourke
4.   Theobald Bourke
5.   Richard Bourke

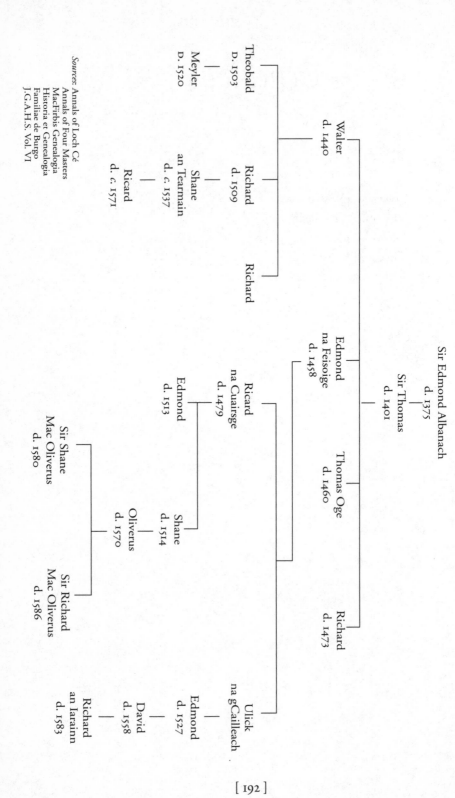

The Lower MacWilliam Succession

Sir Edmond Albanach
d. 1375

Sir Thomas
d. 1401

Edmond
na Feisoige
d. 1458

Thomas Oge
d. 1460

Richard
d. 1473

Walter
d. 1440

Theobald
D. 1503

Meyler
D. 1520

Richard
d. 1509

Richard

Shane
an Tearmain
d. c. 1537

Ricard
d. c. 1571

Ricard
na Cuairsge
d. 1479

Edmond
d. 1513

Shane
d. 1514

Oliverus
d. 1570

Ulick
na gCailleach

Edmond
d. 1527

David
d. 1558

Richard
an Iarainn
d. 1583

Sir Shane
Mac Oliverus
d. 1580

Sir Richard
Mac Oliverus
d. 1586

Sources: Annals of Loch Cé
Annals of Four Masters
MacFirbis Genealogia
Historia et Genealogia
Familiae de Burgo
J.G.A.H.S. Vol. VI

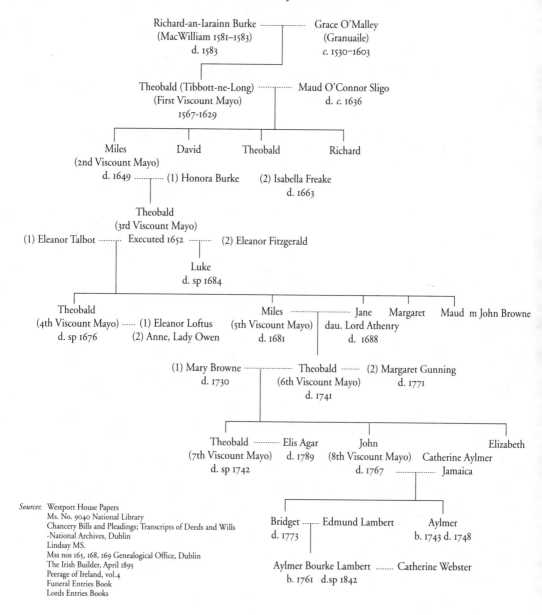

Viscount Mayo Succession

Richard-an-Iarainn Burke ······· Grace O'Malley
(MacWilliam 1581–1583)   (Granuaile)
d. 1583   c. 1530–1603

Theobald (Tibbott-ne-Long) ······· Maud O'Connor Sligo
(First Viscount Mayo)   d. c. 1636
1567-1629

Miles   David   Theobald   Richard
(2nd Viscount Mayo)
d. 1649 ··········· (1) Honora Burke   (2) Isabella Freake
                                            d. 1663

Theobald
(3rd Viscount Mayo)
(1) Eleanor Talbot ········ Executed 1652 ········· (2) Eleanor Fitzgerald

Luke
d. sp 1684

Theobald   Miles ··············· Jane   Margaret   Maud m John Browne
(4th Viscount Mayo) ······ (1) Eleanor Loftus   (5th Viscount Mayo) dau. Lord Athenry
d. sp 1676   (2) Anne, Lady Owen   d. 1681   d. 1688

(1) Mary Browne ················ Theobald ········ (2) Margaret Gunning
d. 1730   (6th Viscount Mayo)   d. 1771
                              d. 1741

Theobald ·········· Elis Agar   John   Elizabeth
(7th Viscount Mayo)   d. 1789   (8th Viscount Mayo) Catherine Aylmer
d. sp 1742   d. 1767 ················ Jamaica

Bridget ······· Edmund Lambert   Aylmer
d. 1773   b. 1743 d. 1748

Aylmer Bourke Lambert ········ Catherine Webster
b. 1761 d.sp 1842

Sources: Westport House Papers
          Ms. No. 9040 National Library
          Chancery Bills and Pleadings; Transcripts of Deeds and Wills
          -National Archives, Dublin
          Lindsay MS.
          Mss nos 165, 168, 169 Genealogical Office, Dublin
          The Irish Builder, April 1895
          Peerage of Ireland, vol.4
          Funeral Entries Book
          Lords Entries Books

DAVID

2nd. Son of First Viscount Mayo

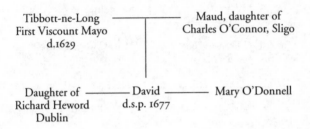

Tibbott-ne-Long ——————— Maud, daughter of
First Viscount Mayo   Charles O'Connor, Sligo
d.1629

Daughter of ——— David ——— Mary O'Donnell
Richard Heword   d.s.p. 1677
Dublin

THEOBALD

3rd. Son of First Viscount Mayo

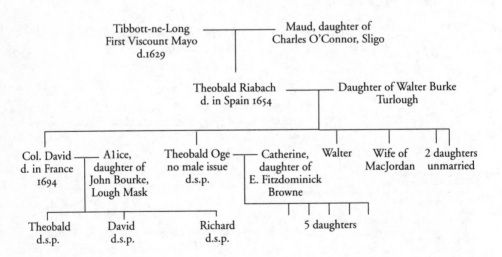

Tibbott-ne-Long ——————— Maud, daughter of
First Viscount Mayo   Charles O'Connor, Sligo
d.1629

Theobald Riabach ——————— Daughter of Walter Burke
d. in Spain 1654   Turlough

Col. David —— Alice,   Theobald Oge —— Catherine,   Walter   Wife of   2 daughters
d. in France   daughter of   no male issue   daughter of   MacJordan   unmarried
1694   John Bourke,   d.s.p.   E. Fitzdominick
               Lough Mask   Browne

Theobald   David   Richard   5 daughters
d.s.p.   d.s.p.   d.s.p.

RICHARD
4th Son of First Viscount Mayo

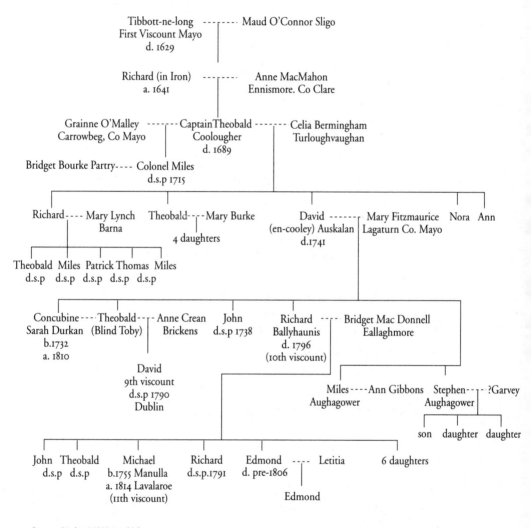

Tibbott-ne-long ---┬--- Maud O'Connor Sligo
First Viscount Mayo
d. 1629

Richard (in Iron) ---┬--- Anne MacMahon
a. 1641 .... Ennismore. Co Clare

Grainne O'Malley ---┬--- CaptainTheobald ---┬--- Celia Bermingham
Carrowbeg, Co Mayo ... Coolougher .... Turloughvaughan
.... d. 1689

Bridget Bourke Partry ---- Colonel Miles
.... d.s.p 1715

Richard ---- Mary Lynch ... Theobald ---┬-- Mary Burke .... David ------┬ Mary Fitzmaurice ... Nora ... Ann
.... Barna .... (en-cooley) Auskalan ... Lagaturn Co. Mayo
.... 4 daughters ... d.1741

Theobald Miles Patrick Thomas Miles
d.s.p ... d.s.p ... d.s.p ... d.s.p ... d.s.p

Concubine ---- Theobald ---┬- Anne Crean ... John .... Richard ---┬- Bridget Mac Donnell
Sarah Durkan ... (Blind Toby) ... Brickens ... d.s.p 1738 ... Ballyhaunis ... Eallaghmore
b.1732 .... d. 1796
a. 1810 .... (10th viscount)

David
9th viscount
d.s.p 1790
Dublin

Miles ----Ann Gibbons ... Stephen ---┬- ?Garvey
Aughagower .... Aughagower

son ... daughter ... daughter

John ... Theobald ...... Michael .... Richard ...... Edmond ---- Letitia .... 6 daughters
d.s.p ... d.s.p ... b.1755 Manulla ... d.s.p.1791 ... d. pre-1806
.... a. 1814 Lavalaroe .... Edmond
.... (11th viscount)

Sources: Lindsay MS National Library
Ms 168,159 National Library
Funeral Entries Books (various)
Lodge's Peerage, vol. 2
Stafford's Inquisition (Mayo)
Lord's Entries, vol.1
Westport House papers
Freeman's Journal (various)

References

CHAPTER ONE

1. *Pacata Hiberniae*, preface.
2. *The Celtic People and Renaissance Europe*, p.42.

CHAPTER TWO

1. *Discovery of the True Causes, Why Ireland was Never Entirely Subdued*, p.199.
2. *The Chronicle of Ireland*, p.16.
3. *The Course of Irish History*, p.48.
4. *Discoverie of the True Causes, Why Ireland was Never Entirely Subdued*, p.166.
5. *Social History of Ancient Ireland*, vol. II, p.11.
6. *The Irish Law of Kinship*, Proceedings RIA, vol. XL, p.186.
7. *Gaelic Society in Ireland in the Late 16th Century*, p.56.
8. *A Treatise of Ireland*, p.9.
9. *The Course of Irish History*, p.50.
10. *Gaelic and Gaelicised Ireland in the Middle Ages*, p.146.
11. *Historia et Genealogia Familiae de Burgo*, folio, 2.
12. *ibid.*
13. *History of the County Mayo*, p.144.

CHAPTER THREE

1. *Hibernia Dominicana*, p.319.
2. *Course of Irish History*, p.175.
3. *New History of Ireland*, vol. 3, p. LXII.
4. *Calendar of Carew MSS*, vol. I, p.235.
5. *Description of Ireland*, p.1.
6. *Course of Irish History*, p.182.

7. *History of the County Mayo*, p.174.
8. *Gaelic and Gaelicised Ireland in the Middle Ages*, p.79.
9. *Discovery of the True Causes, Why Ireland was Never Entirely Subdued*, p.178.
10. *De Rebus Hibernicus*, Cork Historical and Archaeological Society, vol. 26, p.41.
11. *ibid.*
12. *ibid.*
13. *The Course of Irish History*, p.183.
14. *New History of Ireland*, p.91.
15. *ibid*, p.99.
16. *C.S.P.I.*, vol. CLXX, p.284.
17. *S.P.I. 63/19*, no.56.
18. *History of the County Mayo*, p.188 .
19. *ibid.*
20. *ibid.*
21. *Westport House MSS.*
22. *ibid.*
23. *ibid.*
24. *ibid.*
25. *Calendar of Carew MSS*, p.50.
26. *C.S.P.I.*, vol. CLXX, p.132.
27. *Annals of the Four Masters*, vol. IV, p.1805.
28. *ibid.*
29. *C.S.P.I.*, vol. CLXX, p.133.

CHAPTER FOUR
1. *Westport House MSS.*
2. *Galway Archaeological and Historical Society*, vol. 28, p. 28.
3. *History of the County Mayo*, p.359.
4. *S.P.I. 63/171*, no.62.
5. *History of the County Mayo*, p.207.
6. *Titus B XIII*, p.236.
7. *ibid.*
8. *C.S.P.I.*, vol. CLXX, p.132.

9. *Cork Historical and Archaeological Society*, vol. XXVI, p.382.
10. *Westport House MSS.*
11. *ibid.*
12. *ibid.*
13. *ibid.*
14. *Calendar of Cecil Mss*, vol. 3, p.401.
15. *C.S.P.I.* vol. CXLVIII, p.417.
16. *TITUS b XIII*, p.446.
17. *ibid.*
18. *ibid.*
19. *Calendar of Salisbury MSS*, vol. 9, p.423.
20. *History of the County Mayo*, p.250.
21. *ibid.*
22. *ibid.*

CHAPTER FIVE

1. *S.P.I. 63/171*, no. 62-66.
2. *C.S.P.I.*, vol. CLXXIV, p.105.
3. *S.P.I. 63/171*, no. 62-66.
4. *ibid*, no.81.
5. *C.S.P.I*, vol. CLXXIX, p.315.
6. *ibid*, vol. CLXXIII, p.198.
7. *S.P.I. 63/179*, no.81.
8. *Life of Hugh Roe O'Donnell*, preface, p. lvi.
9. *S.P.I. 63/179*, no. 81.
10. *ibid*, no. 75.
11. *ibid*, no. 81.
12. *C.S.P.I.*, preface, p. xxvi.
13. *New History of Ireland*, p.122.
14. *Calendar of Carew MSS*, vol. III, p.505.
15. *S.P.I. 63/184*, no.23.
16. *Life of Hugh Roe O'Donnell*, p.111.
17. *ibid.*
18. *History of the County Mayo*, p.265.
19. *S.P.I. 63/190* no.371.

20. *C.S.P.I.*, vol. 6, p.186.

21. *Annals of the Four Masters*, vol. IV, p.2013.

22. *Calendar of Carew MSS*, vol. III, p.265.

23. *ibid.*

24. *Annals of the Four Masters*, vol. IV, p.2013.

25. *Calendar of Carew MSS*, vol. II, p.265.

26. *S.P.I.*, 63/199, no.66IV.

27. *ibid.*

28. *ibid.*

29. *C.S.P.I.*, vol. CXCIX, p.285.

30. *ibid*, p.294.

31. *S.P.I. 63/199*, no.145.

32. *ibid.*

33. *C.S.P.I.* vol. 6, p.324.

34. *ibid*, p.410.

CHAPTER SIX

1. *New History of Ireland*, p.123.

2. *Calendar of Carew MSS*, vol. III p. 270.

3. *ibid.*

4. *S.P.I. 63/200* no.233.

5. *ibid*, no.358.

6. *Calendar of Cecil MSS*, vol. 3, p.270.

7. *ibid.*

8. *Chronicle of Ireland*, p.143.

9. *C.S.P.I.*, p.332.

10. *Moryson's Itinerary*, p.230.

11. *ibid.*

12. *Annals of the Four Masters*, vol. IV, p.2123.

13. *C.S.P.I.*, vol. CLVI, p.332.

14. *Annals of the Four Masters*, vol. IV, p. 2124.

15. *C.S.P.I.*, vol. 8, p.119.

16. *ibid*, p.120.

17. *ibid*, p.121.

18. *ibid*, p.136.

19. *ibid* p.331.
20. *ibid.*
21. *ibid.*
22. *Moryson's Itinerary,* p. 390.
23. *Annals of the Four Masters,* vol. IV, p.2145.
24. *ibid,* p.2184.
25. *C.S.P.I.,* vol. 9, p.446.
26. *ibid,* p.67.
27. *ibid,* p.69.
28. *S.P.I.* 63/207, pt 6, no.207.
29. *C.S.P.I.,* vol. 9, p.68.
30. *Calendar of Carew MSS,* vol. 3, p.490.
31. *C.S.P.I.,* vol. 9, p.69.
32. *ibid,* p.224.
33. *ibid,* p.135.
34. *ibid,* p.105.
35. *ibid.*
36. *Annals of the Four Masters,* vol. IV, p.2265.
37. *Pacata Hibernia,* preface.
38. *ibid.*

CHAPTER SEVEN
1. *Making of Modern Ireland,* p.13.
2. *Moryson's Itinerary,* vol. III, p.205.
3. *C.S.P.I.* 1601-03, p.418.
4. *Moryson's Itinerary,* vol. III, p.214.
5. *ibid.*
6. *C.S.P.I.* 1601-03, p.497.
7. *New History of Ireland,* p.221.
8. *Lodge's Peerage,* vol. IV, p.202.
9. *Repertory of the Enrolements on the Patent Rolls of Chancery,* vol. I, p.239.
10. *Discovery of the True Causes, Why Ireland was Never Entirely Subdued,* p.277.
11. *Chancery Bill,* no. B.B7.

12. *ibid,* no.R.63.
13. *ibid,* no.I.209.
14. *ibid.*
15. *Westport House MSS.*
16. *ibid.*
17. *ibid.*
18. *ibid.*
19. *Advertisements for Ireland,* p.19.
20. *C.S.P.I.,* vol. 14, p.254.
21. *ibid, p.*291.
22. *ibid,* p.415.
23. *ibid,* vol. 15, p.55.
24. *ibid.*
25. *ibid.*
26. *ibid,* 1610, p.464.
27. *ibid.*
28. *ibid.*
29. *ibid,* 1611, p.272.
30. *Westport House MSS.*

CHAPTER EIGHT
1. *Historical Tracts,* p.211.
2. *Moryson's Itinerary,* vol. III, p.342.
3. *Irish Life in the 17th century,* p.195.
4. *Analecta Hibernia,* vol. 8, p.97.
5. *Calendar of Patent Rolls, James I,* p.398.
6. *Chancery Bill,* A-E, no.46.
7. *New History of Ireland,* p.222.
8. *ibid.*
9. *Calendar of Patent Rolls,* James I, p.318.
10. *ibid.*
11. *Rural Society in Connacht 1600-40,* p.193.
12. *Liber Munerum,* vol. I, p.55.
13. *S.P.I.* 63/236 no.195.
14. *ibid.*

15. *ibid.*
16. *C.S.P.I.,* 1621, p.316.
17. *Chancery Bill,* AA no.137.
18. *Irish Life in the 17th century,* p.47.
19. *S.P.I.* 63/241, no.93.
20. *ibid.*
21. *PRO London,* ms. no.501 (001131).
22. *ibid.*
23. *C.S.P.I.,* vol. CCXLVII p.385.
24. *ibid.*
25. *Ordnance Survey: Mayo,* p.102.
26. *Rural Society in Connacht,* p.29.
27. *ibid.*
28. *Funeral's Entries Book,* vol. 5, p.147.

CHAPTER NINE
1. *Inquisitions of the County Mayo,* p.186.
2. *Irish Life in the 17th century,* p.280.
3. *ibid.*
4. *Inquisitions of the County Mayo,* p.40.
5. *ibid.*
6. *C.S.P.I.,* vol. LLLI, p.590.
7. *Lords Journals,* vol. I, p.25.
8. *Course of Irish History,* p.195.
9. *ibid,* p.200.
10. *Lodge's Peerage,* vol. IV, p.238.
11. *Hickson,* vol. I, p.377.
12. *ibid,* p.378.
13. *ibid.*
14. *ibid,* p.382.
15. *ibid.*
16. *ibid.*
17. *ibid,* p.397.
18. *ibid,* p.394.
19. *ibid,* p.393.

20. *Lodge's Peerage*, vol. IV, p.243.
21. *Course of Irish History*, p.202.
22. *Owen Roe O'Neill*, p.336.
23. *ibid*, p.337.
24. *Lodge's Peerage*, vol. IV, p.243.
25. *Iar-Chonnacht*, (notes) p.241.
26. *Course of Irish History*, p.202.
27. *Lodge's Peerage*, vol. IV, p.244.
28. *ibid*, p.245.
29. *Life of Ormond*, vol. III, p.399.
30. *Ormond MSS*, vol. III, p.39.
31. *Lodge's Peerage*, vol. , p.245.
32. *ibid*, p.246.
33. *Westport House MSS.*
34. *ibid.*
35. *Lodge's Peerage*, vol. IV, p.246.
36. *Westport House MSS.*
37. *ibid.*
38. *ibid.*
39. *ibid.*
40. *Westport House and the Brownes*, p.13.
41. *The Irish Builder*, 1 April 1895.
42. *ibid.*
43. *Monumental Inscriptions of Jamaica.*
44. *Westport House MSS.*
45. *Lindsay MSS*, no.6.
46. *Westport House MSS.*

CHAPTER TEN
1. *Westport House MSS.*
2. *MS 169*, GO.
3. *Books of Survey and Distribution*, p.112.
4. *MS 165, (pt. II)* GO.
5. *MS 159*, p.196, GO.
6. *ibid.*

7. *Westport House MSS.*
8. *MS 159,* GO.
9. *ibid.*
10. *ibid.*
11. *Lindsay MSS,* no.6.
12. *ibid.*
13. *ibid.*
14. *ibid.*
15. *ibid.*
16. *Champagne and Silver Buckles,* p.58.
17. *Lindsay MSS.*
18. *ibid.*
19. *Freeman's Journal,* 27 April 1790.
20. *Lindsay MSS.*
21. *Westport House MSS.*
22. *ibid.*
23. *Sligo Correspondence, Yale, letter 2.*
24. *ibid.*
25. *Westport House MSS.*
26. *State of Ireland* (1808) p.29.
27. *MSS.* p.1370 National Library if Ireland.
28. *Lindsay MSS.*
29. *Westport House MSS.*

Bibliography

MANUSCRIPT SOURCES

Westport House Papers (courtesy of the Marquess of Sligo)
Yale Beinecke, *Sligo Correspondence* (ed. P. Cochran)
Genealogical Office, Dublin
MSS. nos. 159, 165, 168, 169
Funeral Entries Book, vols. 2, 5, 14
Lords Entries, vol. I, 1681, vol. I 1702
Irish Folklore Department, UCD
MSS. nos. 1181, 693
National Library of Ireland, Dublin
State Papers of Ireland, nos.
    63/91;56;63/88;34;63/71;62/66;81;63/179;36;38;81;75;63/190;114;63/11
    9;66;145;63/200;233;358;353;63/235;195;63/241;93;63/185;23;25
MSS. nos. D3375. D3650-3
Private Collection, Sir John Ainsworth, nos. 138, 204, 306
National Archives, Dublin
Chancery Bills nos. AA137,150; A150; BB7; G79; I209; R55,63, 65;
Calendar of Fiants, Charles 1
Chancery Pleadings, 1559-1618; 1627-30; 1633-48
Repertory to the Decrees of Chancery, 28 Henry to 1624
Transcripts of Deeds and Wills, Mayo
Inquisitions in Offil. Rot. Canl. R/C 4/14-15, vol. 15 MSS, nos. 12/L;
    5/30, M2793-4; M5788; M3442; M2798
Graves MSS Irish Baronage
Lindsay MSS, no.6
Royal Irish Academy
MSS. nos. 744, AV2, 3CI3,
Proceedings vols. XL, XVV, XXXVI

Trinity College, Dublin
MSS nos. 1440; 6403
Public Office, London
MSS no. 501 1 1001131
British Museum
Cotton Titus, BXIII, BXVII

PUBLISHED PRIMARY SOURCES

Analecta Hibernica, nos. 8, 26
Annals of Loch Ce, ed. B MacCarthy (Dublin, 1893)
Annals of the Kingdom of Ireland by the Four Masters, ed. and trans. John
     O'Donovan (Dublin 1851)
Army Historical Research, vol. XI
Books of Survey and Distribution, 1636-1703, vol. II, Mayo
Calendars of the Carew Manuscripts, ed. J.S. Brewer and W. Bullen
     (London 1869)
Calendars of the Cecil Manuscripts, Historical Manuscripts Commission
     (1883-1899)
Calendars of Patent Rolls, vols. I, II, III, ed. J. Morrin (Dublin 1861-
     1863)
Calendars of the Patent and Close Rolls of Chancery in Ireland, ed. J.
     Morrin (London 1863)
Calendars of the State Papers of Ireland, 1509-73; 1574-85;1588-92;1596-
     97;1598-99;1599-1600;1600;1601;1601-03;1603-06;1606-08;1608-
     10;1625-32
Chronicle of Ireland 1584-1608, Sir James Perrot, ed. H. Wood (Dublin
     1933)
Compossion Booke of Conought, trans. A.M. Freeman (Dublin 1936)
Description of Ireland, ed. E. Hogan (Dublin 1878)
Government of Ireland, Sir John Perrot (London 1626)
History of the Commoners of Great Britain and Ireland (London 1834)
History of the Life of James, Duke of Ormond, T. Carte (London 1834)
Letters and Papers relating to the Irish Rebellion, 1624-1646, ed. J. Hogan
     (Dublin 1936)
Liber Munerum Publicorum Hiberniae

Moryson, F. *An Itinerary* (London), Facsimile edition Glasgow 1907-8

Ordnance Survey: Letters relating to the Antiquities of the County Mayo,
    vols. I, II J. O'Donovan (Dublin 1862)

Patent Rolls of James I, ed. W. O'Sullivan (Dublin 1958)

Peerage and Baronetage, Burke (London 1834)

Repertory of the Enrolments on the Patent Rolls of Chancery, vol. I

Reports of the Royal Society of Antiquarians of Ireland, vols. VII, XVIII

Stafford Inquisition of the County Mayo, ed. W. O'Sullivan (Dublin
    1958)

SECONDARY SOURCES

Bagwell, R. *Ireland under the Tudors,* vols. I, II, II (London 185/90)
    Ireland under the Stuarts, vols. I, II (London 193)

Beckett, J.C. *The Making of Modern Ireland, 1603-1923* (London 1966)

Chambers, A. *Granuaile: Ireland's Pirate Queen (Grace O'Malley) c.
    1530-1603* (Dublin 1998 new edition) .

Corkery, D. *The Hidden Ireland* (Dublin 1979)

Curtis, E. *A History of Ireland* (London 1937)

Davis, J. *A Discovery of the True Causes why Ireland was Never Entirely
    Subdued* (Shannon 1969)

Derricke, J. *Image of Irelande* (London 1581)

Dolley, M. *Anglo-Norman Ireland* (Dublin 1972)

Edwards, E.D. *Ireland in the Age of the Tudors* (London 1977)

Ellis, S. G. *Tudor Ireland* (London 1985)

G.E.C. *The Complete Peerage, vol. VIII* (London 1932)

Graham, W. *The Spanish Armadas* (London 1972)

Hardiman, J. *History of the Town and County of Galway* (Dublin 1820)
    Irish Minstrelsy, vol. II (London 1831)

Hayes-McCoy, G. *Scots Mercenary Forces in Ireland* (Dublin 1939)

Hickson, M. *Ireland in the 17th century, vol. I* (London 1884)

Jones. F. M. *Mountjoy: The Last Elizabethan Deputy* (Dublin 1958)

Joyce, P. *Social History of Ancient Ireland, vols. I, II* (Dublin 1913)

Knox, T. H. *History of the County Mayo* (Dublin 1908)

Lydon, J. *Ireland in the Later Middle Ages* (Dublin 1973)

MacCalmont, R. E. *Memoirs of the Binghams* (London 1915)

MacCurtain, M. *Tudor and Stuart Ireland* (Dublin 1972)

MacLysaght, E. *Irish Life in the 17th Century* (Cork 1939)

Maxwell, C. *The Stranger in Ireland* (London 1915)

Moody, T. W. and F. X. Martin (eds.) *The Course of Irish History (revised edition),* (Cork 1994)

Moody, T. W., F. X. Martin and F. Byrnes (eds.) *A New History of Ireland, vol. III* (Oxford 1976)

Moryson, F. *An Itinerary, 3 pts.* (Glasgow 1907-08)

Nicholls, K. *Gaelic and Gaelicised Ireland in the Middle Ages* (Dublin 1972)

O'Brien, G. *Economic History of Ireland in the 17th Century* (Dublin 1919)

O'Cahan, T. S. *Owen Roe O'Neill* (London 1968)

O'Ciannan, T. *The Flight of the Earls* (Dublin 1916)

O'Connor, C. *The O'Connors of Connaught* (Dublin 1846)

O'Flaherty, R. A. *Chorographical Description of West Connaught* (Dublin 1846)

O'Raghallaigh, T. *Fili agus Filidheacht Chonnacht* (Dublin 1938)

Robbins, J. *Champagne and Silver Buckles: The Viceregal Court at Dublin Castle, 1700-1922* (Dublin 2001)

Scott, A. E. *Everyone A Witness: The Stuart Age* (Hampshire 1974)

Silke, J. J. *Ireland and Europe 1559-1607* (Dundalk 1966)

Sligo, Marquis of, *Westport House and the Brownes* (1981)

Trimble, W. L. *History of Enniskillen* (Enniskillen 1919)

NEWSPAPERS AND PERIODICALS

Cork Historical and Archaeological Society, vol. XXVI

Galway Archaeological and Historical Society, vols. I – XIV, XXI, XXVII

Historical Studies, vol. IV

Irish Book Lover, April 1941

Irish History Series, no. 8

Reports of the Royal Society of Antiquarians of Ireland, vols. XII, XVIII

The Irish Builder, various issues

The Freeman's Journal, various issues

The Times, various issues

Index

A

Achill, 52, 61

Agar, Ellis, Countess of Brandon, 162,
    163, 169, 170, 171, 173

Aille Castle, 32

Anglo-Normans, the 14, 19, 52

Aquila, Don Juan, 101

Argyle, duke of, 30

Armada, 57, 58

Armagh, 30

Asgalan, 166, 167, 169, 172

Askeaton castle, 41, 41

Athenry, lord, 30

Athlone, 79, 146

Athlone Castle, 69, 70, 104, 116, 127,
    136

Aughagower, 66, 160, 175

Aylmer, Sir, 164
    Bridget, 164
    Catherine, 163, 164
    Whitgift, captain, 163

B

Bagnell, Sir Henry, 89

Ballinahinch, barony of, 153

Ballinakill, 152

Ballinaloob Castle, 63

Ballinrobe Castle, 22, 44, 79

Ballintobber Abbey, 132, 136, 145, 158

Ballyhaunis, 147, 172, 173
    Abbey, 148, 173

Ballyknock Castle, 32, 41, 42

Ballymote Castle, 52, 89

Belcarra, 84, 104, 115, 124, 128, 130,
    143, 149

Bellabourke, 46

Berwick, 159

Bingham, Sir George, 52, 53, 55, 57,
    69, 72,
        Captain George, 56, 74, 75
    Henry, 52, 148
        Sir John, 52, 121
        Sir Richard, 49, 52, 53, 54, 55,
            56, 57, 58, 60, 61, 62, 63,
            64, 65, 66, 68, 69, 70, 71,
            75, 76, 80, 82, 83, 87

Bermingham, Francis, 163
        Richard,

Blackwater fort, 72, 74, 86, 89

Blake, Valentine, 145

Bourke,
        Bridget, 164
        Caitriona, 26
        David, 26
        David mac Tibbott-ne-Long,
            104, 125, 128, 136, 139,
            140, 141
        David mac Ulick, 105, 116
        David, 9th viscount Mayo,
        166, 167, 168, 169, 170,
        171, 172
        Edmond (Castlebarry), 47, 51,
            54, 56
        Edmond, (Cong), 78
        Edmond (of the Owles), 148,
            149, 150
        Edmond mac Richard-an-
            Iarainn, 26, 55, 65, 66, 75

Elizabeth, the honourable, 168
Honora, 124, 125, 128,
  136
James, 164
John, 26
John, 8th viscount Mayo, 163,
  164, 165, 167, 168
John mac Richard, 78
Katherine, 56
Luke, captain, 152, 155, 159
Margaret, 104, 125, 128, 136
Mary, 104, 124, 125, 136
Maud, 152, 157
Michael, 11th viscount Mayo,
  173, 174, 175
Moyler,
Miles, 2nd viscount Mayo, 60,
  72, 83, 104, 114, 116, 118,
124, 127, 128, 129, 130,
131, 132, 133, 134, 135,
136, 140, 141, 142, 143,
147, 148, 149, 150, 151,
152, 166
Miles, 5th viscount Mayo, 155,
  158, 160
Oliverus, mac John, mac Oliver,
  78
Richard-an-Iarainn, 12, 25, 26,
  30, 39, 40, 41, 42, 43, 44,
45, 46, 47, 170
Richard, 10th viscount Mayo,
  172, 173
Richard Og, 62
Richard Roe, 56
Richard mac Oliverus, 42, 43,
  47, 48, 49
Richard mac Tibbott-ne-Long,
  104, 125, 128, 136, 139,
140, 141, 166, 167, 170

Richard, The Devil's Hook, 55,
  56, 59, 69
Richard, son of The Devil's
  Hook, 70, 71, 78, 82, 83, 99, 10
Shane mac Oliverus, 39, 41, 42
Shane mac Moyler, 62, 110
Theobald (Blind Toby), 172,
  174, 175
Theobald, 3rd viscount Mayo,
  124, 144, 149, 150, 151,
152, 154
Theobald, 4th viscount Mayo,
  154, 155, 156, 157
Theobald, 6th viscount Mayo,
  158, 160, 161, 162, 167,
168, 169, 171
Theobald, 7th viscount Mayo,
  162, 164, 165, 167, 168
Theobald mac Tibbott-ne-long,
  104, 125, 128, 136, 139,
140, 141
Theobald of Tirawley
(O'Donnell's MacWilliam), 78,
  79, 81, 82, 83, 86, 87, 88,
89, 90, 93, 94
Thomas, Sir, 120
Tibbott Reagh, 55
Ulick, 26, 110
Ulick mac William, 26, 55, 62
Walter, 26
Walter Fada, 26
Walter Kittagh, 65
Walter mac Edmond, 59
Walter ne Mully, 65
William, The Blind Abbot, 26,
  51, 59, 60, 64, 84
William of Shrule, 78
Bowen, William, 112
Brabazon, Sir Anthony, 76, 7

Brehom law, 17, 18, 19, 24, 31, 36, 42, 44, 51, 54, 112, 114
Broadhaven Bay, 132
Browne, Bridget, 163
    John I, sheriff of Mayo, 49, 55, 58, 59, 62, 63, 158
    Col. John, 121, 149
    John III
    Mary, 160, 161
Bunowen castle, 57, 87, 132, 153
Burghley, Lord, 74
Burrishoole, barony of, 15, 23, 31, 32, 42, 45, 48, 52, 60, 66, 89, 127, 140, 158, 160, 167
    castle, 23, 32, 41
Burke, Honora, 104, 115, 130, 140
    Rev. Patrick, 145
    Richard, 96, 97
    Sir Thomas, 116
    Ulick, 74, 75
    Ulick Finn, 24
Burgh, Lord, 81
Burgos, de, 14, 17, 32
    Edmund Albanach, 16, 20, 21
    Elizabeth, 16
    Richard Mor, 15, 16, 45
    Richard O'Cuaraisge, 23
    Thomas, 21
    William I, 15
    William II, 16
    William Liath, 16,
Burgo, de, lordship of, 15
    earldom of, 16
Butlers (Botiller), 15, 31, 32
Butler, John, 31

C
Carew, Sir George, 36, 94, 96, 97, 98
Carnacon, 145

Carra, barony of, 15, 22, 23, 33, 44, 45, 46, 75, 89, 110, 127, 128, 140, 158, 160, 167
Carra Castle, 45, 112, 141
Carrichahowley Castle (Rockfleet), 32, 48, 59, 60, 104
Carrickfergus, 72
Carrickennedy Castle, 32
Carrick-on-Suir, 74
Castle Barry (Castlebar), 22, 47, 51, 64, 65, 66, 82, 83, 105, 121, 148, 149
Castlebourke (Kilboynell), 46, 113, 158, 161, 162, 164, 165, 173
Castlecoote, 174
Castleleaffy, 32, 33, 41, 129
Cathair-na-Mart (Westport), 41, 48, 127, 141
Cecil, Sir Robert, 36, 98, 100
Charles I, 131, 133, 134, 141, 143, 146, 151, 152
Charles II, 155
Chichester, Sir Arthur, 115, 116, 117, 118, 120, 123
Clandonnells, 32, 41, 55, 59, 64, 65, 77, 83, 87, 118
Clangibbons, 41, 55, 59
Clanmorris, 59
Clan Philpin, 55
Clanrickard, 23
    earl of, 24, 29, 30, 31, 33, 41, 42, 58, 66, 91, 129
Clare, 153
Clare Island, 26, 58, 110
Clew bay, 9, 23, 30, 31, 33, 41, 42, 58, 66, 91, 129
Clifford, Sir Conyers, 80, 81, 82, 83, 86, 87, 88, 89, 90, 91, 92, 110
Cloghans, 125, 128, 141
Clogher Castle, 32

Cloonagashel Castle, 65
Collooney, 86, 90, 91
Comerford, Garret, 59, 60
Cong, 65, 150
Conn, Lough, 64
Connaught, composition of 10, 15, 50, 51, 52, 53, 56, 62, 83, 126
Connemara (Iar-Chonnacht), 25, 37, 59, 153
Conroys, 26
Corrib, Lough, 59
Cork, 118
Corraun, 55
Cromwell, Oliver, 152, 153, 156
Crean, Anne, 166, 168
   William, 166
Crowe, Reverend, 149
Cichulainn, 11,
Curlew Mountains, 11, 91

D
Davies, Sir John, 107, 119, 122
Desmond, 36, 37
   Eleanor, Countess of, 96, 125
   Gerald, Earl of, 40, 41, 42, 71, 96
   James, Earl of, 96, 98
Dillon, Justice, 58
   Sir Theobald, 47
Docwra, Sir Henry, 95, 101
Donamona Castle, 53, 56, 124, 154
Dowdall, John, 7
Dublin, 28, 30, 57, 117, 118, 121, 132, 155
Dublin Castle, 41, 57, 65, 68, 106, 116, 122, 131, 132, 133, 135

E
Edward I, King, 15

Edward III, King, 16
Edward IV, King, 16
Elizabeth I, Queen, 29, 30, 40, 43, 50, 53, 57, 61, 64, 69, 70, 76, 90, 101, 106
Ennis, 135
Enniskillen, 72
Erris, 48, 64, 70, 127, 140, 160
Essex, Robert, Earl of, 90, 93
Everard, Sir John, 122, 123

F
Falkland, Lord Deputy, 132, 142
Fenton, Sit Geoffrey, 75, 80
Fingall, Earl of, 142
Fitzgerald, Eleanor, Countess of Mayo, 152, 154, 155, 156, 158, 159
   James FitzMaurice, 37
   James FitzThomas (Sugan Earl), 96, 97
   Margaret, 96
   Thomas, 135
FitzWilliam, Sir William, 58, 60, 62, 63, 64
Fitton, Sir Edward, 37
France, 29
Freake, Isabella, 140, 152

G
Gallen, barony of, 75, 127, 140, 160
Galloglass (Scots), 21, 30, 34, 42, 43, 55, 56, 63, 64, 69, 118
Galway, 22, 24, 39.40, 42, 58, 61, 62, 63, 75, 86, 90, 91, 92, 94, 105, 149, 152
Gardiner, Chief Justice, 89
Garvey, John, 150
Gormanstown, Viscount, 142
Graces, the, 142

Grey, Sir Leonard, 28
Gunning, John, 161, 173
    Margaret, 161, 174
    Maria, 161
    Elizabeth, 161

H
Hag's Castle, 54
Hawkins, William, 167
Hely, Bishop, 65
Henry VIII, King, 24, 28, 50

I
Iniskea, 70

J
Jamaica, 163, 164
James I, King, 101, 106, 107, 109, 110,
    120, 123, 126, 131
James II, King, 159
John, King, 15
Jordan, Edmund, 164
Joyce, clan, 55

K
Kelly, William, 124, 154
Kildare, Earl of, 24, 28
Kilgeever, 166
Kilkenny, 150, 151
Kilmaine, 22, 23, 44, 59, 64, 77, 82,
    99, 127, 140
Kinlough, 22, 44, 149
Kinsale, 9, 10, 12, 13, 101, 103, 104,
    105, 108, 114
Kinturk Castle, 33, 45, 46, 74, 113,
    114, 116, 124, 125, 132, 135, 139, 145,
    147, 152, 155, 161,
    165

Knallagh, 159
Knockdoe, 24

L
Lambert, Aylmer Bourke, 164, 173
    Edmund, 164, 170
    Sir Oliver, 105
Lewis, Elizabeth, 144, 152
Lisgowell Castle, 141
Loftus, Archbishop, 89, 158
    Ellen, 158
Lough Mask,
London, 69, 74
    Tower of, 40, 96, 97
Lough Mask, 22, 54, 82
    Castle, 44, 64, 84
Luccopp, Robert, 129, 130
Lynch, Sir Henry, 152, 169

M
MacCormack, Bishop, 145
    Sarah, 145
MacCostello, 77
MacDonnell, Randall, 172
    Bridget, 172
MacEvilly, Edmond, 113
    Ever, 113
    Myles I, 15, 33, 35, 45, 46, 47,
        108, 110, 112
    Myles II 140
    Sarah, 113
    Walter, 4
MacGeoghegan, Art, 153
MacGibbons, 32, 111
    Tibbott, 66
MacJordan, 77
MacMurrough, Dermot, 14
MacMyler, 32, 84
MacPhilbin, 32, 140

MacSweeney, 89
MacTibbott, 32, 33, 66
MacWalter Boy, 32
MacWilliam Lower, 16, 17, 20, 21, 22, 23, 24, 28, 29, 30, 37, 38, 44, 48, 51, 77
MacWilliam, Upper, 16, 20, 21, 23, 24, 28, 48
Maeve, Queen, 11,
Maguire, Hugh, 68, 69, 70
Malby, Sir Nicholas, 41, 42, 43, 48, 49
Manulla, 46, 113, 174
Maxwell, Bishop, 149
Mayo, earls of, 172, 175
Mellifont Abbey, 106
Monaghan, 72
Moone, 45
Moore, John, 140
Mountjoy, Lord Charles, 9, 10, 11 94, 95, 96, 101, 103, 105, 106, 115
Moy, 56
Moyne, 30
Munster, 37, 40, 41, 49, 50, 73, 96, 104
Murrisk, 31, 111, 127, 128, 139, 141, 158, 160, 162, 165, 166, 167
    Abbey, 145

N
Naas, 172
Neale, the, 49, 64, 149, 152
Newport (Ballyvechin) castle, 48, 52
Newry, 72
Nova Scotia, Baronet of, 134

O
O'Brien,
    Daniel Mor, king of Munster, 15

O'Boyle, Bishop, 65
O'Cahan, 106
O'Carolan, Turlough, 162
O'Connor, Anthony, 172
    Dermot, 96, 97, 98, 99
O'Connor Don, 30, 45, 91
    Charles, 124
    Sir Hugh, 125
O'Connor Roe, 28
O'Connor Sligo, 28, 30
    Dermot, 135
    Sir Donal, 53
    Donough, 53, 80, 81, 90, 91, 93, 94, 96, 97
    Maud (Maeve), 53, 104, 130, 136, 139, 145
O'Donnell, Hugh (Red) 9, 10, 11 12, 23, 65, 66, 68, 69, 70, 73, 74, 75, 76, 77, 78, 79, 80, 86, 87, 88, 89, 90, 91, 92, 93, 94, 95, 98, 99, 100, 101, 103, 117, 141
    Mary, 141
    Rory, 105, 106, 115, 116
O'Dowd, 26
O'Flaherty, 24, 26, 37, 41, 55, 68, 74, 118
    Donal-an-Chogaidh, 25
    Donal macOwen, 74, 110
    Margaret, 25, 55, 57
    Murrough-na-Doe, 59, 60
    Murrough-na-Mart, 133, 153, 154
    Murrough-na-Maor, 25, 57, 74, 82, 87, 91, 110, 116, 130, 132, 133
    Murrough (Aughnanure), 128
    Owen, 25, 56, 74
    Patrick, 133
    Roger, 152
O'Malley, 24, 25, 26, 31, 32, 51, 55, 68,

74, 77, 111, 118, 173
   Dermot, 141
   Dermot mac Teig Roe, 16
   Donal-na-Piopa, 69, 70, 82, 127
   Dowdara mac Cormac Og, 25,
     111
   Edmond, 83
   Grace (Granuaile), 12, 19, 25,
     35, 39, 40, 41, 42, 43, 46,
     52, 54, 56, 57, 60, 66, 69,
     70, 73, 87, 89, 91, 94, 104,
     109, 111, 132, 145
   Hugh, 111
   Margaret, 19
   Sir Owen, 51, 169, 170, 171
   Sabina, 16
   Teig, 111
   Thady, 158
O'Mulconry, Archbishop, 117
O'Neill, 56
   Art, 74
   Henry, 151
   Hugh (Earl of Tyrone), 9, 10,
     11, 19, 67, 68, 73, 74, 75,
     86, 87, 88, 89, 92, 93, 94,
     95, 96, 97, 98, 99, 101, 103,
     104, 106, 107, 115, 116, 131
   Owen Roe, 151
   Sir Phelim, 146
   Shane, 30
O'Rourke, Brian, 68, 69, 105
   Tadhg, 141
Ormond, earls of, 31, 151
   Duke of, 155, 172
   Black Tom, 70, 73, 74, 89, 130
Oxford, 140
Oxfordshire, 164

P
Perrot, Sir John, 49, 50, 54, 57, 62
Peyton, Thomas, 121
Philip II, King, 67, 75, 80
Plantation, 28, 126, 128, 144
Prendergast, 20

R
Raleigh, Sir Walter, 27
Ranelagh, Viscount, 146
Recusants, 120, 122, 123, 134, 135, 146
Reformation, the, 29
Rinucini, 151
Rome, 142
Roscommon Castle, 55
Ross Abbey, 150
Russell, Sir William, 81

S
Sarsfield, Patrick, 159, 160
Savage, Sir Arthur, 97
Scotland, 21, 25, 29, 42, 63, 129
Scots (see galloglass)
Shrule, 37, 44, 64, 149, 150, 154
Sidney, Sir Henry, 25, 30, 31, 36, 39
Slane, Lord, 142
Sligo, 87, 90, 92, 105
   Castle, 74, 75
   Marquess of, 165, 173
Spain, 25, 27, 67, 72, 75, 95, 100, 103,
   115, 116, 129, 131, 135, 141
Spaniards, 58, 59, 103
Spanishtown, 163
Spenser, Edmund, 49
St. Lawrence, Christopher, 115
St. Leger, Anthony, 116
   Warham St. 79
Staunton de, Adam, 15, 45, 112
   Adam II, 45

Bernard, 46
Edmund, 140
Miles, 74
Philip, 45
Rev. Philip, 145
Strongbow, 14
Surrender and re-grant, 28, 50

T
Thomand, 90, 96
Earl of, 64
Tirawley, 22, 23, 44, 59, 64, 70, 75, 77, 81, 128, 140
Townsend, Lord, 168, 171
Trimblestown, Lord, 45, 112
Tuam, Archbishop of, 32, 55
Tullahoghe, 104
Tyreconnell, Earl of, 159

U
Ulster, 9, 19, 42, 56, 57, 68, 72, 74,

103, 105, 115, 126, 146, 147
Earl of, 16
Umhall, 22, 23, 25, 31, 51, 75

V
Varges, Dean, 149

W
Wentworth, Sir Thomas, 133, 139, 141, 142, 143, 144, 145, 146
West Indies, 163
Westmeath, Earl of, 142
Westport, 160, 166
House, 43, 44, 46, 113, 118, 134, 144, 151, 152, 157, 159, 160, 166
White, Sir Nicholas, 62
Wild Geese, 160

Y
Yellow Ford. 11, 89